Long-Run Economics

The authors would like to thank Butterworths Ltd for permission to re-use material which appeared in an earlier article in *Futures*, and IEEE inc., New York and North Holland Ltd for permission to reproduce graphical material.

Long-Run Economics

An Evolutionary Approach to Economic Growth

Norman Clark and Calestous Juma

Pinter Publishers, London and New York

First published in Great Britain in 1987 by
Pinter Publishers Limited
25 Floral Street, London WC2E 9DS

British Library Cataloguing in Publication Data

Clark, Norman
Long-run economics: an evolutionary approach to economic growth.
1. Economic development 2. Technological innovations — Economic aspects
I. Title II. Juma, Calestous
339.5 HD82

ISBN 0-86187-903-1

Library of Congress Cataloging in Publication Data

Data applied for.

ISBN 0-86187-903-1

Filmsetting by Mayhew Typesetting, Bristol, England
Printed by Biddles of Guildford Ltd.

Contents

List of tables and figures

Tables

Figures

[the] power of the computer is merely an extreme version of a power that is inherent in all self-validating systems of thought. Perhaps we are beginning to understand that . . . abstract systems — [for example] the games computer people can generate in their infinite freedom from the constraints that delimit the dreams of workers in the real world — may fail catastrophically when their rules are applied in earnest. We must also learn that the same danger is inherent in other magical systems that are equally detached from authentic human experience, and particularly in those sciences that insist they can capture the *whole* man in their abstract skeletal frameworks.

Joseph Weizenbaum, *Computer Power and Human Reason*

the ideas of economists and political philosophers, both when they are right and when they are wrong, are more powerful than is commonly understood. Indeed the world is ruled by little else. Practical men, who believe themselves to be quite exempt from any intellectual influences, are usually the slaves of some defunct economist. Madmen in authority, who hear voices in the air, are distilling their frenzy from some academic scribbler of a few years back. I am sure that the power of vested interests is vastly exaggerated compared with the gradual encroachment of ideas.

John Maynard Keynes, *The General Theory of Employment, Interest and Money*

Preface

The quotations on the previous page illustrate a theme which runs throughout the argument of this book: ideas, and the models/metaphors in which they are encased, are both powerful and dangerous — powerful because in an important sense all of our understanding of the world is metaphoric; dangerous because to the extent that this understanding is faulty, our capacity to damage our environment is considerable. Such is the power of modern science and technology. And the most powerful and dangerous of all metaphors are those of economics.

We began writing this book because we wanted to explore why it is that the world described in most economic models is not the world in which we live, at least not without the most extreme suspension of disbelief. Professional economists inhabit a simple world described in terms of a narrow range of variables connected by an equally narrow range of linear equations. It is a world of determinate solutions to pre-specified problems, where 'economic' phenomena (i.e. those to which property rights may be assigned) can be separated off from everything else and where there is no uncertainty. It is a world of homogeneous, irreducible analytical units such as 'firms' and 'households' which operate according to simple behaviour postulates over short time horizons (the 'short run'). Above all, it is a world which always tends towards equilibrium. But it is not the world in which most people live. That is a world of complexity, relative ignorance and interrelatedness, where our present state has an evolutionary history and where our 'long-run' future is important. Indeed, it is the only future we shall have. It is an 'open system', non-linear, indeterminate world and is certainly not one that can be described meaningfully in equilibrium terms.

Very soon, however, we came to realize that the apparent disjunction is a reflection of a much deeper phenomenon — namely, the incorporation into research of tacit and unquestioned intellectual values which are particularly common amongst social scientists but which are also often present amongst other scholarly communities, even on occasion those of the natural sciences themselves. Such values reflect the desire to quantify even where the basis for quantification is weak, to build models which are virtually untestable, to reduce heterogeneity to homogeneity and thence to describe resultant entities in mathematical terms. It is a peculiar form of intellectual corruption which has at its root very probably the great success of Newtonian dynamics combined with the philosophies of Bacon and Descartes, but which has come to substitute a superficial intellectualism for values of traditional scientific scholarship. This would not be so bad (i.e. it would merely reflect academic inefficiency) were it not for the fact that reality is often recreated to fit the needs of the models, and where (as in the case of many social sciences) there is difficulty relating modelling to evidence it is all too often the empirical work which is sacrificed rather than the models themselves, no matter how unrealistic they may be.

Thus the problem is really one of epistemology, and accordingly we have tried to set out what we feel the major difficulties to be. If one is dissatisfied with existing theory, then surely it is necessary to begin the debate by laying out the criteria against which argument may take place. People may disagree with these criteria, but at least the level of argument has been raised from mere scholastic confrontation to one where the roots of disagreement may be laid bare more explicitly. Conventional economists show a marked distaste, however, for questioning the nature of their abstractions. There is only one 'theory' and that is 'economic' theory. It is a homogeneous, inviolate edifice, and to question its inner foundations is often resented deeply. Rather like religious faith, beyond a certain stage ones does not go, unless, as Guy Routh once pointed out, you have reached an elevated professional position in an appropriate learned society, in which case you are permitted once a year to inveigh against the shortcomings of economics on the occasion of your presidential address.

And yet we believe that it is precisely the implicit content of economics which brings about its frequent misuse, since what is, in the hands of a skilled practitioner, a powerful and serviceable analytic tool *given complementary skills and a suitable context*, is often treated as if it were the *whole* story. We argue that this is particularly the case where time horizons are beyond the 'short run' as conventionally defined (hence the book's title), where environmental degradation is threatened and where it is difficult to separate out non-economic factors in any given social problem. The difficulty is, however, that the world is rapidly becoming a very complex place indeed. The power of modern technology means that any changes in our ecology have ramifications through space and time which are likely to be both far-rèaching and irreversible. They are also likely to be incapable of anticipation. In short, it is becoming less and less true (if it ever were true) that we can realistically model our world in simple equilibrium terms. We need a science of complex dynamic systems.

Our aim has been to make a start in this direction by applying our own variation of the evolutionary metaphor to the process of technological change and economic development. By portraying the evolution of new technologies as complex and unstable systems based upon flows of information and guided by socially agreed paradigms, not only is it possible to open up the 'black box' of technical change (normally reduced to an exogenous 'catch all' in standard economic models), it is also possible to give economic growth and development a content of detailed causation. New institutions, for example, may be viewed as necessary vehicles for bringing about (and controlling) economic change rather than as obstacles to the free play of market forces, which is how they tend to be viewed in conventional economics. And although our modelling is qualitative rather than quantitative, we feel that it provides a more realistic basis for 'long-run', or strategic, policy advice compared to the narrow instrumentalism of monetary and fiscal policy, whose main area of application has in any case been that of short-run national income stabilization.

Many colleagues and friends within and outside the Science Policy Research Unit have helped in the evolution of the ideas contained in this book, even if in some cases they do not altogether agree with the overall argument. We are grateful especially to Peter Allen, Martin Bell, Albert Cherns, Martin Fransman, Christopher Freeman, Neil Kay, Christopher Thomson, Nicholas von Tunzelmann, William Walker and other members of the SPRU Development Research Centre (innovation) and Developing Countries groups who kept us on the right lines at various stages. We should like to thank also the Canadian International Development Research Centre, which funded part of the contributary research, and Andrew Barnett, Geoffrey Oldham and Christopher Smart for their unfailing support and encouragement. We are also particularly grateful to Alison Field for her patience and encouragement during the difficult moments of research and writing.

Finally, we should like to thank Sally Marjoram, who typed and in many other ways supervised the preparation of the manuscript, and Heather Page, who prepared the bibliography.

Part I

Introduction

Chapter 1

Epistemological Issues

In a recent article in which he compares the respective 'visions' of Marx and Schumpeter, Nathan Rosenberg concludes that in a number of important respects both authorities saw the world in very similar ways.[1] Both, for example, paid note to the role of science and technology within it. Both emphasized its highly productive character. And both, with some reservations on the part of Schumpeter, favoured an economic interpretation of historic change. Nevertheless, as Rosenberg goes on to point out, while Marx was quite content and consistent with his own 'vision', in the case of Schumpeter there is an evident tension between his view of capitalism as a living, organic system on the one hand, and his profound respect for conventional economics on the other:

> In Schumpeter's case, though he never faced up to it, his analysis [of capitalist development] really amounted to a wholesale rejection of some of the basic tenets of neo-classical reasoning. Schumpeter believed that neo-classical analysis did not provide an adequate framework for understanding the essential aspects of capitalist reality. In spite of [his] numerous expressions of filial piety to Walras, including his description of Walras' *Elements* as '. . . this Magna Charta of exact economics . . .', his rejection of neo-classical reasoning is profound.[2]

Here, then, we have a fundamental paradox in which a man, deeply committed to an understanding of the essentials of capitalist development, is at one and the same time also committed to a conceptual schema which not only is of little help in such an endeavour but is also in many respects actually antagonistic. Rosenberg ends his article on this note of paradox.

It is a major purpose of this book to explore precisely that theme — namely, the fundamental disjunction in much contemporary economics writing between the nature of the phenomena requiring explanation on the one hand, and the conceptual tools used for the task on the other. The argument that we shall make depends upon the proposition that the kinds of theories which economists make about the world they are investigating depend upon more deeply held commitments, which in turn condition the effectiveness of their theories. Such commitments are partly *ideological*, in the political sense; partly *professional*, in that they comprise what is acceptable to the peer group to whom they are addressing their work; and partly *functional*, in that they must be acceptable to those who finance their endeavours. But above all, such commitments are *cerebral* in that they correspond to deeper, metaphysical beliefs about nature, how it functions and how it may be understood.

And it is here that the nature of Rosenberg's paradox surely lies. For Schumpeter's passionately sought grasp of the inner workings of capitalist development was confronted with a body of doctrine which described a different type of world — a world where such development could not take place. What he was groping towards was an organic theory which encapsulated uncertainty, evolution, cybernetic process and dynamic change. Subconsciously, however, he was wrestling with quite a different perception of economic systems — one which postulated perfect knowledge on the part of consumers and producers, where market prices were the only operant variables, where technology was given and where behavioural adjustment was instantaneous. Such a mechanistic, almost clockwork, world fitted in well with a prevailing *zeitgeist* heavily influenced by the apparent success of classical physics, but attempts to make it square with the real world of socioeconomic change, which Schumpeter to his credit did not attempt, are still taking place today — with results which are as unreal and contrived as they ever were.

As with Marx and Schumpeter, this book is also concerned with economic *change*, with how economic systems transform themselves through time both in terms of their structural characteristics and their capacity to produce goods and services. Several points follow from this broad objective. First, we are concerned with economic growth but not in the formal sense of 'growth economics', which we do not regard as useful for our purposes. Rather, we are concerned with that complex of economic, institutional and organizational relationships which together transform economic systems. Second, technological change and innovation are clearly central features of such relationships, not merely because of their role in a 'causal' or 'productivity-improving' sense, but also because they transform irreversibly organizational structures of economic production and distribution. Third, we focus upon scientific research and development (R&D) and associated public policy (or science policy) issues since their relations with the process of economic change are clearly very close, if only very imperfectly understood. Fourth, we are concerned with *strategic issues*, with the *long run*, and not with questions of allocative efficiency amongst a given set of productive resources. Indeed, we argue that a major related problem with prevailing economic theory is that while it is a useful conceptual organizer of *short-run*, allocative questions, its tools are very much more limited when it comes to *long-run*, strategic questions. Finally, our perspective is *interdisciplinary* in the sense that we believe an adequate theory of long-run economic change cannot be built around any one academic discipline but should make use of a variety of disciplinary tools in an integrative fashion. Our starting point is within the evolutionary tradition of economic theory because that tradition in many ways has developed its ideas from an interdisciplinary perspective.

1.1 Time

It follows, therefore, that we see little future in 'rewriting economic theory' to cope with the analysis of the long run. The conceptual trappings of conventional economic theory — its static orientation, its focus on equilibrium paths, its treatment of time and uncertainty, its focus upon a very small range of analytic units, its reductionism — represents methods of abstraction which are too far divorced from the realities of economic change to provide more than a very limited scientific function. This can be seen most clearly in treatments of time since economic and technological changes take place irreversibly over considerable time periods and hence any conceptual structure purporting to model it needs to pay close attention to temporal considerations. A major problem of conventional economics, as Hicks and others have pointed out, is that in order to provide a satisfactory theory of *markets* (in the sense of reaching determinate conclusions to the problems of what sets of prices and quantities will clear markets), one has to abstract from an explanation of *economic growth*. On the other hand, an explanation of how and why growth takes place inevitably means that a determinate resource allocation theory of markets does not work. One way out of this problem appeared to be the rediscovery of the 'steady state', the temporal path along which economic systems could be hypothesized to move:

> A Stationary State, as found in the Classics or in Wicksell, was a very poor instrument for the study of saving and investment, even in the long run; for in a Stationary State both net saving and net investment must by definition equal zero. The Steady State, with its constant growth rate, admitted positive saving, so it looked much better. It could be tidied up, on equilibrium lines, just as well as the Stationary State; for though the quantities of inputs and outputs did not remain unchanged over time, their ratios did. In ratio terms, the Steady State was still quite stationary. Thus, so long as attention was fixed on ratios (and the growth rate itself is a ratio) the Steady State could be absorbed into full-blown equilibrium economics, in which one point of time is just like another. It was just as much 'out of time' as the Stationary State itself.[3]

In both cases 'real' or 'historic' time is ruled out *ex hypothesi*, and in the second case interest then focuses on a description of growth paths under specific boundary conditions concerning preference orderings, technology, resources and institutions: 'The better defined are the boundaries of the problem, the more tractable is the corresponding model and the more completely characterized is the set of solutions; i.e. the nearer the model is to closure the less ambiguous are the solutions to the model'.[4]

Hicks sees two problems in all this: first, the 'impression that has been given to non-economists (through the mediation of statisticians) that there is something natural about a constant growth rate';[5] second, the increasing complexity of growth models is often both misleading and unproductive. Faber and Proops are more specific, arguing that since boundary conditions cannot be held constant, 'economic theory has become divorced from economic history'.[6] In addition, the treatment of innovation, resource depletion and environmental degradation can only be handled by *ad hoc* assumptions.

And yet time in economics is a fundamental quantity. It is the variable against which all resource flows are judged. The production function, for example, represents a relationship between flows of output as a function of input flows *per unit of time*. The demand schedules of households are supposed to represent how much of a given commodity will be demanded at each putative price *over a given period*. Similarly with industrial supply schedules, liquidity preference, the *rate* of investment, and so on. There is no relationship in standard economic theory which is not dependent in a fundamental sense upon time. Why is it then that time is treated in such an artificial manner? It is our view that the answer can only be metaphysical. Only a very deep belief in the ultimate necessity of reaching determinate solutions to mathematically describable relationships could possibly lead to time being treated either as something that does not exist (statics or comparative statics) or as reversible (where the future and the past are treated symmetrically as with the notion of 'rational expectations', for example).[7]

There may be many facets of such a value system — perhaps the psychological need to establish a set of absolute truths to aim for in investigating a complex and intractable nature, *or* possibly it reflects a religious need in an age of avowed materialism, *or* even the uncomprehending admiration that even a minor facility with mathematics appears to invoke in university communities. We suspect that all are important, but guess (and it *is* only a guess) that underlying everything there is a deep desire to emulate the nostrums of classical physics, the theories which have been so successful in explaining the gross behaviour of natural macro-systems and have had so much influence upon all modern academic disciplines.

1.2 The Influence of Classical Physics

The authority best known for the argument that intellectual endeavour in the nineteenth and twentieth centuries has been unduly influenced by classical physics is A.N. Whitehead. In his Lowell Lectures, brought out as *Science and the Modern World* in 1926,[8] he made his argument in terms of the following broad propositions:

(1) Intellectual thought in any field is always conducted through a process of abstraction whereby 'reality' is expressed in terms of specific entities and their relationship to each other.
(2) This process of abstraction both excludes what is felt to be unimportant for the analysis in question and gives the entities specific characteristics.
(3) Provided these abstractions are used carefully — i.e. constantly confronted by experience — then they have great scientific usefulness. Where, however, they get taken for reality itself they will have a profoundly deadening effect on scientific development.
(4) It is the job of philosophy (and philosophers) to make sure that this does not happen by constantly reviewing the nature of the abstractions made within any given context both conceptually and empirically.

However, it is all too easy to get caught in the grip of one's abstractions, a relic or throwback, according to Whitehead, of medieval rationalism:

> We all know those clear-cut trenchant intellects, immovably encased in a hard shell of abstractions. They hold you to their abstractions by the sheer grip of personality. [Nevertheless] . . . the disadvantage of exclusive attention to a group of abstractions, however well-founded, is that, by the nature of the case, you have abstracted from the remainder of things. In so far as the excluded things are important in your experience, your modes of thought are not fitted to deal with them. You cannot think without abstractions; accordingly, it is of the utmost importance to be vigilant in critically revising your *modes* of abstraction. It is here that philosophy finds its niche as essential to the healthy progress of society. It is the critic of abstractions. A civilisation which cannot burst through its current abstractions is doomed to sterility after a very limited period of progress. An active school of philosophy is quite as important for the locomotion of ideas, as is an active school of railway engineers for the locomotion of fuel.[9]

Whitehad argues that much of the history of science from Greek times may be epitomized as the relentless search for what William James called 'irreducible and stubborn facts'. This was brought to a head by Galileo, who insisted that scientists should restrict themselves to those vital properties of material bodies that could be expressed in shapes, numbers and movements. If it could not be measured, it did not count.[10] Whitehead stresses also that the very great success of Newtonian physics has tended to obscure the degree to which its fundamental abstractions are contingent upon a view of nature which at best is crude and at worst simply wrong. Fundamental particles, for example, are not 'corpuscular' or atomistic but exhibit different qualities depending upon the context they find themselves in. They are probably best conceived of as packets of energy fluctuating in an unknown medium (or media). Moreover, they do not traverse four-dimensional space-time in response to fields of force (as they should do according to Newtonian mechanics) but rather appear to inhabit worlds of much wider dimensionality exhibiting behaviour which to us is simply incomprehensible (it can of course be described mathematically, but the mathematics does not correspond to our everyday reality). Finally, although classical physics has been very successful in describing inert macro-systems — and therefore is useful in large areas of economic production — it has, as we shall see, been singularly unsuccessful in explaining living systems at whatever level of size or complexity. Nor does it always explain very well changes of form and structure even in inert macro-systems. And yet despite all this there is still a remarkably strong desire in many of these non-physical fields to theorize in ways which emulate classical physics.

Allen, from a modern standpoint, puts the same problem in a rather different way.[11] The foundations of classical physics are based upon two fundamental ideas:

(1) That the movement and behaviour of all entities can be 'explained' by forces which in turn are determined by universal potential force-fields. At the macroscopic level there are two such potential fields, gravitational and electro-magnetic, though Newton of course argued his cosmology in terms of gravitation.
(2) That although Newton's Laws work reasonably well at the level of the planets, on earth *pure* mathematical movement is vitiated by factors such as air resistance or friction, so that the behaviour of any entity becomes an empirical question. Nevertheless, although the general movement of entities cannot be predicted, what *can* be said with absolute certainty is that any macroscopic system which is isolated or maintained in a uniform environment, will move towards a thermodynamic equilibrium. This is the famous Second Law of Thermodynamics.

Together these ideas permitted the formation of a theoretical basis for all science:

> First came the extension of this to macroscopic physical objects and the development of thermodynamics. In systems where there was no dissipation, then the laws of conservation, and the form of the potential energy field gave the correct answers. In systems where there was dissipation (by far the overwhelming category of course) then provided that the boundary conditions imposed on the system permitted it to go thermodynamic equilibrium, then it would do so, and the precise properties at that final state could be calculated correctly. The 'potentials' which governed the evolution of the system to the

equilibrium state, and allowed the prediction of its properties, were the *thermodynamic potentials*. For an isolated system, this was the *entropy*, while for other situations where energy and matter could flow into or out of the system, it was the appropriate *free energy*. And this fulfilled the promise of Newtonian science. The concept of a deterministic evolution, governed by a potential function had been found to be applicable to macroscopic *complex* systems. But always with the proviso that they were placed in a *uniform* environment which permitted them to evolve towards thermodynamic equilibrium. Physics had almost nothing to say about systems for which the boundary conditions did not allow thermodynamic equilibrium! And of course, all living things (even economists!) fall into this category.[12]

It is interesting to note how closely the modern tradition in economics echoes precisely this mechanistic framework set out most clearly by early economists like Walras.[13] Economic systems are conceived of in terms of *units of production* (firms) and *units of consumption* (households) exchanging commodities and factor services in *markets*, at *prices* which reflect the forces of supply and demand. Markets are always predisposed to clear since competition amongst buyers and sellers ensures that prices will *equilibrate* at precisely the point at which there is no excess or deficiency of goods or services in the market place. The system is then 'idealized' to reveal the conditions under which it will function in a 'perfect' way — there are many buyers, many sellers, perfect knowledge of all alternatives, no production/ consumption complementarities, and so on. Under such an idealized system all economic actors will behave perfectly predictably. The force-fields involved are those of competition, themselves determined by specific behavioural postulates of a psychological character and by technical conditions. Prices provide all the necessary information to allow the entities (households and firms) to behave optimally, and provided the system is suitably isolated, its internal behaviour can be described mathematically in a deterministic way. Finally, historic time is effectively abolished in the sense that markets are assumed to clear instantly, there are no transactions costs, and future states of nature are either perfectly known or can have probabilities of their occurrence assigned to them.

Where system conditions are not such as to allow the economic system to behave in this idealized way, economists tend to talk in terms of 'market imperfections'. And of course that is what reality is all about. The point is, however, that the idealized system becomes the ultimate reference point against which all real states of the system are judged. In Whitehead's language, a set of logical abstractions becomes a normative standard. The idealized system is turned from an analytic device into what nature *really is*. Where the evidence does not seem to support such a view, which is practically all the time, then 'institutions' are routinely wheeled in to explain deviations from the mechanistic ideal. *Quod erat demonstrandum!*

But why should the economics profession behave like this? What indeed can explain this apparent hold of classical physics on the collective minds of all disciplines at a time when physics itself has changed so markedly as a result of the theory of relativity and that of quantum mechanics?

The answer is, we simply do not know. It may be, as Whitehead argued, that the scientific revolution, despite its great liberating effects on medieval dogma, carried with it some essential metaphysical trappings from the earlier epoch and that these are embedded deeply in our psyches. The notion, for example, that there is an ultimate order to nature which is permanent and ultimately discoverable by man lent itself very well to the new inductive methods based on the atomism of scientific materialism and the idea of nature behaving like a clockwork mechanism. Or the notion of an individual's *value*, developed during the period of the reformation in response to the unbridled authoritarianism of the Roman Church, became conflated with the notion of the individual as the *only ultimate fact* leading to the rise of a subjectivist philosophy in the hands of Descartes and the rampant individualism of the modern industrial period, so well suited to the neoclassical tradition in economics.

What is certain is that intellectual life in many modern fields has become professionalized and differentiated to such a degree that it is ceasing to comprehend nature as a unity, but tries to confine it within preconceived and differentiated categories – often with extreme difficulty. It will be our argument in this book that this is precisely what professional economics tries to do. The more it tries, however, the more it disenfranchises itself from everyday problems which in themselves know nothing of the 'discipline' but merely cry out for resolution. Our focus will be on science, technology and public policy, partly because this is an area where we have special interests but partly also because it is our area where Rosenberg's 'paradox of Schumpeter' is illustrated most clearly.

Above all, the influence of science and technology on society is one of long-term structural change. Scientific discoveries get translated into inventions and innovations which profoundly alter established patterns of economic production and institutional organization, and do so *irreversibly*. Moreover, at any point in time future states of nature are simply unknowable. Science policy decisions are therefore *strategic* — they are taken in the knowledge only that their consequences will need to be articulated within the context of conditions which have yet to evolve. 'Rational expectations' have no place in such a world. It is also likely, although we do not know for certain, that future states of the world economic system will be more complex, differentiated and yet more integrated than has been the case in the past, so that any given set of events will impinge more widely on the world as a whole.

1.3 Criteria for Scientific Choice

It will be evident from the discussion so far that our quarrel with conventional economics is at bottom an epistemological one. It fails as an adequate theory of long-run economic change. For example, a key to Rosenberg's identification of the Schumpeterian 'paradox' is his explicit separation of the visionary act from that of scientific research. 'Vision' is a pre-analytic cognitive process which is not to be confused with 'science'. It is 'not science but rather a pre-condition for the conduct of science'.[14] Rosenberg has taken an epistemological stand. By explicitly drawing his own boundaries around what is to be regarded as legitimate scientific activity he is thus able to identify a paradox in Schumpeter's writings, something that he can only explain in terms of the surmise that Schumpeter himself is a 'lover of paradox'.

However, there are few contemporary philosophers of science who would accept such a bald distinction between pre-scientific and scientific activity. Toulmin, for example, shows how our appreciation of reality is heavily conditioned by more fundamental beliefs about 'natural order'.[15] To Aristotle and his followers, since the natural tendency of all objects is to be at rest, what required explanation is why objects moved *at all*. His conclusion that the force acting upon a body is directly proportional to its speed was therefore a direct consequence of his view that bodies *need* a force to get them into motion. To Newton, on the other hand, who accepted the view that bodies naturally continued in inertial motion, what required explanation was why bodies deviated from this norm. And his proportional law between force and *acceleration* followed from this different perception of the way the world *naturally* works. Similarly, Kuhn's notion of 'paradigm'[16] and Lakatos' 'negative' heuristic'[17] are both used in part to include metaphysical influences on the creative act, while Popper includes 'bold speculation' as an intrinsic property of good science.[18] Hence we prefer to adopt a more general definition of the scientific quest whose function it should be to provide an adequate explanation of existing phenomena, to explain *reality* in ways which are held to be valid according to established canons of enquiry.

However, reality is a slippery concept. It is not something which can be somehow separated from the visionary act but is, on the contrary, at least to some degree a function of our own cognitive processes. It is mediated by prior belief inherited from past writing and acculturation, providing a context within which explanation is to be sought and validated. By separating the two concepts, Rosenberg (probably unwittingly) is falling into precisely the trap which bedevils so much of conventional neo-classical economics, thereby in effect allowing two apparently irreconcilable 'realities' to exist. Rosenberg's Schumpeterian paradox is merely but one example of a much wider intellectual problem, which is that economists tend to behave more like theologians than like scientists. Conversely, what gives expression to the scientific quest, and distinguishes it from dogmatic controversy, is the use of experimental evidence to test, falsify or validate, propositions. And however halting and spasmodic the process has been, there is an important sense in which theory and practice in many of our natural sciences have built upon each other in a symbiotic fashion — the ultimate success of any given theory consisting, *first*, in how well it stands up to repeated experimental testing and *second*, upon the extent to which such experimental procedures result in further refinement and extension of theory. We argue that the lack of such a close interdependence between evidence and theory is a major deficiency in much of social science in general, and in economics in particular.

A second characteristic of scientific activity is its varied nature. Kuhn, for example, has pointed out that most individual sciences are in a constant state of evolution (and have reached different levels of maturity), and there are also wide variations in how the scientific 'craft' is practised. Some disciplines, like geology, for example, are heavily *taxonomic* in the sense that much activity tends to be classificatory, while others, like nuclear physics, are also very much concerned with the *interaction* of phenomena — and hence with cause and effect. Some, like computer science, are very young compared to the molecular sciences, like chemistry and biology, and there are important differences in how sciences are institutionalized and professionalized. Given this heterogeneity of scientific activity it is clear that there is no *one* means of categorization which can subsume the whole endeavour under *one* generic description.

A third feature of science is the well-known difficulty of postulating a homogeneous set of standards by which scientific work may be judged. Thus Toulmin argues that while 'philosophers are often tempted to offer portmanteau characterisations of science, finding in some one requirement (such as predictive success) the unique test of a scientific hypothesis',[19] they are generally unsuccessful. For example, Darwin's theory of evolution became widely accepted despite the fact that it was able to predict nothing. Similar problems arise with other criteria, such as falsifiability, richness of an ensuing research programme, instrumentality and many others. Indeed, Kuhn has shown that historically science has progressed by rules which are as much sociological as they are cerebral, and Lakatos portrays science as advancing heuristically — namely, by scientists specifically accepting certain basic truths which are themselves unquestionable and which determine the sorts of 'lower-level' questions that it is legitimate to ask. This is perfectly acceptable *provided* that scientists are fully aware that they are to that extent 'culture bound' — that the nature of what Lakatos called 'the negative heuristic' is fully appreciated, and that where the ruling research programme is running into great difficulty, scientists are willing to retreat to first principles, as it were, and ask fundamental questions about such tacit knowledge. Unfortunately, very often for professional and other reasons, many scientists are unable or unwilling to do this. On the whole, social scientists, particularly economists, are the worst offenders — partly for narrow reasons of vested interests but also because their own values intrude heavily into their analyses.

Given these features of science — namely, its attempt to model reality using logic and experiment, its typological heterogeneity and the lack of any universally accepted criterion for theoretical choice — what can we say which will allow us to make any progress whatsoever with respect to the social sciences? Here we suggest two fundamental propositions:

(1) One must be less ambitious with respect to what one *expects* from social science theory — and in particular it is advisable to substitute the notion of 'metaphor' (or 'model') for that of 'theory'.

(2) One should, however, be prepared to lay down general *norms* for what one expects from such a metaphor. We shall put forward our own position on this.

On the first proposition it is useful to start with Beloff's distinction between 'strong' and 'weak' theory using the capacity to predict as the essential discriminant: 'For any doctrine to qualify as a theory in the strong sense it must be possible for us to derive predictions from it which could not have been anticipated in the absence of that 'theory'.[20] Beloff goes on to cite the discovery of the planet Neptune (astronomy) and that of the elementary particle, the neutrino (nuclear physics), in both cases before they had been observed, as examples of what could happen in sciences which are theoretically advanced. In contrast, most social sciences, including psychology and economics, can at most employ 'weak theory', which he defines in terms of a 'model' or 'metaphor'. Such a model 'serves to guide us in forming our hypotheses but they are not strict deductions from it and if they are falsified we are not obliged to scrap the model; we can merely tinker with it and readjust it'. It will continue to be used 'as long as it supplies a framework into which we can fit our observations and by reference to which we can conceptualise our knowledge [but] . . . sometimes a model may be little more than an extended analogy'.[21]

Not everyone would accept his equation of strong theory with predictive power (as we have seen, for instance, Darwin's theory of evolution, which underpins most of contemporary biology and genetics, would fail the test), but there is an important sense in which most social science theory is 'weak' in Beloff's definition. Much of conventional economics is clearly metaphoric, and the gap between its attempts to model economic life on the one hand, and empirical evidence on the other, is very great indeed. However, it seems to us that Beloff is altogether too restrictive in his epistemology, since no criteria are provided which would allow us to discriminate amongst competing metaphors. Here philosophers like Lakatos provide more help in so far as they postulate the importance of the *research programme* which flows from any given metaphoric tradition (or in Lakatos' terminology, its negative heuristic). A *progressive* research programme is one in which there are constantly new problems being thrown up which inform and enhance theory. Theory and evidence reinforce one another in a symbiotic fashion. Conversely, a *degenerative* research programme is one where no such progress (indeed regress) is made and where controversy declines, in the limit, into scholastic debate. Toulmin comes to similar conclusions in his search for the 'meaning of scientific theory', and there are distinct echoes of Kuhn's 'crisis of normal science'. Such a degenerative programme is clearly proceeding nowhere, producing no new results of interest and often making conceptual points in ever more abstruse ways. Also, interaction between evidence and theory becomes increasingly weak. Readers of some of our contemporary economics journals may recognize the symptoms.

Two important metaphoric properties follow immediately from this discussion. First, models must correspond as closely as possible to reality so as to permit a point of departure for relevant empirical work. The further the departure from reality, the weaker they are from an empirical standpoint. Second, they should be *progressive* in the Lakatos sense, that is, they should have the potential to produce new and relevant propositions which may then be tested empirically so as to further inform theory, and so on until, as it were, the heuristic runs out of steam.

To these fundamental properties we add two further ones relating to social science in particular. First, any adequate metaphor should be capable of *discriminating amongst socioeconomic units*. For example, 'a' theory of 'the firm' will only amount to an adequate metaphor where firms are in reality relatively homogeneous. Where they are not, the appropriate metaphor may have to encompass several such 'theories'. In this connection McKelvey has pointed out that a major weakness in contemporary social science is the lack of attention paid to *classifying* populations *prior to* the task of developing appropriate conceptual accounts. Within the context of organization theory, he argues that

> systematic studies are crucial to the orderly progression of organizational science. Other sciences such as physics, chemistry, mineralogy, and biology all have systematic studies as a significant feature of their past, and in high-energy physics and biology the advent, respectively, of particle accelerators and electronic computers caused a reawakening of interest in classification. I would go as far as to say that the search for laws and principles in these sciences did not flourish until prerequisite work in systematics was completed.[22]

Second, an adequate social metaphor should have the capacity to produce results of *relevance to policy*, in the sense that the propositions derived from it, once validated, are of direct relevance to policy concern and may be activated institutionally. We realize that this is the most problematic criterion of all since there is traditionally a wide gap between social policy and social theory. Nevertheless, it would appear difficult to justify the funding of much social science research were there to be no such policy focus, and clearly the closer one can get to policy relevance the better. One interesting example in relation to innovation and technological change, which we shall return to later, is the emphasis placed by Nelson and Winter on the importance of institutions in the development of a theory of innovation. They point out that unless the behaviour of relevant institutions is specifically 'built into' such a theory (or metaphor), it will have little chance of informing policy, since policies operate through, and by means of, these very institutions.[23]

We have now outlined four properties which, arguably, an adequate social science metaphor ought to have. These are realism, heuristic progressiveness, discriminatory power and policy relevance. We have deliberately not included 'rigour' amongst our criteria, since we believe that this has become a much-abused term. Popper once put it in terms of the gap between 'interesting' and 'uninteresting' truth. And Duns Scotus and the medieval schoolmen demonstrated immense rigour in their arguments about how many angels could balance on the head of a pin, though they were in the end unable to agree. The point of course is that rigour in social science is essentially a secondary property, understood to be a necessary function of *all* scholarship, and not to be conflated with the practice of putting conceptual propositions in mathematical form. Where it takes over (in a crude) form, from more fundamental criteria for good science (as we believe it has in the case of economics), then clearly something is wrong.

1.4 Summary of the Argument

Given this general philosophical position, it will be our purpose in this book to explore these problems with a view to suggesting that an evolutionary approach based on general systems theory is likely to prove a better conceptual organizer of the economic change process. More specifically, we shall argue in Part II three broad propositions: (1) that existing approaches to the analysis of technological and economic change fail on theoretical grounds and that this is probably due to their mechanical underpinnings; (2) that evolutionary approaches to economic change (which have a long history) despite having developed many useful insights, have never engaged systematically with technological change as a process and have, instead, tended to erect an evolutionary canopy over a conceptual structure which remains fundamentally a mechanistic one; (3) that a combination of evolutionary and general systems theory shows much greater promise as a theoretical framework for the analysis of technological change viewed as a social process. In particular, it allows for the direct integration of information flows, and therefore information technology, into the analysis of economic change.

Our approach follows the inductivist tradition of the institutional economists. In the words of Wilber and Harrison, it is 'holistic, systemic and evolutionary' — *holistic* in the sense both that the whole evinces behaviour which cannot be deduced merely by aggregating that of its constituent parts *and* that the parts themselves cannot be individually understood separate from the relationships they maintain with each other to make up the whole; *systemic* and *evolutionary* in the sense that the socioeconomic system under investigation is conceived of as always in a state of flux as its constituent elements alter their behaviour in relationship to each other and to the extra-systemic environment. Such an approach represents a metaphysical position which is antithetical both to the hypothetico-deductive formalism of the early neoclassical tradition for which logical rigour was the only scientific criterion of value, as well as to its more recent logical positivist variant which allows for the use of empirical evidence so as to test the predictive powers of the formal model. However, as Wilber and Harrison point out, the criterion of predictive power is on the whole an empty one because the inherently poor experimental design and the nature of the subject-matter make prediction very difficult to achieve. Since economic data cannot be handled using the experimental methods of the natural sciences, resort is had to *ceteris paribus* clauses which are routinely blamed when predictions fail — as they usually do. Therefore not only is positive economics 'perfectly insulated from refutation', it does not, indeed it cannot, proceed in ways common to the natural sciences where, however imperfectly, evidence and theory build upon each other in a symbiotic manner.

Chapter 2 summarizes some of the major problems we find with conventional treatments of economic change and suggests an alternative broad conceptual framework based upon a variant of general systems theory. Chapter 3 explores the evolutionary tradition in economic analysis. Much of this tradition is neo-Darwinian in tone and is thus still too mechanistic for our purposes. However, the modern neo-Schumpeterian literature, particularly in the form developed by Freeman and Perez, takes a much more organic perspective, which we then use as a point of departure for the development of our own qualitative model of economic and technological change.

In Chapter 4 we outline a range of necessary conceptual 'building blocks' starting with Prigogine's theory of dissipative structures in macroscopic chemical systems later extended by Jantsch to describe the co-evolutionary development of all natural systems. We suggest that the development of socio-economic systems follows a precisely analogous pattern with, however, one important variation: the much more pronounced role played by information flows in systemic communication. The importance of informational exchange is developed further through a brief discussion of evolutionary epistemology which explores the relations between 'information' and 'knowledge' and argues that knowledge itself follows an evolutionary logic. Finally, we review some recent developments in the sociology of science which explore in more detail some of the ideas originally put forward by Kuhn. On this view the pursuit and validation of all scientific knowledge is primarily a function of social interaction rather than one of objective dialogue between experiment and nature.

Finally, Chapter 5 sets out our own qualitative model of economic and technological change which we see essentially in terms of a complex set of information interactions amongst economic actors (producers and consumers) and the science/technology system — those bodies both within and outside the productive system whose function it is to conduct research which may at some point produce useful economic results. Since information flows are very complex, they require some form of economic guidance. This is provided by the technological 'paradigm' or 'system' which provides a social and cognitive framework within which innovation takes place. Finally, innovation and technical change respond to two broad types of social pressure: that arising from market demands and that associated with the institutional interests of scientific and technological communities. The important science policy questions then revolve around how to intervene in such a complex techno-economic system so as to further the attainment of social goals.

Part III of the book consists of two case studies (fuel ethanol, photovoltaics) which give some comparative ideas about how our qualitative model may work in practice. They are each concerned with the evolution of the technology itself rather than with just the consequence of any specific change, and each highlights the very complex interactions which take place in this evolutionary process. Also, in both cases it is clear that institutional structures and government regulation play important roles in enabling the technologies to penetrate the economic arena and to diffuse successfully throughout the economic system. Finally, the lack of predictability inherent in technological changes is highlighted, giving point to the assertion that much modern economic change is setting in train ecological and social trends which may be both dangerous and irreversible. It is important, therefore, to try to understand the essential nature of new technology before putting it into socioeconomic practice. It is also important to monitor technological changes closely, which in turn requires adequate institutional machinery at government level.

Finally, Part IV demonstrates how our qualitative model is consistent with recent empirical literature on technical and economic change in industrialized and in less-developed countries. We close the book with two messages. First of all, an organic and evolutionary view of economic change certainly makes it difficult to apply mathematics to derived models (although by no means impossible). But we question the stress placed on the building of deterministic models. If the *essential reality* of nature is indeed that of co-evolutionary, dynamic open systems, then that must be our analytical starting point, however great the intellectual difficulty involved. Second, if we are to cope with the pace and complexity of modern technology, we must begin to think and act in a truly interdisciplinary way, at all levels. Modern technology does not respect institutional or bureaucratic boundaries but requires, on the contrary, a flexible social response. To bring this about will mean big structural changes at all levels in society. It is our argument that if we are to cope successfully with economic change in the long run, we must begin the process now.

Notes and References

1. N. Rosenberg (1986), 'Schumpeter and Marx: How Common a Vision?' in R. MacLeod (ed.) *Technology and the Human Prospect* (London: Frances Pinter), pp. 197–213.
2. Ibid., p. 208.
3. J.R. Hicks (1976) 'Some Questions of Time in Economics' in A.M. Tang *et al.* eds, *Evolution, Welfare, and Time in Economics* (Lexington, Mass.: D.C. Heath).
4. M. Faber and J.L.R. Proops (1986), 'Time Irreversibilities in Economics: Some Lessons from the Natural Sciences' in M. Faber (ed.), *Studies in Austrian Capital Theory, Investment and Time* (Heidelberg: Springer), p. 3.
5. Hicks, op. cit., p. 143.
6. Faber and Proops, op. cit., p. 3.
7. Strictly speaking, as von Tunzelmann has pointed out to us, the theory of rational expectations simply argues that the past has no significance in determining the future. However, we would argue that such an argument is tantamount to treating past and future symmetrically, that is treating time as 'reversible'.
8. A.N. Whitehad (1985), *Science and the Modern World* (London: Free Association Books).
9. Ibid., p. 73.
10. This attachment to quantification was later refined to the Kelvin dictum: 'When you cannot express it in numbers, your knowledge is a meagre and unsatisfactory kind', quoted in D. McCloskey (1983), 'The Rhetoric of Economics', *Journal of Economic Literature,* **21**, see p. 484. Hume

expressed the same view: 'When we run over libraries . . . what havoc must we make? If we take in our hand any volume — of divinity or school metaphysics, for instance — let us ask, Does it contain any abstract reasoning concerning quantity or numbers? No. Does it contain any experimental reasoning concerning matter of fact and existence? No. Commit it then to the flames, for it can contain nothing but sophistry and illusion' (ibid., p. 485).

11. P.M. Allen (1986), 'Evolution, Innovation and Economics'. Paper presented at the IFIAS Workshop on Technical Change and Economic Theory (Lewes, Sussex, 18–20 October 1986), mimeo, SPRU.
12. Ibid., p. 4.
13. See, for example, L. Walras (1984), *Elements of Pure Economics* (Philadelphia: Orion Editions).
14. N. Rosenberg, op. cit., p. 198.
15. S. Toulmin (1961), *Foresight and Understanding* (London: Hutchinson), Chs 3 and 4.
16. See T.S. Kuhn (1970), *The Structure of Scientific Revolutions*, 2nd edn (Chicago: Chicago University Press), Ch. 2 and Postscript.
17. See I. Lakatos (1972) 'Falsification and the Methodology of Scientific Research Programmes' in I. Lakatos and A. Musgrave (eds) *Criticism and the Growth of Knowledge* (Cambridge: Cambridge University Press), see pp. 132–8 particularly.
18. Ibid., p. 92.
19. S. Toulmin, op. cit., p. 15.
20. J. Beloff (1972), 'The Place of Theory in Parapsychology' in R. van Over (ed.), *Psychology and Extrasensory Perception* (New York: Mentor), p. 380.
21. Ibid., p. 381.
22. B. McKelvey (1982), *Organizational Systematics: Taxonomy, Evolution, Classification* (London: University of California Press), see p. 2. McKelvey uses the generic term 'systematics' to comprise all the activities normally understood by the word 'classification'. Actually, however, as Albert Cherns has pointed out to us, there is usually an interaction between classification and experiment as recent events in nuclear physics have shown.
23. R. Nelson and S. Winter (1977), 'In Search of a Useful Theory of Innovation', *Research Policy*, **6** (1): 36–77.
24. See C.K. Wilber and R.S. Harrison (1978), 'The Methodological Basis of Institutional Economics', *Journal of Economic Issues* **XII** (1): 61–89, at p. 71.

Part II

New Approaches to Technical Change

Chapter 2

The Economistic Paradigm

This chapter sets out our objections to the way in which conventional economics explores the problem of the behaviour of economic systems through time, bearing in mind the general epistemological criteria set out in the previous chapter. We start by examining briefly the conventional conceptualization of technology and technological change, where the predominant starting point has been as an adjunct to the economics of growth and production theory. Although there are a number of problems with this approach, they appear to boil down to three basic difficulties — namely, the treatment of time, information and heterogeneity — which together give the analysis an artificial flavour.

We hypothesize two reasons underlying such rationalism. The first, intellectual conservatism, is almost inevitable in the analysis of an interdisciplinary topic which has only recently begun to receive widespread attention. In a sense, one must expect a 'cognitive lag' if only for reasons associated with vested interests. However, potentially much more significant is (as pointed out in the previous chapter) an underlying Cartesian or mechanistic rationality that attempts to force socio-economic complexity into the kinds of reductionism associated with the classical dynamics of Newton. It is at least arguable that much of the artificiality of economic analysis, especially when applied to technical change, is associated with a deep-seated desire to view the economic universe as subject to a small number of timeless, or clockwork, laws similar to those of Newtonian cosmology — to imagine the economy as a kind of 'machine' powered by a range of behavioural and technological forces whose ultimate nature is discoverable, and in the meantime whose proper functioning may only be serviced by those who have been appropriately trained — that is, professional economists. We believe that ultimately it is the need for this kind of psychological security that drives the current paradigm.

As an alternative approach, therefore, the second half of the chapter sets out a version of general systems theory which may provide a more suitable metaphor for the analysis of economic systems through time. There have in fact been a variety of systems approaches put forward in different contexts, but we have chosen Koestler's 'nested hierarchy' structure because it provides a neat way of conceptualizing economic systems both *synchronically* (i.e. as a set of linked sub-systems at a point in time) and *diachronically* (as that same economic system moving through time). Indeed, we shall see that there are *a priori* grounds for believing that technological change itself operates in an evolutionary manner leading to a continuous organizational flux in the pattern of economic change. Thus it is that we prefer to model the socioeconomic system organically rather than mechanistically and argue later on that although there may be resultant disadvantages in terms of deterministic model-building, nevertheless, such an approach brings the analyst closer to the realities of economic life and to a more sensible basis for policy advice.

2.1 Economic Analysis and Technological Change

How then has the dominant neoclassical tradition in economics attempted to conceptualize technological change? It is arguable that modern interest in the technology factor has been a by-product of the economics of growth — the study of how and why economic systems grow through time in terms of their capacity to produce goods and services. The starting point for one strand of this tradition is undoubtedly Harrod's famous paper published in 1939 which extended Keynes's macroeconomic concepts (developed for his short-run analysis of instability) into the long run.[1] Harrod showed how advanced industrial systems would normally grow in a highly unstable manner given a range of initial assumptions about the behaviour of productive and household sectors. His work led to controversy about the precise degree of this instability — about the conditions under which stabilization would automatically come about, about the rate of fluctuation obtaining and about the proper role of government in ensuring reasonably steady growth through time.

The simplest exposition of the Harrod instability problem (and the associated conditions for a 'steady state' equilibrium growth path) may be seen using a simple model of two linear equations one of which, the investment function, has a single period lag. The exposition also has the advantage of showing how typically economists tackle such questions. Using Sen's notation[2] we have

$$I_t = (X_t - Y_{t-1})\, C \tag{1}$$

$$Y_t = \frac{1}{s} \cdot I_t \tag{2}$$

where the subscript, t, refers to the time period, I is investment, X and Y expected and actual output respectively, s the marginal propensity to save out of current income and C is the capital–output ratio. The boundary conditions of this model are particularly severe. Its parameters (C and s) are assumed to be constant through time, there is no labour force, no foreign trade, no government sector and no technical change.[3]

Moreover, economic behaviour is not influenced by other factors, like for example the rate of interest. In any given time period the model is assumed to achieve an instantaneous equilibrium before its own internal operations drive it to a new equilibrium in the following time period — and so on. Provided these conditions are satisfied, equation (1) tells us that investment in any period is determined by the difference between expected and (lagged) actual output multiplied by the capital–output ratio, while equation (2) relates income instantaneously to investment expenditure. Since national income is identically equal to national output it is simple to show that

$$\frac{Y_t}{X_t} = \frac{C}{s}\left[\frac{X_t - Y_{t-1}}{X_t}\right] \tag{3}$$

or $\dfrac{Y_t}{X_t} = \dfrac{C}{s} \cdot \hat{g}_t$

where $\hat{g}_t = \dfrac{X_t - Y_{t-1}}{X_t}$ = the expected rate of growth.

It follows that expectations are realized only where $\dfrac{C}{s} \cdot \hat{g}_t = 1$

or $\hat{g}_t = \dfrac{s}{C}$.

Harrod called this the *warranted* rate of growth. Now let

$g_t = \dfrac{Y_t - Y_{t-1}}{Y_t}$ = the actual rate of growth.

Then it can be shown that

$$g_t = 1 - \left[\frac{1 - \hat{g}_t}{\hat{g}_t}\right] \cdot \frac{s}{C}$$

from which it follows that

$$g_t \gtreqless \hat{g}_t \text{ according as } \hat{g}_t \gtreqless \frac{s}{C} \tag{4}$$

In other words, if our economy moves off its equilibrium path, $\dfrac{s}{C}$, it will not be self-correcting but will be inherently unstable.

Much of subsequent work in this field has revolved around relaxing the assumptions and exploring the conditions under which the outcomes might be different. The analysis can become very complex, but it is probably fair to state that most of this literature is still very much what Harrod and his colleagues initially intended it to be — namely, an extension of macroeconomic instability controversies from the short into the long period. Certainly, its predisposition to describing the properties of various classifications of growth paths within an integrated industrialized economy, the classifications being dependent upon arbitrary initial assumptions and subsequent behavioural postulates, give it a distinctly artificial flavour. 'Technology', for example, is simply defined in terms of ratios of real inputs of factor services per unit of output, and 'technical change' then becomes an assumption (or set of assumptions) about how technical conditions change in specific factor-saving directions. There is, however, no real sense in which we can imagine technology as a living process, alterations to which, by government policy, will bring about changes in growth rates. Putting it more explicitly, modern growth economics has little or no empirical power and therefore policy relevance in any precise sense.

It was partly as a result of this deficiency that a second strand of analysis developed, again from within the neoclassical tradition, but this time based upon direct empirical measurement of the aggregate production function. Much of this literature rests upon formal production theory, a branch of economics which attempts to model the productive process as the conversion of resources (inputs) into goods and services (outputs) using a production method (or 'technique') which may be defined in terms of combinations of inputs at a point of time. In effect, the so-called 'short-run' production function purports to describe a range of combined factor proportions (or 'techniques') which are available in the 'given state of knowledge' for the productive act in question. Notice that the definition of technique is again in terms of factor input ratios at a point in time.

A useful way of portraying this type of treatment of technical change is to review Solow's attempt to fit time series data to an aggregate production function for the non-farm US economy between 1909 and 1949.[4] Solow's problem was to discover how much of observed growth in output per head was due to increases in capital stock per head compared with 'technical change', defined in forms of shifts in the aggregate production function. It is interesting from our point of view precisely because it represents a 'stretching' of a short-run relationship into the long run, thus allowing time to vary. The conventional aggregate production function describes output simply as a three-variable relationship involving homogeneous output Q, capital K and labour L:

$$Q = F(K, L) \tag{5}$$

where Q, K and L represent *flows* of resources per unit of time. 'Capital', for example, is conceived as being 'used up' to a degree sufficient to produce a given quantity of goods when combined with a certain input of labour power over the period in question. The relationship at bottom is therefore an energetic one, with 'technology' being understood as the means through which transformation takes place — or more accurately, the underlying knowledge which tells us how ideally economic production could take place. Thus the production function portrayed in Figure 2.1 represents also an 'efficiency frontier'. Any point (A) above the curve is not feasible in the given state of knowledge. Any point (B) below it indicates an inferior method of production, dicounting of course the case where the economic system attempts to use the current best practice technology but fails due to its own inefficiency.

There are several points of potential ambiguity here. To begin with it is important to distinguish between 'technique' and 'technology'. The former represents a point on the aggregate production function while the latter defines the spectrum of possible techniques in the given state of knowledge. 'Technology' therefore has a *time* dimension since production possibilities are consistently improving. A major defect in

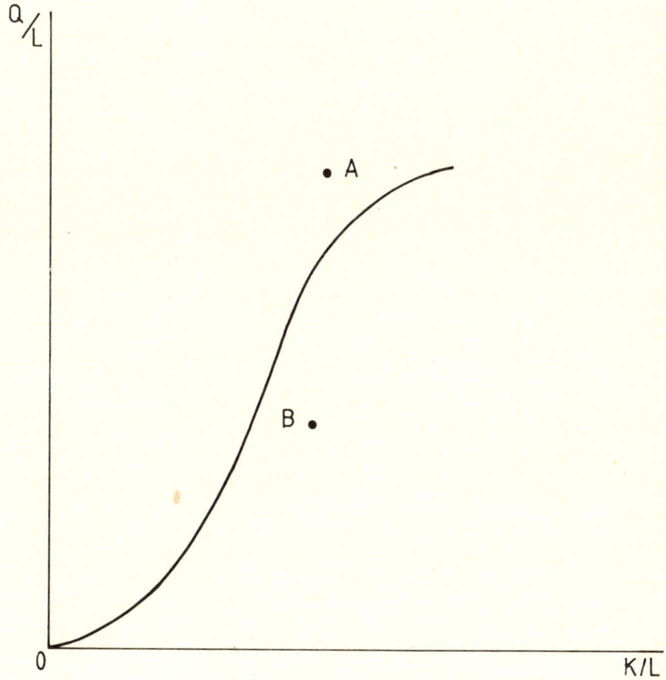

Figure 2.1 The production function

conventional economic analysis was the relegation of such improvements to an *exogenous* status — an unexplained influence on temporal variations in economic systems, often schematized in the following mathematical form with 'technology' defined identically with 'time':

$$Q = F(K, L; t) \tag{6}$$

There is also a logical distinction between a switch in techniques along a given function and a wholesale shift in the function itself, but notice that this distinction carries an inherent ambiguity. 'Time' has to be long enough to allow the productive act to take place with the vintage of equipment available at the point of installation, but since 'time' is also a continuous variable acting as a proxy for technical progress, no production would ever be possible under such functional conditions. Finally, there are important conceptual problems in defining capital flow as a homogeneous quantity. To the businessman, capital represents a stock of equipment from which produce flows. To the economist, it can only be defined as a financial flow derived by normalizing a heterogeneous collection of physical inputs by prices and then making difficult assumptions about depreciation. The resulting 'values' are more than a little ambiguous, where the degree of aggregation is that of the entire economy of a country. Like so much in economics, the reader is routinely invited to suspend disbelief in order to render further analysis possible.

Solow, however, did not attempt to tackle all of these problems. Broadly speaking, he accepted the aggregate production function as a useful tool of analysis and confined himself to investigating the influence of the variable hitherto regarded as exogenous: technological change. His problem may be seen as follows. Actual empirical observations of production conditions for any economic system over time involves, in effect, selecting only one observation (R_1, R_2, . . .) from each of a number of sequential production functions out of an infinite possible number (t_1, t_2, t_3, . . .). This has to be the case because 'technology' is conflated with 'time' so that during any time period there can only be one aggregate technique actually chosen. Labour productivity is denoted by $q = Q/L$ and 'technique' by $k = K/L$. Improvements in labour productivity are then functionally caused by two influences, namely changes in the aggregate technique and changes in overall factor productivity. The question was how important relatively was each influence. If sequential production functions are as portrayed in Figure 2.2(ii), changes in k tend to be more important compared to the situation portrayed in Figure 2.2(i).

Assuming neutrality of technical change (i.e. technical change is not inherently biased in any factor-saving direction abstracting from price influences) allowed Solow to rewrite expression (6) as

$$Q = A(t) \cdot F(K, L) \tag{7}$$

(i)

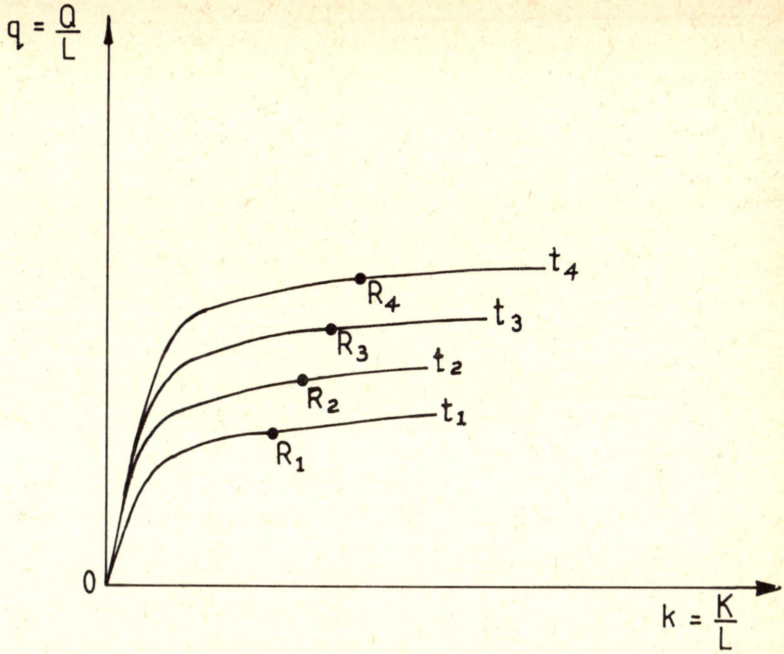

(ii)

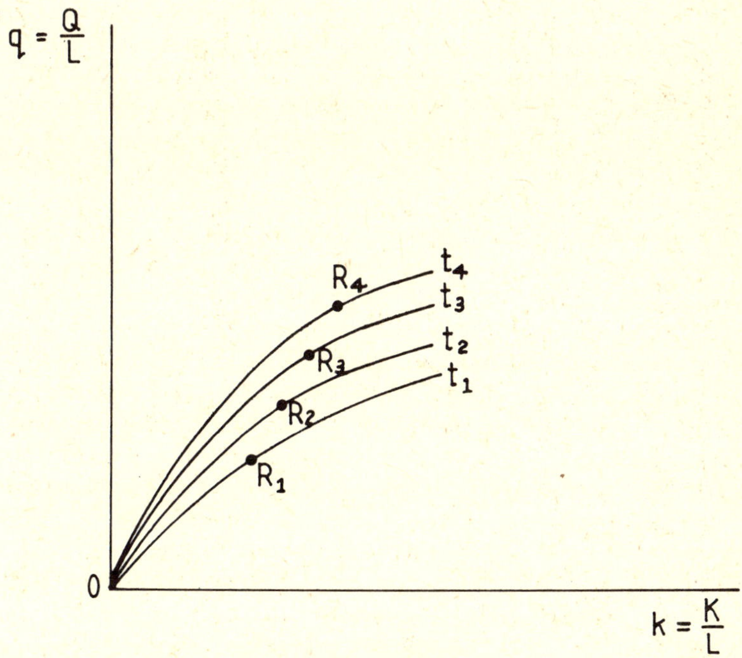

Figure 2.2 Temporal shifts in the aggregate production function

where $A(t)$ represents the overall shift in the production function. Some straightforward mathematical manipulation then produced the following differential equation

$$\dot{q}/_q = \dot{A}/_A + w_k \cdot \dot{k}/_k \qquad (8)$$

where W_k is the share of capital in total output and the dots represent first partial differentials with respect to time. Collecting discrete year-to-year data for capital, output and capital share and reverting from the continuous function (8) to its discrete analogue, allowed Solow to conclude that around 87 per cent of the observed shift in labour productivity was due to technical progress and only around 13 per cent to increased investment. Relaxing the assumption of neutrality and performing similar calculations for different production function specifications did not significantly alter the results.

Solow's results (and corresponding conclusions reached by others, such as Abramovitz, Fabricant and Massell) proved somewhat of a bombshell since they indicated that the bulk of observed improvements in the economic performance of a macroeconomic system could not be explained by the established economic variable, the rate of investment.[5] It was the efficiency of investment which was the important factor, and that remained unexplained. Moreover, subsequent attempts by Jorgensen, Griliches, Denison and others either to resuscitate the rate of investment as the important explanatory variable *or* to split the unexplained residual into its component parts, failed to deal with the basic policy problem, namely what should a government do to raise the rate of growth of its economic system?[6] Clearly, there was little in standard production theory which could provide appropriate policy guidelines.

More recently, a third strand in the conventional literature has been to eschew analysis of macroeconomic systems and to confine attention to the behaviour of microeconomic units particularly with respect to inventive and innovative activity within the firm. Here emphasis is placed upon R&D expenditures as a surrogate for such activity and many attempts made to relate R&D both to microeconomic output performance (with mixed success) and to its determinants (such as expected sales, levels of present profits, market structure and the like). Sometimes also we find regression analyses carried out at international level to determine whether export performance is related to investment in innovative activity on the part of firms. A lot of this work has provided interesting insights but has nevertheless often left us with considerable problems of interpretation.[7]

We know, for example, that innovative success is not simply due to R&D expenditures but is usually a function of complex interactions within and amongst institutions. User–supplier contact and applications engineering are known also to be significant in many spheres of capital goods innovation, while government purchase decisions and the funding of scientific research in universities often affect the economic performance of the productive sector. Furthermore, there is evidence that organizational and structural features are often instrumental in determining a firm's innovative performance. In short, it is difficult to see how statistical exercises amongst a narrow range of 'economic' variables can take us very far in understanding the sheer complexity of the technical change process since what is really needed is a conceptual structure which is capable of interpreting this evidence in such a way as to suggest new policy insights and thence new empirical problems. Conventional economic theorems do not appear to be capable of doing this in the field of economic and technical change.

2.2 The Major Problems

It is useful at this stage to set out what the major problems appear to be:

(1) *Reversible time*. Within the conventional paradigm, time is treated as reversible in so far as it is assumed that a deterministic equilibrium path may be postulated for any dynamic economic system. Moreover, this path may be conceived of in terms of a small range of homogeneous variables. If the resultant model is reversed — run backwards through time — then it is the case that you will arrive back at your initial conditions. We believe that whatever innovation may be, it is not determinate through time in this sense, and to model it in this way is simply to fly in the face of reality.

(2) *Uncertainty, risk and ignorance*. Most economic theorems require the assumption of perfect knowledge of possible outcomes, otherwise it is not possible to make optimal decisions. At the very least a probability distribution under conditions of 'risk' is required. However, since innovation by definition is at best conducted under conditions of 'uncertainty' (defined in terms of knowable outcomes which are incapable of being evaluated), there is a clear conceptual hiatus. Actually, writers like Collingridge go further in stressing that conditions of ignorance (unknowability of the outcomes themselves) normally apply, in which case determinant optimizing behaviour cannot take place by any stretch of the imagination.[8]

(3) *Causation and comparative statics*. Since most economic theorems are built up using comparisons of static equilibria, they do not engage with complex causality. Dynamic theory tends to be conspicuous by its absence (or by its conceptual oversimplicity). Since innovation is a continuous process through time, there are

therefore major problems in using conventional economic theorems to model it.

(4) *Information*. Lack of information is not a problem in conventional economic theory either because complete knowledge is assumed (see item 2, above) or because all necessary information is provided by prices. Conversely, we shall argue that the search for, storage, processing and dissemination of information plays a fundamental role in determining the structure and extent of technological change.

(5) *The firm as the basic productive unit*. Although considerable work has been carried out into investigating firm behaviour, much of it does not bear on the larger theoretical questions associated with technical change. Here the profit-maximizing firm is treated as the basic unit of analysis. Similar assumptions of homogeneity are made about the household. We shall argue in contrast that units of productions are often much more diffuse and complex, and have to be treated as such for analytical purposes.

(6) *Definition of technology*. 'Technology' and 'technique' are often very loosely defined, but for modelling purposes are based upon formal production theory, as a series of factor input ratios per unit of output. We argue that such practice drastically oversimplifies and misleads. It implies, for example, a false contiguity between technology and the productive unit, and tends to play down the complex and pervasive nature of real-life technological practice. Conversely, a definition which emphasizes technology as a 'system' is much more realistic, but of course cannot be handled within the scope of conventional economic theory.

(7) *Pervasiveness of technical change*. A related point is that technological change varies widely depending upon the sector under analysis. It also impinges across industrial sectors depending upon complex upstream–downstream relations and user–supplier interactions. Because of this it is difficult to make realistic statements about relationships between innovative activity and firm performance of the kinds that are amenable to the conventional regression analysis adopted in applied economics research (e.g. 'firms that spend x per cent of sales on R&D will improve their performance by y per cent, etc.).

(8) *The flux of innovation*. Innovation does not simply 'happen' as a once-and-for-all occurrence, with 'diffusion' of this homogeneous entity throughout the economic system in response to economic signals. Although regarding it as such suits requirements for formal modelling and the generation of 'S' curves, in reality innovation is a continuous activity constantly altering the nature of both process and product through time, so much so that often the final innovative form is barely recognizable as the rough-and-ready

innovation it once was. Any metaphor that does not take such morphological considerations into account is bound to misconstrue the analysis of technical change.

(9) *Equilibrium*. Most economic theorems are developed on the basis of distance from putative equilibria, or equilibrium paths to which the economic system is assumed to gravitate. However, most of what we know about innovation and technical change appears to indicate 'open system' behaviour. Far from seeking natural equilibria, innovations appear to 'swarm' in ways which cannot be defined in terms of pre-specified equilibrium paths.

(10) *The interdisciplinary nature of technical change*. In reality there is no good reason why economics as a discipline should be able to model complex economic change. Causality is complex and involves a variety of institutional/organizational factors, including, importantly, the structure of the scientific community.

It is factors such as these which have forced many analysts to conclude that the prevailing tradition in economics, when applied to the analysis of technological change, cannot do what a science is supposed to do, namely describe reality and show how to use that reality for action. In the social sciences such action implies policy decisions which therefore cannot be informed significantly by economic analysis as conventionally practised. In fact, what appears to have occurred is that an intellectual system, or philosophical construct, designed as a pedagogical tool (or set of tools) has had altogether too heavy a burden placed upon it. A metaphoric system purporting to model interrelationships amongst a narrow range of variables at a point in time, *given* very restrictive assumptions about the world, is being asked to 'explain' complex socioeconomic change through time where economic and institutional conditions (including the very nature of commodities themselves) are constantly changing in ways which cannot be predicted — surely an impossible task, indeed almost a contradiction in terms, since only by assuming the important problems away can the theory, *qua theory*, begin to operate.

It follows, therefore, that the problem is really one of epistemology. No one is arguing against the use of analytic abstractions, since without abstractions it is virtually impossible to make sense of society. But abstractions need both to approximate to reality and to lead to productive empirical work which improves the verisimilitude of our models. To the extent that such conditions do not obtain then model-building becomes an exercise of ritual rather than science, and debate takes on a dogmatic character — orthodoxy confronting heterodoxy. We believe that this is precisely what has happened in the application of conventional economic ideas to socio-economic change.

2.3 Hierarchies and Systems

2.3.1 *Social Organization*

A useful alternative way of viewing dynamic change in economic production is as a function of the systemic behaviour of social and technological hierarchies. In contrast to the deductive, artificial constructs of conventional economic analysis, we propose as a metaphoric descriptor the organism viewed as a synthesis of lower-level cellular structures and itself part of higher-level structures. In this context the notion of the 'holon' has been suggested by Koestler as the fundamental building block for a general systems theory of a fairly ambitious kind.[9] However, our interest in it is much more limited — that is, to use it as an element in a suggested organic metaphor for technological change in economic systems — although it is necessary to explain the idea in some detail to begin with.

In Koestler's view, all cohesive social systems may be approximated as interlocking social hierarchies which are constantly in a state of flux but which at the same time show a measure of stability. The way they are able to do this is because their structure allows for 'unity in diversity' and for adaptive response within certain fundamental constraints. At each *level* of the hierarchy individual social units (or holons) obey certain rules of conduct which define and give meaning to their social role, and which permit integration within a framework laid down by a higher authority. At the same time, such units are permitted a certain room for manoeuvre with respect to exactly how they fulfil their functions, and which have therefore 'knock on' effects at lower levels of the hierarchy.

An example might be that of an army where at the apex of the hierarchy the decisions of a command HQ are formulated and from where instructions are then fed down to lower levels for implementation. Thus the decision to capture an enemy stronghold and the overall strategic battle plan are made at the apex, while the lower-level decisions, like the supply of necessary munitions and tactical procedures, are relegated to progressively subordinate levels. On any given level, however, the operant social unit has a certain degree of freedom in deciding exactly how its particular piece of the jigsaw is to be fulfilled, and this is true both with respect to particular tasks *and* for general organizational behaviour (Fig. 2.3).

Each social holon, therefore, has a certain social role assigned to it which defines its function and separates it from other holons on the same level of the hierarchy and on other levels. On a given level the differentiation is a function of the division of labour and the logic is akin to that of economic specialization. On the vertical plane the metaphor is explicitly biological (or more accurately organic) with each level

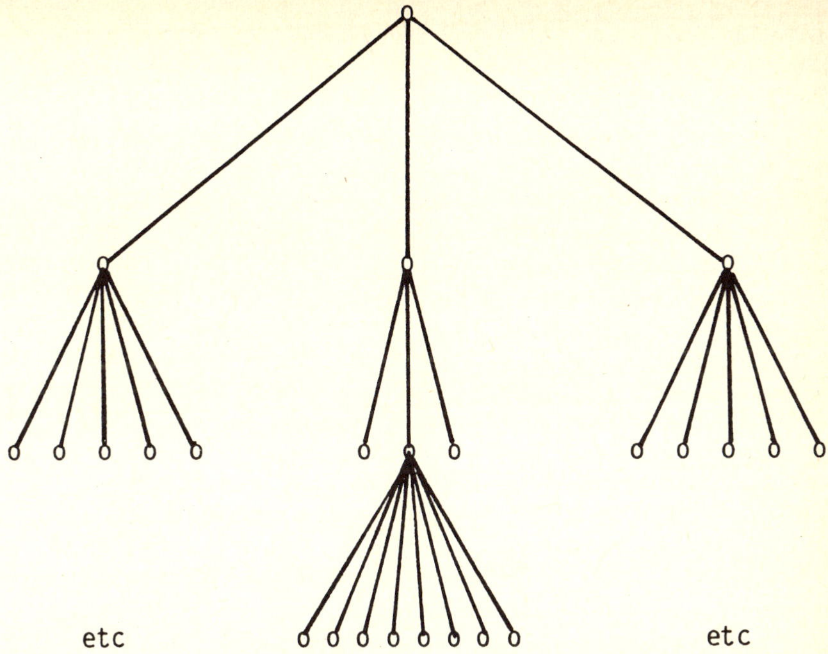

Figure 2.3 A nested hierarchy

exhibiting both an *integrative* tendency (within its own level and according to the rules laid down at higher levels) and a *self-assertive* tendency — freedom to pursue courses of action and to relate with the environment in ways which are consistent with the laid-down heuristic but which at the same time act as an outlet for dynamic drives, such as competition, aggression, creativity, protection, and so on. In Koestler's own words, 'the self-assertive tendency is the dynamic expression of the holon's wholeness, the integrative tendency the dynamic expression of its partness'.[10] Finally, social hierarchies are not independent but interlock and interrelate on a variety of 'levels' so as to create social structures which are exceedingly complex:

hierarchies do not operate in a vacuum, but interact with others. This elementary fact has given rise to much confusion. If you look at a well-kept hedge surrounding a garden like a living wall, the rich foliage of the entwined branches form horizontal networks at numerous levels. Without the individual plants there would be no network. Without the network, each plant would be isolated, and there would be no hedge. 'Arborisation' and 'reticulation' (net-formation) are complementary principles in the architecture of organisms and societies. Thus the circulatory system controlled by the heart and the respiratory system controlled by the lungs function as quasi-autonomous, self-regulating hierarchies, but they interact on various levels. In the subject-catalogues in our libraries the branches are entwined through cross-references. In cognitive hierarchies — universes of discourse — arborisation is reflected in the 'vertical' denotation (classification) of concepts, reticulation in their 'horizontal' connotations in associative nets.[11]

How, then, can we transcribed this general metaphor into the economic analysis of technological change? The obvious place to start is to apply the tree formulation to an economic system E_1 which itself is one of a number (n) of economic systems within the world economy $E_2, E_3, \ldots, E_n$.[12] E_1 is governed by a set of rules (laws, customs, etc.) which lay the ground-plan for the various sectors which go to make it up ($S_1, \ldots S_m$). In turn each sector, say industry, may be split up into a variety of industrial 'types' (electronics, textiles, food, etc.) which themselves consist of a range of 'firms' defined as legal entities in *economic space* whose function it is to undertake the productive act ($F_1, \ldots, F_j$). Again each firm is itself made up of various components, which we may classify as 'divisions' ($D_1, \ldots, D_k$) for want of a better expression, each of which has a degree of autonomy within some overall corporate policy laid down at the centre. Such autonomy is often used to influence corporate policy, but in terms of our schema it is best to regard the production process as fixed.

For any *given* product, then, a representative firm F_1 may be viewed as behaving within the constraints laid down by its industry of primary relevance I_1 which involves (1) legal constraints (e.g. law pertaining to firm behaviour as laid down by government), (2) customary constraints (informal sanctions laid down by tradition), (3) technological constraints (those relating to the ruling technological system in vogue) and (4) economic constraints (e.g. market structure). What economic analysis conventionally does is to describe a set of interrelationships under these circumstances with F_1 attempting to maximize (or optimize) some objectives function in relation to a limited range of variables.

In reality, of course, contextual conditions are not invariant. F_1 is constantly aware of threats coming from rivals ($F_2, \ldots, F_j$) any or all of whom may be in a position to capture its markets (or a share of its markets) through a variety of courses of action (of which technological change represents a very important category but not the only one). This being the case, F_1 will normally take care to alter its own environment in such a way as to reduce the threat to itself, through such mechanisms as advertising, investment in R&D, control over factor supplies, taking over rivals, and so on. Where all possible F's are behaving similarly — at least within the overall framework provided by I_1, we have a situation of constant flux in which the environment is constantly changing in unpredictable ways. All that F_1 can reasonably do is to make sure that it remains abreast with what is happening and maintains the capacity to react quickly if things go wrong. Life is inherently and unavoidably uncertain. Determinate outcomes are certainly not the order of the day in a holarchic system which has a high degree of vulnerability like this one. Conversely, everything revolves around reducing the corporate threat.

2.3.2. *Phylogeny and Technological Trajectory*

Where, then, does technology fit into this story? Clearly, it is a central vehicle for operant action on the part of the firm. Expenditure upon R&D creates the possibilities for competitive growth through the development of new products and processes within the established technological paradigm. At the same time it provides the firm with the capacity to respond to unexpected competitive threats. A useful analogy might be made with the concepts of *ontogeny* (the process by which the individual develops) and *phylogeny* (the process by which the species develops). The latter has an analogue with the 'technological trajectory' (the path along which a given technological system moves), while the former has an analogue with a given innovation, gradually maturing until it arrives at the stage of a fully fledged mature product.[13] Let us explore these analogies a little further.

According to Koestler, evolution is not a function of chance — random mutations mediated by environmental selection — but should rather be regarded as *purposive* with a certain chance element thrown in. What is purposive is partly a function of a genetic past encoded within the biochemical structure of the embryonic cell but is also partly a function of how far the species has evolved in terms of its own specialization. The history of zoology is one in which certain species come up against evolutionary 'dead ends'; they are regressive, while others are progressive. Julian Huxley has put it as follows:

> The course followed by evolution appears to have been broadly as follows. From a generalized early type, various lines radiate out, exploiting the environment in various ways. Some of these comparatively soon reach a limit to their evolution, at least as regards major alteration. Thereafter they are limited to minor changes such as the formation of new genera and species. Others, on the other hand, are so constructed that they can continue their career, generating new types which are successful in the struggle for existence because of their greater control over the environment and their greater independence of it. Such changes are legitimately called 'progressive'. The new type repeats the process. It radiates out into a number of lines, each specializing in a particular direction. The great majority of these come up against dead ends and can advance no further: specialization is one-sided progress, and after a longer or shorter time, reaches a biomechanical limit . . ..
>
> Sometimes all the branches of a given stock have come up against their limit, and then either have become extinct or have persisted without major change. This happened, for instance, to the echinoderms, which with their sea-urchins, starfish, brittle-stars, sea-lilies, sea cucumbers, and other types now extinct had

pushed the life that was in them into a series of blind alleys: they have not advanced for perhaps a hundred million years, nor have they given rise to other major types.

In other cases, all but one or two of the lines suffer this fate, while the rest repeat the process. All reptilian lines were blind alleys save two — one which was transformed into the birds, and another which became the mammals. Of the bird stock, all lines came to a dead end; of the mammals, all but one — the one which became man.[14]

Koestler then goes further, arguing that the *mechanism* of evolutionary change acts through paedomorphosis (Garstang 1922) — that is, by evolution retracing its steps, as it were, along the path which led to the dead end, and making a fresh start in a new more promising direction. This occurs through a process named *neoteny* — the speeding-up of sexual maturation relative to the development of the rest of the body such that a 'race may become rejuvenated by pushing the adult stage of its individuals off from the end of their ontogenies . . . [with the result that it] may then radiate out in all directions . . . until racial senescence sets in again (gerontomorphosis)'.[15] In this way evolutionary innovation occurs through a process of returning to first principles, of drawing back so as to set off in a new direction — 'reculer pour mieux sauter'. But this is not a return to a blank sheet of paper since the genetic basis of the species will often remain the same in many respects. Conversely, new development channels are explored on the basis of a given genetic 'heuristic', the successful one becoming established through environmental selection.

2.3.3. *From Synchronic to Diachronic Structures*

We have now explicitly introduced a dynamic flavour to our metaphor. Let us now explore in some more detail how these ideas might describe the process of technological change. At first blush it might appear that a given technological 'system' or 'family' might act as a phenotypic stereotype providing the basis for similar evolutionary development. Thus transistor technology provided the basis for radically new and cheaper products throughout the 1950s and 1960s using the molecular structure of certain chemical elements as a channel for electronic signals which was markedly superior in many economic *and* technical respects to the older valve-based technology, which had gradually become increasingly clumsy and costly when incorporated in sequential forms of production. In terms of its 'productive evolution', valve technology had reached a dead end and the techno-economic response was to retrace the technology to first principles, as it were, and to strike off in a new direction.

In this case the basic phenotype — the set of scientific and technological principles which underlie the conversion of electrical power to artefacts which provide a range of services to the consumer — remained substantially the same. But the use of the transistor provided a means of reducing unit costs, size and bulkiness, *and* of improving the applicability of these artefacts to further areas of economic production. Of course, this new technological system required articulation. Mistakes were made, blind alleys gone down and firms went out of business; but nevertheless, a new 'trajectory' was evolved which turned out to be very successful indeed. A similar story might easily be told about the integrated circuit and about microprocessor technology.

What we have, then, is a view of technological change which operates according to an evolutionary pattern which is *not random*. There are clear 'genetic links' between successive technological systems which provide an important element of innovative coherence through time. The role of entrepreneurship becomes one of 'guiding' or 'channelling' this trajectory in productive ways subject to the exigencies of an environment which is unpredictable, much in the same way as the embryonic cells have to constantly test out their biochemical environment in order to determine whether or not they are in the correct location of their developmental hierarchy. To put things differently, technological development is a function of fixed rules and flexible strategies. Entrepreneurial activity applies to the latter and not to the former. Entrepreneurial *success* is determined at least in part by how well the economic unit moves along the trajectory.

Notice that we have now changed the metaphoric description to give organic properties not only to the economic organization as a productive category but also to the ruling technology itself. And although this may appear to smack of determinism, in reality it is arguably quite a good description of what often obtains in fact. Thus Atkinson and Stiglitz, for example, point out that for any industrial grouping the range of efficient techniques (in terms of relative factor intensity per unit of output) is often very small, sometimes reaching the limit of one technological system which rules at any point of time.[16] And we shall see in the following chapters that much modern research treats the technological 'paradigm' or 'system' as a basic growth heuristic. For all firms in an industry at any point in time, it provides the 'focus' for R&D, in effect telling engineers and designers how to carry out their innovative activities in the most productive way.

In a somewhat related fashion, McKelvey has postulated that viewing organizations (firms) as organisms, their capacity to adapt and change is determined very much by their own internal competences (or 'comps') which play a role akin to DNA in molecular biology and genetics[17] (see also Nelson and Winter's 'routines').[18] Since such competences are very strongly influenced by technological skills and other knowledge, technological factors play a very important role in determining how firms adapt to their environment through time. And notice that such dynamic change is Lamarckian rather than Darwinian in the sense that firms can create new genetic material on the basis of past learning and in response to expected *future* environments, thus changing the basis of their own behaviour and, by extension, the environment of other firms. Burton Klein has argued that it is largely through this sort of technological mechanism that firms 'internalize risk' and bring about their own, and their industry's, economic growth.[19]

For these reasons, therefore, it seems quite legitimate to model organically not only the behavioural unit (the firm) but also the technology itself. Indeed, from a policy perspective there are distinct advantages in so doing since, as we shall argue, it widens the range of policy options, and may lead to better decision-making. There is evidence from Japan that this is precisely what has taken place in the post-war period, with great success; policy-makers taking decisions that are based as much on technological variables (the likelihood of investments in given technologies succeeding) as they are on conventional economic variables.[20] Having made this point, however, let us now return to the firm as the behavioural unit, recognizing that technological development does not occur in a vacuum but as a result of the interplay of social and technical forces with, in the case of economic production, an important 'market' element.

2.3.4. *The Firm and Industry as Social Units of Analysis*

The 'fixed rules' for the firm are first of all 'legal'. Second, they are 'behavioural' — the firm's action must conform in definable ways to the dictates of its ownership structure and internal managerial hierarchy. Third, they are 'technological'. Since economic production is a matter of converting resources into saleable goods using a 'technology' which in some sense defines the process of conversion, most firms will be operating within a relatively narrow systemic range which itself will relate to certain product types and will be very much a function of accumulated skills inherited from the past.

But how firm-specific are these 'rules'? Given the apparently high degree of variation in behavioural, structural and technological factors, is it ever possible to define given 'phenotypes' of firm which will respond in predictable ways to competitive forces? For the opposite side of the coin is represented by the flexible strategies which allow firms the freedom to pursue their goals in autonomous ways, and at first blush the degree of autonomy seems very wide indeed — certainly far wider than that permitted to the liver tissue cell seeking its natural habitat amongst its fellows. The answer to this question is that we simply do not know. Pavitt's 'taxonomy' of firms, broadly according to crude industrial phenotype, is an attempt to be a litle more systematic about the analysis of innovation,[21] but the quality of his data does not enable more than very general statements to be made.

Part of the problem lies in how the firm itself has been defined, since although it is the conventional unit of production, its analytical use is often confused because it is defined in terms of distribution rather than production, that is as a legal and financial entity in economic space. Kay has suggested that for purposes of production analysis it may be more suitable to regard the firm as a bundle of purchased resources transforming these into other resources which are then disposed of in the market

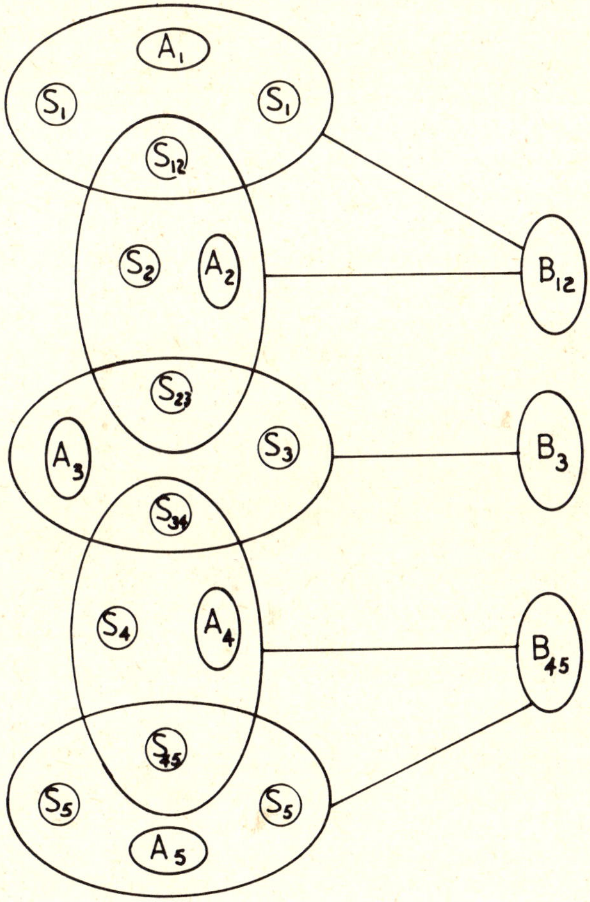

Notes: Subscripts refer to relevant model of car.
A = Assembly firms
B = Financial firms
C = Supply firms

Figure 2.4 Shifting forms of economic organization in the car industry

place.[22] Defined in this more general way it becomes rather less important how the input resources are legally bounded. A number of different solutions are clearly possible depending upon a rationality of productive efficiency. For example, in the Japanese automobile industry the 'productive unit' for any given car is a complicated arrangement of assembler, satellite component makers and sources of finance, but any or all of these may shift arrangements where producing another car is involved.[23] Indeed, there is now considerable evidence of technical changes occurring alongside shifting boundaries through merger, joint venture, subcontracting and other organizational devices across a wide range of modern industry production, as firms vie with each other to attain competitive advantage (Fig. 2.4).

A second and related point lies in the heterogeneity of organizations. Traditionally, industries have been classified in terms of *type of commodity* produced, to which the technological basis of production is not at all congruent. Thus within a given industry, firms may be large or small; they may vary widely in terms of their internal organization; they may be multi-product or single-product; they may be technological leaders or followers; they may appropriate their technologies from other firms or they may create technologies largely for themselves. In short, the attempt to *classify* by industrial phenotype so as to provide a more secure basis for policy analysis is fraught with complexity and will no doubt require the collection of richer data.

However, having made this point, it is at least clear that there *are* differences. Possibilities for technological change are not independent of the type of firm involved, and hence the purely economistic approach breaks down. For example, from a policy perspective it is no longer advisable to await 'entrepreneurs' who will generate innovations simply through the force of their personalities, since the context within which they are able to operate will vary widely, as we have seen. Similarly in industries closely related to a science base, the degree to which firms are receptive to extramural work will often relate as much to organizational factors as to the entrepreneurial quality of senior staff. Hence, for example, R&D work accompanied by close links with the scientific system will often be a necessary determinant of how successfully entrepreneurs will be able to innovate and commercialize new ideas. A different but equally important example might well relate to patterns of public purchase on the part of large institutions like defence departments of state.[24]

2.4 Some Concluding Points

We began this chapter by arguing that conventional formal treatments of technological and economic change suffer from a number of weaknesses which are really epistemological. Existing economic theory does not appear to provide a realistic account of the process of complex technological change, according to the epistemological criteria set out in our opening chapter. Because of this, it cannot provide an efficient guide to public policy. The second half of the chapter set out a different way of viewing dynamic change in economic production, namely, in terms of the systemic behaviour of social and technological hierarchies. Although at this stage these ideas are speculative, nevertheless we believe that they show promise of being capable of synthesis into a more general theory of economic change which satisfies our epistemological criteria. We shall attempt to do this in Chapters 4 and 5. Meanwhile, in the following chapter we shall show that such ideas are consistent with the evolutionary tradition in economic theory, particularly in its Schumpeterian perspective. By grafting recent developments in Schumpeterian analysis to general systems theory it may well be possible to integrate technological change as a socioeconomic process more convincingly with the analysis of economic events.

Notes and References

1. R. Harrod (1939), 'An Essay in Dynamic Theory', *Economic Journal,* **49**: 14–33.
2. See A.K. Sen (ed.) (1970), *Growth Economics* (Harmondsworth: Penguin), pp. 9–39 for a useful summary account of Harrod's treatment.
3. Harrod introduces a labour force and technical change later in his model to describe the 'natural' rate of growth.
4. See R. Solow (1957), 'Technical Change and the Aggregate Production Function', *Review of Economics and Statistics*, August, pp. 312–20.
5. See M. Abramovitz (1962), 'Economic Growth in the United States', *American Economic Review,* **52**: 762–82; S. Fabricant (1959), 'Basic Facts on Productivity Change', Occasional Paper 63, National Bureau of Economic Research, New York; B. Massell (1961), 'A Disaggregated View of Technical Change', *Journal of Political Economy,* **69**: 547–57.
6. See E. Denison (1962), *The Sources of Economic Growth in the US and the Alternatives Before Us*, Supp. Paper 13, (New York: Committee for Economic Development); D. Jorgenson and Z. Griliches (1967), 'The Explanation of Productivity Change', *Review of Economic Studies*, **34**: 249–83.
7. A very good example of this genre is M. Kamien and N. Schwarz (1982), *Market Structure and Innovation* (Cambridge: Cambridge University Press).
8. See, for example, D. Collingridge (1980), *The Social Control of Technology* (Oxford: Oxford University Press). Collingridge argues that it is essential to build a capacity to correct for future mishaps into large projects since you can never anticipate them *ex ante*.
9. A. Koestler (1970), *The Ghost in the Machine* (London: Pan Books), pp. 62–76. See also A. Koestler (1982), *Bricks to Babel* (London: Picador), Chs 36–41, for a useful summary discussion of Koestler's ideas on the intellectual sterility of behaviourism in psychology, which also have a

wider social significance. We realize that Koestler's (Lamarckian) views are controversial within biology. However, they do appear to have direct relevance to our own purposes here.

10. Koestler, *The Ghost in the Machine*, op. cit. p. 74.
11. Koestler, *Bricks to Babel*, op. cit., p. 463.
12. For purposes of exposition we excluded multinational firms. Thus our hierarchical network describes for all countries separately (a) a division of labour, (b) a categorization of output and (c) a loose power structure.
13. Thus we shall argue in Chapter 5 that innovations do not suddenly appear at a point in time and thence diffuse unchanged throughout the economic system, as they are described in much of the diffusion literature. On the contrary, innovations have their own morphology. Like any organisms they grow, develop and change their structure. They do not diffuse. They become!
14. J. Huxley (1964), *Man in the Modern World* (New York), pp. 12–13, cited in Koestler, *The Ghost in the Machine*, op. cit., p. 190. It should be noted, however, that we do not subscribe to Huxley's anthropomorphism, nor necessarily to his view of evolution.
15. Koestler, ibid., p. 193. Here he refers to W. Garstang (1922), 'The Theory of Recapitulation: A Critical Restatement of the Biogenetic Law', *Journal of the Linnean Society, London, Zoology,* **35** (81).
16. A. Atkinson and J. Stiglitz (1969), 'A New View of Technological Change', *Economic Journal* 79: 573–8.
17. B. McKelvey (1982), *Organizational Systematics* (London: University of California Press), pp. 243–6.
18. R. Nelson and S. Winter (1982), *An Evolutionary Theory of Economic Change* (Cambridge: Harvard University Press).
19. See B.H. Klein (1977) *Dynamic Economics*. (Cambridge, Mass.: Harvard University Press). Klein argues also that in order to bring about technical change, governments must create conditions appropriate to this type of behaviour.
20. See G.C. Allen (1981), 'Industrial Policy and Innovation in Japan', in C. Carter (ed.), *Industrial Policy and Innovation* (London: Heinemann), pp. 68–87.
21. K. Pavitt (1983), *Patterns of Technical Change: Evidence, Theory and Policy Implications*, Papers in Science, Technology and Public Policy, SPRU, University of Sussex (No. 3).
22. N. Kay (1982), *The Evolving Firm* (London: Macmillan), see Chs 3–5. See also Ch. 2 for an interesting critique of conventional neoclassical economics, particularly with respect to the treatment of time and aggregation.
23. See, for example, D.T. Jones (1985), *A Revolution in Automobile Manufacturing? Technological Change in a Mature Industry*, Papers in Science, Technology and Public Policy, SPRU, University of Sussex (No. 9).
24. See M. Fransman (ed.) (1986), *Machinery in Economic Development* (London: Macmillan).

Chapter 3

Evolutionary Approaches in Conventional Economics

This chapter undertakes a critical review of the development of evolutionary notions in traditional economics. It will show that the history of economic thought has been marked by persistent efforts to graft evolutionary notions on to traditional views. However, the efforts to break away from the traditional world-view have been unsuccessful. This tendency is clear in Adam Smith, Marx and Marshall and is also manifested in the emerging neo-Schumpeterian school.

3.1 Classical Antecedents: From Smith to Marshall

Evolutionary views of socioeconomic development in general, and technological change in particular, are not a recent academic enterprise. Their antecedents are to be seen in the work of the classical economists. For example, Darwin's work was inspired by reading Malthus's *Essay* on human population, and according to Schumpeter, 'the terms static and dynamic were . . . introduced into economics by John Stuart Mill. Mill probably heard them from Comte, who, in turn tells us that he borrowed them from the zoologist de Brainville'.[1]

Darwin's *Origin of the Species* consolidated a long tradition of evolutionary thought. But the application of Darwin's theory to economic development was impeded by three main factors. First, the limited knowledge on evolution and human behaviour opened the way to arguments by analogy; such arguments are often fallacious. Second, social change was not obviously gradualist, and therefore the theory was not particularly consistent with the observations of social historians (especially of the Marxists). Third, the rules of the hard sciences (especially Newtonian physics) combined with the Cartesian philosophy of nature as automata and the Baconian appeal to empirical rigour, had become the legitimate view of reality. And economics readily adopted this mechanistic world-view.

Classical economists did not know as much as we do today about evolutionary concepts.[2] However, they recognized the dichotomy of static and dynamic systems. But this recognition was influenced more by mechanical dynamics than by organic evolution. It is in this context that the dynamics of Mill and Smith can be understood. Much of Smith's use of the terms 'equilibrium', 'laws of motion' and 'scientific objectivity' are drawn from Newtonian physics. The economic sphere was a microcosm of the celestial arena; forces of supply and demand, guided by the invisible hand, would generate a near-instantaneous balance, as market forces gravitated in the right direction. The ideal social welfare balance, like that of Newtonian celestial objects, could be realized through some form of Pareto optimality. And, of course, Ptolemy lives through the pages of mainstream economics — the individual was, and still is, at the centre of the economic universe.

Smith was obviously not at home with biological metaphors. He stressed that, unlike animals, human beings had specific attributes which enabled the division of labour to emerge — the ability to truck, barter and exchange. These abilities could be brought into a common stock 'where every man may purchase whatever part of the produce of the other man's talent he has occasion for'.[3] But not for animals: 'The strength of the mastiff is not . . . supported by either the swiftness of the greyhound, or by the sagacity of the spaniel, or by the docility of the shepherd's dog. The effects of those different geniuses and talents . . . cannot be brought into a common stock, and do not . . . contribute to the better accommodation and conveniency of the species.'[4]

Darwin's influence on economic thought is particularly interesting in the context of the development of Marx's concept of technological change. When Marx first read Darwin's *Origin* in 1860, he wrote to Engels that 'although it is developed in the crude English style, this is the book which contains the basis in natural history for our view'.[5] But later, Darwin and his followers became victims of Marx's hostility. There are two main reasons for this. First, the Malthusian content of the theory was inconsistent with Marx's own ideological position. He saw Malthusianism as an apologia for the establishment and Engels asserted that Darwinism was more scientific without its Malthusian content. Second, Marx and Engels contended that their conception of history as a series of class struggles was much richer in content than the 'weakly distinguished phrases of the struggle for existence'.[6] Marx therefore rejected the application of Darwinian views to socioeconomic evolution, preferring a Hegelian approach. However, he adapted Darwinian concepts to his analysis of technological change.[7]

His view of socioeconomic evolution involved the transition from one mode of production to another. These transitions resulted from internal antagonisms or conflicts which resolved themselves in a new synthesis where the ultimate transformation (e.g. from feudalism to capitalism) was seen as a dialectical leap. This is clearly inconsistent with Darwin's evolutionary gradualism, though not with modern notions of punctuated evolution. Indeed, Marx was committed to the overthrow of the political system and therefore any appeal to gradualism was not welcome. And Darwin was equally uninterested in his revolutionary ideas.[8] But despite this hostility towards Darwinian concepts, Marx consistently used biological or organic metaphors in his analysis of socioeconomic transition in general and technological change in particular. Technology evolves from crude designs to more refined manufacturing systems that benefit from scientific disciplines:

The power loom was at first made . . . of wood; in its improved modern form it is made of iron . . . It is only after considerable development of the sciences of mechanics, and an accumulation of practical experience that the form of a machine becomes settled entirely in accordance with mechanical principles, and emancipated from the traditional form of the tool from which it emerged.[9]

This evolution occurs in a social and economic environment. Both the technology and the environment influence each other:

Social relations are closely bound up with productive forces. In acquiring new productive forces men change their mode of production; and in changing their mode of production, in changing the way of earning their living, they change all their social relations. The handmill gives society with the feudal lord; the steam mill, society with the industrial capitalist.[10]

In this process, the role of individuals adds little to the broader pattern of evolution: 'A critical study of technology would show how little any of the inventions of the eighteenth century are the work of a single individual.'[11] Marx equates the development of technology with that of organs in species:

Darwin has directed attention to the history of natural technology, i.e. the formation of the organs of plants and animals which serve as the instruments of production for sustaining their life. Does not the history of the productive organs of man in society, or organs that are the material basis of every particular organisation, deserve equal attention?[12]

His view of technological change is akin to the evolution of species in a given ecosystem and their mutual transformations.

As simple tools evolve, they are adapted to the requirements of particular applications and used by specific workers:

In Birmingham alone 500 varieties of hammer are produced, and not only is each one adapted to a particular process, but several varieties often serve exclusively for the different operations in the same process. The manufacturing period simplifies, improves and multiplies the implements of labour by adapting them to the exclusive and specific functions of each kind of worker.[13]

This function differentiation, according to Marx, creates a combination of simple instruments that forms one of the material conditions for the existence of machinery. Here we see evolutionary theory applied to technical change. But where does technical change come from? Marx himself reveals the source. Darwin's law of variation:

As long as the same part has to perform diversified work, we can perhaps see why it should remain variable, that is, why natural selection should not have preserved or rejected each little deviation of form so carefully as when the part has to serve for some one special purpose. In the same way that a knife which has to cut all sorts of things may be of almost any shape; whilst a tool for some particular purpose must be of some particular shape.[14]

Marx recognized that technical evolution continued long after the machinery had been installed, a fact that underscores the evolutionary nature of technological progress. As noted elsewhere, he paid particular attention to the role of working experience, or the accumulation of disembodied technical change. But he also anticipated modern studies of technical change in the capital goods sector by pointing to plant-level technical improvements: 'When machinery is first introduced . . . new methods of reproducing it more cheaply follow blow by blow, and so do improvements which relate not only to individual parts and details of the machine, but also to its whole construction.'[15] He was able to blend Darwin's notions of random mutation with Hegelian dialectics to provide a methodological analysis of technical change that is unparalleled among classical thinkers. Studies which have ignored this fact have missed the vital interactions and feedbacks between technology and social change and have erroneously viewed Marx as a technological determinist. These studies have also alluded to some imagined ambiguity in Marx's analysis of technological change. The perceived ambiguity is a result of confusing the role and position of technology in the various transitional stages along the path of socioeconomic evolution.[16]

The main problem with Marx is that he recognized the significance of evolutionary factors but returned to a classical Newtonian world-view, especially in his prognosis for future social systems. In Marx's world, the socioeconomic system tends to move from moments of extreme fluctuations, of class struggles, towards social equilibria governed by socialist principles — classless societies in which the sources of fluctuations and struggle are eliminated. Like Newton's cosmology, society settles into an equilibrium, as the underlying social laws that Marx sought to lay bare, prevail over individual action. A similar type of ambivalence is also manifested by Marshall.[17]

For Marshall, the 'Mecca of economics lies in economic biology rather than economic dynamics'.[18] He argued that economics was like biology because they both dealt with 'a matter, of which the inner nature and constitution, as well as the outer form, are constantly changing'.[19] For Marshall, the subject-matter was 'human beings who are impelled, for good or for evil, to change and progress'.[20] However, although he advocated the use of biological concepts, his own work paid only token allegiance to the approach. Much of his *Principles of Economics* is non-evolutionary except for the sections which deal with industrial organization and the division of labour where he draws on the concepts of survival of the fittest and the physiological view of human behaviour. He sees large-scale industries as trees of the forest which grow, compete for light and water, lose vitality, grow old and die; except for 'vast joint-stock companies, which often stagnate, and do not readily die'.[21]

Marshall's evolutionary views also differed from Marx's in terms of their 'gradualist' content. In Marx we find cumulative transition mediated through class antagonism which reaches a critical moment and makes a dialectical leap, a revolutionary overthrow of one class by another. In contrast, Marshall adopts Darwinian gradualism: 'Economic evolution is gradual. Its progress is sometimes arrested or reversed by political catastrophies: but its forward movements are never sudden'.[22] Nevertheless, both Marx and Marshall agree that the contributions of individuals add only little to the cumulative changes which have been in the making long before them. Thus:

> an inventor, or an organizer, or a financial genius may seem to have modified the economic structure of a people almost at a stroke; yet the part of his influence which has not been merely superficial and transitory, is found on inquiry to have done little more than bring to a head a broad constructive movement which has long been in preparation.[23]

Marshall's biological metaphors led him to visualize some form of equilibrium in the growth of firms. He states that 'a business firm grows and attains greater strength, and afterwards perhaps stagnates and decays; and at the turning point there is a balancing or equilibrium of the forces of life and decay'.[24] But although such balances appear dynamic, Marshall did not abandon the Cartesian-Newtonian world-view. For a volume of the foundations of economics must 'give a relatively large place to mechanical analogies'.[25] These fragmentary statistical hypotheses were seen as a temporary feature in his work. However, a decade later, he offered an economic methodology under which mechanical analogies would be used in the early stages of economic development and biological explanations take over in later stages:

> There is a fairly close analogy between the early stages of economic reasoning and the devices of physical statics . . . I think that in the later stages of economics better analogies are to be got from biology rather than from physics; and, consequently, that economic reasoning should start on methods analogous with those of physical statics, and should gradually become more biological in tone.[26]

Marshall's insistence on mechanical analogies reflects the influence of the Cartesian-Newtonian appeal to mathematical rigour. Mathematics was only useful to economics if it could throw 'a bright light on some small part of the great economic movement rather than at representing its endless complexities'.[27] As a result, the subject-matter would have to be reduced to entities that validate the use of mathematics, namely steady-state units. Marshall's tone was thus clearly Newtonian in his view of the 'stationary state'. Like celestial bodies, parts change while the whole remains stationary: individuals grow old and die while the population remains the same; grain prices fluctuate with every harvest but the average value of the grain remains stable.

The growing command of mankind over nature changes the character and magnitude of economic and social forces. To Marshall this is analogous with Newtonian mechanics: 'Our planetary system happens . . . to be a stable equilibrium; but a little change in circumstance might make it unstable, might for instance, after a time cause one of the planets to shoot away from the sun in a very long ellipse, and another to fall into it.'[28] And the law of supply and demand also takes on at an early stage a clear Newtonian perspective: 'In the earlier stages of economics, we think of demand and supply as crude forces pressing against one another, and tending towards a mechanical equilibrium; but in the later stages, the balance or equilibrium is conceived not as between crude mechanical forces, but as between the organic forces of life and decay.'[29]

Thus Marshall manifests a commitment to the mechanical thinking of the day despite his appeal to biological analogies. All life is reducible to matter, the hard stuff that all things are supposedly made of. These could be understood through mechanical analogies. At the same time, however, since society is not an ordinary combination of inanimate material, we have to revert to an organic view of economic activity. This ambivalence is reflected in his analysis of competition, leading to some confusion over perfect and imperfect competition. His approach was later reorientated by the neoclassical school, especially with the formulations of monopolistic competition and imperfect competition.[30]

By the late nineteenth century it is clear that economics was being progressively purged of its organic content, prompting Veblen to ask, 'Why is Economics not an Evolutionary Science?'[31] There are several answers, some which have been alluded to above. First, biology was still embryonic at the time economics was consolidating itself. Darwin came to the scene a century after Adam Smith, and development in the biological sciences was partly retarded by the emphasis on classification rather than on measurement and analysis. But even more important were the efforts made in the eighteenth and nineteenth centuries to adopt the Cartesian-Newtonian world-view and its Baconian methodology to economic analysis.

This became the tradition that economists sought to belong to — the tradition of hard sciences, of irreducible and stubborn facts. The post-Smithian economics relied increasingly on particular forms of abstraction or units of analysis, and the best mathematical minds endeavoured to make the discipline an exact science. This process reached a significant peak with the publication in 1874 of Leon Walras' *Elements of Pure Economics*, whose general equilibrium theory had strong mechanical underpinnings. He visualized 'the pure theory of economics or the theory of exchange and value in exchange' simply as a 'physico-mathematical science like mechanics or hydrodynamics'.[32] The need to make economics an exact science was a strong drive during the period. Walras says that 'the establishment . . . of economics as an exact science is no longer in our hands and need not concern us. It is . . . perfectly clear that economics, like astronomy and mechanics, is both an empirical and rational science'.[33] He complained that France produced mathematicians with no knowledge of economics and cultivated men of letters devoid of any notion of mathematics. This, in his view, led to the flourishing of bad mathematicians and bad pure economists. He said the twentieth century would feel the need to entrust the social sciences to men of general culture initiated to inductive and deductive thinking and who are familiar with reason and experience: 'The mathematical economics will rank with mathematical science of astronomy and mechanics; and in that way justice will have been done to our work.'[34]

But the very discipline that set the pace for economics started changing its course in the last century. The attack on Newtonian physics started with the theory of electrodynamics, which replaced the concept of force with that of force-fields. The process was later complemented by the theories of relativity and quantum physics, and with the acceptance of these theories, Newton started to lose his grip on the natural sciences. In the subatomic world there are no irreducible and stubborn facts but relationships, no isolated entities but systems. It can be therefore argued that conventional economics was well ahead of the other social sciences, but in a misleading direction; even the pace-setter, physics, had changed course. Georgescu-Roegen puts it as follows:

> by the time Jevons and Walras began laying the cornerstones of modern economics, a spectacular revolution in physics had already brought down the mechanistic dogma both in the natural sciences and in philosophy. And the curious fact is that none of the architects of 'the mechanics of utility and self-interest' and even none of the latter-day model builders seem to have been aware at any time of this downfall.[35]

No heed was paid to Veblen's argument that if 'economics is to follow the lead or the analogy of the other sciences . . . the way is plain so far as the general direction in which the move will be made'[36] (that is, the evolutionary route). Instead, evolutionary concepts in the post-Marshallian period sought refuge in other theoretical camps and co-existed with Cartesian-Newtonian frameworks.

3.2 The Post-Marshallian Era

Although post-Marshallian economic thought was dominated by mechanistic notions, efforts were made to inject some dynamic elements into its content. One of these areas was market competition. Competition was viewed in conventional economics as analogous with Newtonian motions where resources 'gravitated' towards their most optimal pattern of utilization and prices were 'forced' to the lowest possible levels which could be sustained over the long run. Competition therefore guaranteed order and stability in the market just as gravitation did among Newtonian bodies.[37] However, this view did not adequately account for the competitive behaviour of firms. Economic theory was bedevilled by the paradoxical concepts of monopoly and perfect competition: 'both are situations in which the possibility of any competitive behaviour has been ruled out by definition'.[38]

Chamberlin attempted to reorientate economic theory by introducing dynamic concepts. Although he remained in the orthodox economic mainstream, his work carried elements of evolutionary thinking. His analysis sought to synthesize monopoly and competition in a way that is akin to chemical processes in so far as chemical synthesis requires continuous movement and change in which dynamic and static characteristics may be clearly distinguished.[39] Moreover, the dominant role of continuous product differentiation and the wide range of product possibilities suggests an implicit evolutionary content.

Although product variation plays a significant role in Chamberlin's model, it is not clear whether technology was to be held constant or not. But since he stressed product variation, it is reasonable to assume that innovation would play a significant role. Indeed, he subsequently admitted that an entrepreneur would need to innovate to break away from the established order of things: 'The appearance on the market of any new product creates pressure in some degree on the markets for others, and when products are variable and determined by profit maximization some of this pressure is bound to be exerted on quality in order to maintain prices which people can afford to pay.'[40] Technical change therefore continues to unfold as firms adjust to emerging competitive conditions in the market environment.

Despite these dynamic aspects, Chamberlin did not seek to recast his theory of competition on an explicit evolutionary forge. This was left to Alchian, who sought to replace the notion of profit maximization with the biological concept of natural selection: 'The suggested approach embodies the principles of biological evolution and natural selection by interpreting the economic system as an adaptive mechanism which chooses among exploratory actions generated by the pursuit of "success" or "profit".'[41] Competitive behaviour among firms, he argued, was not determined by the motive of profit maximization, but by 'adaptive, imitative, and trial-and-error behaviour in search for profits'.[42] Success was largely influenced and reinforced by previous success, not motivation. The fact that successful firms were still in the market was not a result of their profit-maximizing behaviour but an outcome of the fact that a whole lot of other firms had been selected out. The situation is clearly Darwinian: 'Those who realize *positive profits* are the survivors; those who suffer losses disappear'.[43] Alchian rejects the relative importance of Schumpeter's entrepreneur because even in a world of fools there would still be profits.

Although Alchian gives a comprehensive assessment of the behaviour of firms in a competitive environment, he does not offer a convincing account of the role of technical change in the process of natural selection. Part of the problem results from excessive emphasis on imitative behaviour to which much of innovation is attributed: 'Adapting behavior via imitation and venturesome innovation enlarges the model. Imperfect imitators provide opportunity for innovation, and the survival criterion of the economy determines the successful, possibly because imperfect, imitators.'[44] But those who pioneer in innovating do so in response to changing market conditions: 'Innovation is provided also by conscious wilful action, whatever the ultimate motivation may be, since drastic action is motivated by the hope of greater success as well as the desire to avoid impending failure.'[45] This view ignores conditions under which technical change becomes a critical tool for competition in so far as it sets in motion the conditions which call for its constant improvement. As in neoclassical approaches, Alchian treats technical change as exogenous to economic evolution. It is merely brought into play for purposes of adaptation to the changing market environment but does not necessarily shape those conditions. Alchian did not seek to reframe all economic theory into an evolutionary outlook. He restricted his analysis to firm behaviour by showing the irrelevance of the notion of profit maximization.

Boulding, on the other hand, attempted to restructure economics and bring it in line with ecological dynamics. He conceived microeconomics as a 'study of particular economic quantities and their determination'.[46] Firms or households are analogous with economic organisms. He builds a theory which attempts to show the functional relationship between the behaviour of these organisms and the external environment. 'By developing a theory of the interaction of organisms through exchange, microeconomics also develops a theory of the determination of the main quantities of the system — prices, outputs, consumption, and so on.'[47] In a similar fashion, macroeconomics is viewed as dealing with the national aggregates of individual quantities.

However, it is difficult to avoid the conclusion that Boulding was interested mainly in adapting neoclassical thinking to evolutionary concepts, to embellishing economic theory with an ecological canopy. Indeed, he was hostile to efforts to expand economic analysis to include the concerns of other social sciences, although this would not necessarily undermine the primacy of prices, outputs and other quantitative elements. His view of the other social sciences was that they were still inadequate: 'A synthesis of inadequate parts may be worse than no synthesis at all'.[48] And institutional economics was 'regarded as a premature attempt at synthesis of the social sciences, an attempt to synthesize bad economics, bad sociology, and bad anthropology in the medium of subconscious emotional bias.'[49] In this way Boulding sought to defend economics as a hard science, a discipline based on a small range of neoclassical abstractions: 'It must never be forgotten that economics is an abstraction, useful and necessary as it is.'[50] The main task of his work was 'to improve the abstraction'.[51]

Boulding therefore sought in ecology those elements which were analogous with existing economic abstractions such as population equilibrium and homeostatic mechanisms. This led him to a 'balance sheet' approach to economic analysis in which he expanded the Marshallian forest to include other organisms: 'It is a complex pattern of organisms, trees, grasses, flowers, birds, mammals, insects, reptiles, bacteria; subsisting, growing, propagating, dying in a maze of complementary and competitive relationships, all founded on the physical environment of earth, air, sun, water.'[52] But this reformulation remained ineffective in explaining economic transition because it sought simply to replace static equilibria with dynamic equilibria. Concepts such as homeostasis became crucial to the theory because they provided arguments for some form of balancing mechanism among economic organisms.

As with celestial bodies, economic organisms drift towards some steady-state situation. In his view, there is some state 'of the organism which is organized to maintain, and any disturbance from this stage sets in motion behaviour on the part of the organism which tends to re-establish the desired state'.[53] This argument suggests that there are some inherent forces in economic organisms which direct them towards 'a homeostasis of the balance sheet'. But these forces are not adequately explained. By insisting on these limited ecological analogies, Boulding does not account for the internal dynamics of economic evolution which are associated with technological change. The homeostasis of the balance sheet may tell us a little, just a little, of what happens in the structure of industry, but does not explain the dynamics of economic evolution. It is therefore not surprising that his work, although paraded as evolutionary, does not examine those crucial factors, such as technological change, which set economic evolution into motion. Institutional economics, which Boulding so much derided, recognized this more than he did.

3.3 The Institutionalist Tradition

Institutional economics, or institutionalism, provided one of the earliest expositions of evolutionary thinking. Institutionalism was not itself a coherent package of analytical tools, but a diverse collection of critical ideas built on a theoretical and methodological rejection of conventional economics. It revolved around Veblen, Mitchell and Commons, although as Blaug says, the three economists had little in common: 'Veblen applied an inimitable brand of interpretative sociology to the working creed of businessmen; Mitchell devoted his life to the amassing of statistical data, almost as an end in itself; and Commons analysed the working of the economic system from the standpoint of its legal foundations.'[54] They were dissatisfied with the narrowness of neoclassical thinking, demanding the integration of other social sciences into economic thought, and rejected the casual empiricism of conventional economics.

Institutionalism was rooted in dissent. In his post-mortem, Boulding sees some elements of suicidal criticism in the movement: 'Veblen is the type of dissenter of the sourest kind, whose weapons are irony and sarcasm and sardonic innuendo, but who . . . almost deliberately brings his own house on his head in the process of general destructiveness.'[55] In his critiques, Boulding generalizes on the basis of other forms of dissent, a type of reasoning which many would find fallacious. What is more important, however, is the fact that Boulding's image ignores Veblen's contribution to evolutionary thinking in general and to the significance of technological change in particular. As with many critical attacks on the establishment, Veblen did not develop his ideas into a solid and consistent analytical framework, but he left behind interesting insights into economic systems that deserve attention.

He argued that economic activity evolves in an unfolding sequence, consistent with the close-knit body of theory required for any evolutionary science. But conventional economics had remained at the stage where 'the natural sciences passed through some time back'.[56] What could then replace the law of supply and demand, the theory of price equilibrium, marginal utility and the rest of the tools in the neoclassical kit? The answer lay in a reformulation of the contextual setting of economics, whose subject-matter had to be seen as an unfolding sequence embodying evolutionary realism: 'There is the economic life process still in great measure awaiting theoretical formulation.'[57]

Industry and technology are the motive power behind this economic life process: 'The active material in which the economic process goes on is the human material of the industrial community. For the purpose of economic science and the process of cumulative change that is to be accounted for is the sequence of change in the methods of doing things — the method of dealing with the material means of life.[58] Veblen was writing at the turn of the century when the role of technological change in economic evolution had become apparent but was largely unexplained. And to him, everyone was intractably trapped in the evolutionary sweep of technological advancement: 'Under the stress of modern technological exigencies, men's every-day habits of thought are falling into the lines that in the sciences constitute the evolutionary method; and knowledge which proceeds on a higher, more archaic plane is becoming alien and meaningless to them. The social and political sciences must follow the drift for they are already caught in it.'[59]

Veblen emphasized the role of technological change, broadly defined to include both hardware and know-how, but his work did not manifest a coherent analysis of the role of technological change in economic evolution. Moreover, he stressed industrial arts to a point that bordered on determinism. The adage 'necessity is the mother of invention' was reversed: invention had become the mother of necessity. Technological change was an inherent aspect of social evolution and took place irrespective of economic factors. This line of reasoning has recently been pursued by Gordon in his attempt to unify the various elements of institutional economics. To Gordon, 'a new scientific discovery generally occurs because it is the next natural step in a technological sequence, not because someone wants to solve such and such a problem and goes out and does it or because the profit motive called for a labour-saving rather than capital-saving innovation'.[60]

To some extent Gordon exaggerates Veblen's position, but that is a different problem. The issue at hand is the self-propelling dynamism that is accorded to technological change. There are several problems with this position. First, it ignores the uneven distribution of technological change; why, for example, some societies develop particular technologies and others do not. Second, it implies a form of technological fatalism based on the inevitability of cumulative change; because technological change is inevitable, there would be no need to do anything about it, except to wait helplessly for its emergence and consequences. Third, and more fundamental, it underestimates the role of external or environmental forces in technological evolution. In this view the external factors which shape the selection process and the unfolding cumulative sequence are excluded from analysis and hence the evolutionary context is weakened. Veblen often suggested new directions for analysis but left them undeveloped. It is in this sense that the role of technological change in the process of economic evolution had therefore to await the analysis of Schumpeter.

3.4 The Schumpeterian Heritage

Schumpeter is one of the few economists who both questioned the static underpinnings of neoclassical economics and at the same time suggested an alternative approach. By locating economic transition within the broad context of social change, Schumpeter adopted, like Marx, an evolutionary model in which technological change and the efficacy of the entrepreneur as an innovative agent played the most significant role. However, because of his Walrasian influence, he modified the notion of equilibrium and presented it in a more sophisticated way than it was presented in the neoclassical tradition. There is, nevertheless, a continuous tension between these two aspects of his writings — a tension which he never really resolved.

The Schumpeterian economic system carried strong evolutionary notions. 'The essential point to grasp is that in dealing with capitalism we are dealing with an evolutionary process',[61] and he goes on: 'The fundamental impulse that sets and keeps the capitalist engine in motion comes from the new customers' goods, the new methods of production or transportation, the new market, the new forms of industrial organization that capitalist enterprise creates.'[62] These changes 'illustrate the same process of industrial mutation — if I may use that biological term — that incessantly revolutionizes the economic structure *from within*, incessantly destroying the old one, incessantly creating a new one. This process of creative destruction is the essential fact about capitalism.'[63]

In his early work, Schumpeter set out to analyse not the process of evolution itself but the dynamics which bring it about: 'Not how the economic process developed historically to the state in which we actually find it, but the workings of its mechanism or organism at any given stage of development, is what we are to analyze.'[64] The influence of Walras and Marx can be noted at this metaphorical level in his reference to the 'mechanism or organism' of the economic process. He attempts to blend the two. Interestingly enough, Schumpeter follows Marx's cue by rejecting the hasty generalizations arising from the Darwinian 'postulate that a nation, a civilization, or even the whole of mankind, must show some kind of uniform unilinear development'.[65] He also rejects the Newtonian view of society by asserting that historical 'changes constitute neither a circular process nor pendulum movements about a centre'.[66]

There is an interesting contrast between Marx and Schumpeter which deserves mention. Marx started his analysis with socioeconomic fluctuations and suggested that society would move towards an equilibrium state as classes disappear and institutions such as the state wither away. Marx in a sense, therefore, collapsed into the Cartesian-Newtonian tradition. Schumpeter, on the other hand, started his analysis by assuming an equilibrium state but devotes much time to the analysis of the manner in which the equilibrium is destabilized. Arguably this was because Marx was more interested in the abolition of capitalism while Schumpeter, at least in his early writings, was interested in the sources and effects of instability in the economic system. For Marx socialism would emerge from the collapse of capitalism, while for Schumpeter it would result from its success as investment opportunities shrink and the role of entrepreneurs becomes obsolete.

Schumpeter's theory of economic development emphasized the endogenous forces which bring about economic evolution. For economic development to occur, a society had to do more than just adapt to changing market conditions. If 'the phenomenon that we call economic development is in practice simply founded upon the fact that the data changed and that the economy continuously adapts itself to them, then we shall say that there is *no* economic development'.[67] In the Schumpeter system, development is understood as 'changes in economic life as are not forced upon it from without but arise by its own initiative, from within'.[68] The transition is both cumulative and preconditional: 'Every concrete process of development finally rests upon preceding development . . . Every process of development creates the prerequisites for the following'.[69]

His evolutionary theory of development thus transcends the notion of circular economic flows and the tendency towards general equilibrium. The changes in the circular flow and the destabilization of equilibrium originate in the sphere of industry and commerce (on the supply side) not in the area of 'wants of the consumers of final products' (on the demand side). The shift is not, by definition, minor; it is one *'which so displaces its equilibrium point that the new one cannot be reached from the old one by infinitesimal steps*. Add successively as many mail coaches as you please, you will never get a railway thereby.'[70] Schumpeter emphasizes further the evolutionary view of economic change in his *Business Cycles*: 'As a matter of fact, it is to physiology and zoology — and not to mechanics — that our science is indebted for an analogous distinction which is at the threshold of all clear thinking about economic matters'.[71] He defines economic evolution as the 'changes in the economic process brought about by innovation, together with all their effects, and the responses to them by the economic system'.[72]

Hence we have a picture which is both *co-evolutionary* and *far from equilibrium*. The creation of 'economic space' or a market niche leads to the swarming towards new innovations by imitators as the copying or modification of newly introduced technologies become increasingly possible. In the Schumpeterian system such opportunities come in clusters and are unevenly distributed, so that the changes which result from these disequilibria are not relatively smooth as a Darwinian curve would tend to show, but proceed in jerks and rushes. Nevertheless, it is still possible to locate their epicentre: 'In every span of historic time it is easy to locate the ignition of the process and to associate it with certain industries and, within these industries, with certain firms, from which the disturbances then spread over the system.[73]

As the capitalist system matures, Schumpeter visualizes a situation where investment opportunities vanish and the entrepreneurial function becomes obsolete, forcing the economy into near-equilibrium socialist practice: 'Technological progress is increasingly becoming the business of teams of trained specialists who turn out what is required and make it work in a predictable way. The romance of earlier commercial adventure is rapidly wearing away, because so many more things can be strictly calculated that had of old to be visualized in a flash of genius.'[74] Finally, Schumpeter delivers his ultimate prognosis: 'Since capitalist enterprise, by its very achievements, tends to automatize progress, we conclude that it tends to make itself superfluous — to break to pieces under the pressure of its own success.'[75] This return of the economic system to a near-equilibrium state associated with socialist organization suggests that Schumpeter's break with classical thought was not as radical as it appears. The appeal to stable or near-stable systems that has characterized the post-seventeenth century intellectual tradition influenced Schumpeter's thinking just as it affected Marx's. Schumpeter's work, however, forms a significant starting point for the analysis of non-equilibrium economic structures and has been built upon by a number of modern economists.

For example, Nelson and Winter have made ambitious efforts to develop an evolutionary model of economic change in the neo-Schumpeterian spirit. Their model rests on three basic concepts. First, firms have a set of organizational routines which set out what is to be done and how it is to be done. Routine is the genetic code of the firm; it carries the adaptive information required for competition and survival. The information in the genetic code changes over time as experiences are selected and retained. Second, firms undertake a search process which includes the evaluation of their routines for possible modification or replacement. Search routines stochastically generate innovations, or mutations. Third, there is a selection environment which includes all the factors which influence the well-being of the firm. This covers the socioeconomic conditions prevailing outside the firm, including the behaviour of other firms: 'Differential growth plays much the same role in our theory as in biological theory; in particular, it is important to remember that it is ultimately the fates of populations or genotypes (routines) that are the focus of concern, not the fate of individuals.'[76]

In addition, the model rejects the concept of profit maximization. It is suggested that firms adopt a satisficing behaviour because firms that are sufficiently profitable do not search for alternative techniques: 'They simply attempt to preserve their existing routines, and are driven to consider alternatives only under the pressure of adversity.'[77] The search process could either be local, concentrating on techniques close to the current ones; or imitative, looking to what other firms are doing. And at firm level, innovation tends to occur in a cumulative way following natural trajectories which are defined by technical interrelatedness.

However, the approach is still very neo-Darwinian. Innovation is seen in terms of stochastic search processes (random mutation) which are then selected out by a market environment, and the modelling of the search process itself is done by using a tool borrowed from classical physics — the Markov chain — a fact that has led David to argue that the model still 'remains fundamentally neo-classical in spirit'.[78] His claim is based on the assertion that since the Markov chain is built on the present and not past situations, it is ahistorical. Put another way, the notion of search and selection, which is central to the model, assumes the pre-existence of technological possibilities; and hence it must assume a historical retroaction. The process of innovation thus involves creating *and* discovering, both of which need a historical basis to take an evolutionary posture.

Nelson and Winter admit as much when they state that 'in many technological histories the new is not just better than the old; in some sense the new evolves out of the old. One explanation for this is that the output of today's searches is not merely a new technology, but also enhances knowledge and forms the basis of new building blocks to be used tomorrow.'[79] However, by avoiding engagement with case histories of firms, the Nelson–Winter model is left with no option but to emphasize the initial conditions which would make the Markov chain applicable. The very appeal to initial conditions presupposes a certain level of certainty. This is in fact the strength of the Newtonian paradigm where the knowledge of the initial conditions makes it possible to work out possible trajectories assuming that the internal parameters of the analytical units do not change. But this is not the case in technology. The issue is therefore not one of differences in the initial conditions, as Elster argues in defence of the Nelson–Winter model,[80] but the impact of past choices on current options and future trajectories. Conversely, David's own approach is Mendelian in so far as it emphasizes heredity. The 'drift of technological developments generated over time within a fairly stable economic environment needs to be viewed . . . as a distinctively *historical* phenomenon, inasmuch as it may arise through the myopic selections *past* producers made from among the different species of techniques within which they originally had to work.'[81]

While Nelson and Winter did not apply their model to any specific firm or technological system, except for computer simulations, Dosi has attempted to apply a modified version of the approach to the study of the semiconductor sector. Dosi's work is interesting because it singles out those elements which are specific to technological change and attempts to synthesize them with other theoretical frameworks so as to arrive at an analytical model that exposes the technological mechanisms which underly structural change. He combines the approach provided by Kuhn with Rosenberg trajectories (modified in Nelson–Winter to become natural trajectories), and with evolutionary concepts. The model reveals continuous progress along a defined technological trajectory which is triggered and pulled by the endogenous mechanisms of Schumpeterian competition. And this is associated with 'the complementarities between different technologies and industries jointly with straightforward economic signals, such as changing relative prices, relative profitabilities and distributive shares'.[82]

Further major contributions to the neo-Schumpeterian tradition have been associated with efforts to understand the occurrence of cycles in economic development. Such cycles, according to Mensch, are associated with a cluster of basic innovations which establish new branches of industry but the resulting economic expansion reaches technological limits. The ensuing stalemate or depression then induces further innovations, which come again in clusters and put the economy back on another growth path. Mensch holds that new basic innovations are called upon during depression to replace those whose growth potential has been exhausted.[83]

This view is rejected by Freeman and his colleagues, who argue that the bunching of innovation is associated with fundamental breakthroughs in science and technology leading to the availability of related families of technological systems. It is this swarming effect that leads to economic expansion, and not depression inducement:

> Once swarming does start it has powerful multiplier effects in generating additional demands on the economy for capital goods (of new and old types), for materials, components, distribution facilities, and of course labour. This, in turn, induces a further wave of process and applications innovations. It is this combination of related and induced innovations which give rise to expansionary effects in the economy as a whole.[84]

Hence, while Mensch emphasizes the clustering of innovations, Freeman and colleagues stress the linking together of basic inventions to bring about new technological systems that then contribute to a Kondratiev upswing. The escape from technological stalemate therefore depends on a combination of innovations made before and during the depression as well as during recovery.

Many of these (and other) neo-Schumpeterian studies, in so far as they attach importance to evolutionary processes, assume technology as given and embodying known characteristics. They therefore do not engage directly with the process of innovation but emphasize its consequences. In particular, there is often little emphasis upon the institutional context within which technological change takes place, how institutional and technological mismatches often produce instability and how institutions may be used as guiding agents for new technological systems.

Schumpeter himself, for example, was mainly concerned with institutional change in so far as it related to the transition towards socialism.

This was the period when society would supposedly drift towards a stationary state. It can be argued, therefore, that although Schumpeter recognized the institutional context of his model, he underestimated the co-evolution between innovation and institutional change. Indeed, the bureaucratization of the innovation process which Schumpeter envisaged, was not simply the decay of capitalism but a reorganization of the internal structure of the economic system. Viewed in this way bureaucracy is not necessarily a sign of decay but rather of increasing complexity. A complex economic system can hardly live off flushes of entrepreneurial genius alone; it needs new and extensive institutional support systems. Indeed, the workings of modern economic systems have demonstrated that the imperatives of complexity, as well as related uncertainty, require non-economic institutional support, reflected in the growing network of industry, government and academic institutions in the process of technological innovation. This network suggests that the social system has its own internal logic which operates in an adaptive way, making equilibrium analysis of little policy relevance.

Conversely, for Schumpeter the decay of capitalism is brought about by non-economic factors such as the obsolescence of the entrepreneur, the destruction of the supporting strata of capitalism, the erosion of capitalist institutions, the rise of an anti-capitalist intelligentsia and the dissolution of the middle class. This mismatch between the economic system and its institutional environment signalled to Schumpeter a dismal picture of the future of capitalism. But why did the economist who believed so much in the efficacy of innovation as to construct a long-wave theory, hold so little future for the revolutionizing power of technological change? Why are we told so little about the business cycle in *Capitalism, Socialism and Democracy?* (1943).

One possible explanation is that Schumpeter reverted to his Marxist influences, especially the appeal to socialist transition. Although this is plausible, there is another possible explanation, namely that Schumpeter drifted back to equilibrium analysis. Indeed, his model starts with the stationary state as a theoretical norm with innovations simply acting as destabilizing forces so that the obsolescence of the entrepreneur suggests a return to a stationary social system. Such an abstraction ignores the fact that an economy is a system which constantly undergoes internal reorganization closely associated with the co-evolutionary links between innovation and institutional arrangements. In this respect, Schumpeter adequately diagnosed the problem but gave a misleading prognosis which underestimated the role of institutions in innovation, especially in a complex economic environment. It is arguable that this failure has led to the kind of analysis presented by Mensch under which hyperindustrialization tends to spring from depression without major institutional reorganization. In contrast, Freeman's approach (and that of Perez) attaches importance to the role of institutions and draws more proactive policy conclusions.

It is ironical that to resolve the institutional impasse which Schumpeter leaves in his analysis of the decay of capitalism, neo-Schumpeterians have had to rely on Schumpeter's own elucidation of the business cycle. As Perez argues, yielding the full growth potential of an economic upswing 'requires a fundamental restructuring of the socio-institutional framework, on the national and international levels'.[85] The essential point that emerges from this view is that a neo-Schumpeterian framework leads us away from equilibrium analysis towards a systems approach. Innovations do not just destabilize the equilibrium, they are involved in the irreversible reorganization of economic systems and their embodied institutions. The appeal for flexibility in economic systems relates to internal adaptive reorganization and not to shifts from or towards equilibria. Furthermore, the use of equilibrium as a theoretical norm also denies us the opportunity to examine the impact of time and institutional hierarchy on technological evolution. Part of the mismatch between the imperatives of technological change and related institutional arrangements results from functional variations as one rises up the institutional hierarchy. The higher institutions are in most cases designed to help in the retention of selected economic paths and the means of getting there.

In slowly changing systems there is a fairly close link between the imperatives of technological change and the retentive mechanisms built into the system. But under rapid fluctuations, the mismatch is more pronounced as higher institutions apply strategies and tactics that evolved under different techno-economic conditions but are currently irrelevant or even counter-revolutionary. The situation is further complicated by a rise in technological diversity. In economic systems with less technological diversity, the institutional requirements could be reduced to a few basic practices which can easily be routinized. However, more complex economic systems contain a diverse range of technologies with different institutional requirements. Evolutionary pressures under such conditions require even more adaptive flexibility with extensive communication between the different sections of the nested hierarchy.

By eschewing equilibrium analysis, we are able to examine those forms of reorganization which do not necessarily result from innovation but necessitate technological responses. A case in point are fluctuations in energy prices which do not necessarily result from the sphere of innovation but set in motion adaptive responses which include the introduction of new technological systems as well as new lines of scientific enquiry and technological search. Such changes can be better understood by viewing the economic sphere as a system with its own internal organization to which technological change and institutional networks are endogenous.

Hence we conclude that while neo-Schumpeterian analyses have a grasp of the long-term dynamics of technological innovation in the context of economic long waves, they have yet to deal more systematically with the process of innovation itself. So far only the *consequences* of innovation have been examined in detail. What is now important, however, is to look more closely at the details of technical change as a *process* and accompanying institutional organization so as to identify the key features which give this process its evolutionary character.

3.5 Conclusions

Our intention in this chapter has been to provide a broad account of how the economics literature has engaged with evolutionary ideas at a conceptual level. Our conclusion is that despite repeated efforts to theorize in a more organic (and we would argue more realistic) fashion, the evidence suggests that a mechanical metaphysic still has a very strong hold upon the ways in which economists think. Put another way, economists simply want to believe in a social universe which is timeless, reversible, certain and subject to a small number of axiomatic 'laws' which can provide determinate solutions to all problems. And they will often go to quite considerable lengths to fit nature to their preconceived world, a world which is analogous to that of nineteenth-century classical physics.

The neo-Schumpeterian heritage, however, offers the opportunity to break from conventional thinking and deal with technological change as an inherently dynamic process. Moreover, from this vantage point it is possible to examine the co-evolution between technology and institutions. Such an analysis could provide a more valuable approach to policy studies. However, this vantage point is only important if it enables us to break away from the trappings of classical thought. The following chapters represent our own attempt to do this.

Notes and References

1. J. Schumpeter (1934), *The Theory of Economic Development* (Cambridge, Mass.: Harvard University Press), p. xi.
2. With the exception, arguably, of Malthus. See, for example, N. von Tunzelmann (1986), 'Malthus' "Total Population System": A Dynamic Reinterpretation' in D. Coleman and R. Schofield (eds) (1986), *The State of Population Theory* (Oxford: Blackwell), pp. 65–95.
3. A. Smith (1961), *The Wealth of Nations* (London: Methuen, Cannon edn), Vol. I, p. 20.
4. Ibid., p. 20. Students of entomology would take issue with Smith for not

considering the division of labour among bees and ants. In fact, in his day Linnaeus had already described aphids as ants' cows, recognizing the division of labour among insect societies. Houthakker (1956) has provided economic arguments showing that the Smithian notion that the division of labour was limited by the extent of the market was analogous to speciation, or the formation of species among animals. See H. Houthakker (1956), 'Economics and Biology: Specialization and Speciation', *Kyklos* 9: 180–9.

5. D. Meek (ed.) (1953), *Marx and Engels on Malthus* (London: Lawrence & Wishart), p. 172.
6. Ibid., p. 187.
7. We shall return to the Darwinian strand in our review of Marshall.
8. See R. Colp (1982), 'The Myth of the Marx-Darwin Letter', *History of Political Economy*, **14** (4): 416–82, for a detailed assessment of the contacts between Marx and Darwin, especially on the myth that Darwin rejected Marx's request to dedicate *Capital* to him.
9. K. Marx (1976), *Capital* (Harmondsworth: Penguin), Vol. I, p. 505. Marx captured the ultimate organic metaphor in the 'attempt made to construct a locomotive with two feet, which it raised from the ground alternatively, like a horse'.
10. K. Marx (1975), *The Poverty of Philosophy* (Moscow: Progress Publishers), p. 102.
11. Marx, *Capital*, Vol. I, op. cit., p. 493.
12. Ibid., p. 493. Marx attempted to develop these ideas in unpublished notebooks. See E. Colman (1971), 'Short Communication on the Unpublished Writings of Karl Marx Dealing with Mathematics, the Natural Sciences and Technology and the History of these Subjects' in N. Bukharin (ed.), *Science at the Crossroads* (London: Frank Cass), pp. 234–5.
13. Marx, *Capital*, Vol. I, op. cit., pp. 450–61.
14. C. Darwin, *Origin of the Species*, quoted in ibid., p. 461. It is interesting to note that while Darwin uses a mechanical metaphor, Marx uses organic ones.
15. Ibid., p. 528.
16. See, for example, A. Hansen (1921), 'The Technological Interpretation of History', *Quarterly Journal of Economics*, **36**: 72–83; R. Heilbroner (1967), 'Do Machines Make History', *Technology and Culture*, **8** (3): 335–45; D. MacKenzie (1984), 'Marx and the Machine', *Technology and Culture*, **25** (3): 473–502; W. Shaw (1979), 'The Handmill Gives you the Feudal Lord: Marx's Technological Determinism', *History and Theory*, **18**: 155–76. For a contrary view, see N. Rosenberg (1982), 'Marx as a Student of Technology', *Inside the Black Box* (Cambridge: Cambridge University Press), pp. 34–51.
17. For a detailed review of Marshall's assertion that economics is a branch of biology, see J. Hirshleifer (1977), 'Economics from a Biological Viewpoint', *Journal of Law and Economics*, **20** (1): 1–52. See also J. Hirshleifer (1982), 'Evolutionary Models' in Economics and Law', *Research in Law and Economics*, **4**: 1–60. For an assessment of the use of economic models in ecology, see D. Rapport *et al.* (1977), 'Economic Models in Ecology', *Science*, **195** (4276), Jan. 28, pp. 367–73.
18. A. Marshall (1959), *Principles of Economics* (London: Macmillan), p. xii.
19. Ibid., p. 637.
20. Ibid., p. xiii.
21. Ibid., p. 263. For an empirical test of these ideas of Marshall, see R. Lloyd-Jones *et al.* (1982), 'Marshall and the Birth and Death of Firms: The Growth and Size Distribution in the Early Nineteenth Century Cotton Industry',

Business History, **24** (2): 141–55.
22. Marshall, ibid., p. xi.
23. Ibid., p. xii.
24. Ibid., p. 12.
25. Ibid., p. 12.
26. A. Marshall (1925), 'Mechanical and Biological Analogies in Economics', in A.C. Pigou (ed.), *Memorials of Alfred Marshall* (London: Macmillan), p. 314.
27. Ibid., p. 313.
28. Ibid., p. 317.
29. Ibid., p. 318.
30. Particularly by Chamberlin and Robinson. See E. Chamberlin (1962), *The Theory of Monopolistic Competition* (Cambridge, Mass.: Harvard University Press) and J. Robinson (1933), *The Economics of Imperfect Competition* (London: Macmillan).
31. T. Veblen (1898), 'Why Is Economics Not an Evolutionary Science?', *Quarterly Journal of Economics*, **12**: 374–97.
32. L. Walras (1954), *Elements of Pure Economics* (London: Allen & Unwin), p. 71.
33. Ibid., p. 47.
34. Ibid., p. 48.
35. N. Georgescu-Roegen (1971), *The Entropy Law and the Economic Process* (Cambridge, Mass.: Harvard University Press), pp. 2–3.
36. Veblen, op. cit., p. 388.
37. P. McNulty (1968), 'Economic Theory and the Meaning of Competition', *Quarterly Journal of Economics*, **82**: 639–56, has extended the physical analogy to equate the concept of perfect competition to that of a perfect vacuum: 'not an "ordering force" but rather an assumed "state of affairs"' (ibid., p. 643).
38. Ibid., p. 641.
39. Chamberlin, op. cit., see p. 3.
40. E. Chamberlin (1957), 'The Product as an Economic Variable', in E. Chamberlin, *Towards a More General Theory of Value* (Oxford: Oxford University Press), p. 131.
41. A. Alchian (1950), 'Uncertainty, Evolution and Economic Theory', *Journal of Political Economy*, **58**: 211. For an enlargement of Alchian's approach, see S. Enke (1951), 'On Maximizing Profits: A Distinction Between Chamberlin and Robinson', *American Economic Review*, **41**: 566–78. E. Penrose (1952), 'Biological Analogies in the Theory of the Firm', *American Economic Review*, **42** (5): 804–19, provides a critique of Alchian's model emphasizing the pitfalls of relying on biological metaphors. The critique did not underline Alchian's main arguments.
42. Alchian, op. cit., p. 212.
43. Ibid., p. 213.
44. Ibid., p. 219.
45. Ibid., p. 220.
46. K. Boulding (1962), *A Reconstruction of Economics* (New York: Science Editions), p. 3.
47. Ibid., p. 4.
48. Ibid., p. 5.
49. Ibid., p. 4.
50. Ibid., p. 3.
51. Ibid., p. 5.
52. Ibid., p. 6.

53. Ibid., pp. 26–7.
54. M. Blaug (1968), *Economic Theory in Retrospect* (London: Heinemann), p. 678. For a detailed review of the history of institutionalism since Adam Smith, see J. Spengler (1974), 'Institutions, Institutionalism: 1776–1974', *Journal of Economic Issues*, **8** (4): 877–96.
55. K. Boulding (1957), 'A New Look at Institutionalism', *American Economic Review*, **47**: Papers and Proceedings, 1–13, at p. 2.
56. Veblen, op. cit., p. 384.
57. Ibid., p. 387.
58. Ibid., p. 387.
59. Ibid., p. 397. Veblen placed his evolutionary conception in an institutional context thus. 'From what has been said it appears that an evolutionary economics must be the theory of a process of cultural growth as determined by the economic interest, a theory of a cumulative sequence of economic institutions stated in terms of the process itself' (ibid., p. 393).
60. W. Gordon (1980), *Institutional Economics* (Texas: Texas University Press), p. 12. We are further told: 'The cures of the common cold and for cancer will come at the appropriate stage in the evolution of our technology, but not because we are desperate for cure for these ailments and a squad of scientists has been assigned the task of finding these cures. If wishing and conscious diverting resources to the task could do the job, we would have had a cure for cancer long ago' (ibid.). This position is not taken by all institutionalists. Ayres points out that social forces can arrest technological progress just as much as technological change can disrupt social institutions. See C. Ayres (1944), *The Theory of Economic Progress: A Study of the Fundamentals of Economic Development and Cultural Change* (Chapel Hill: North Carolina University Press).
61. J. Schumpeter (1943), *Capitalism, Socialism and Democracy* (London: Allen & Unwin), p. 82.
62. Ibid., p. 83.
63. Ibid., p. 84.
64. Schumpeter, *The Theory of Economic Development*, op. cit., p. 10.
65. Ibid., p. 57.
66. Ibid., p. 58.
67. Ibid., p. 63.
68. Ibid., p. 63.
69. Ibid., p. 64.
70. Ibid., p. 64 (emphasis added).
71. J. Schumpeter (1939), *Business Cycles* (New York: McGraw-Hill), Vol. I, p. 37.
72. Ibid., p. 86.
73. Ibid., p. 102.
74. J. Schumpeter (1943), *Capitalism, Socialism and Democracy*, op. cit., p. 133.
75. Ibid., p. 133.
76. R. Nelson and S. Winter (1982), *An Evolutionary Theory of Economic Change* (Cambridge: Belknap Press), p. 401. The genetic analogy is explained in detail in S. Winter (1975), 'Optimisation and Evolution in the Theory of the Firm', in R. Day *et al.* (eds.), *Adaptive Economic Models* (New York: Academic Press).
77. Nelson and Winter, ibid., p. 211. See also K. Gwai (1984), 'Schumpeterian Dynamics', *Journal of Economic Behaviour and Organisation*, **5** (2): 159–90 for a neo-Schumpeterian evolutionary model of innovation and imitation.

78. P. David (1975), *Technical Choice, Innovation and Economic Growth* (London: Cambridge University Press), p. 76.
79. Nelson and Winter, op. cit., pp. 255–6.
80. J. Elster (1983), *Explaining Technical Change* (Cambridge: Cambridge University Press), pp. 156–7.
81. David, op. cit., p. 61 (emphasis in original).
82. G. Dosi (1984), *Technological Change and Industrial Transformation* (London: Macmillan), p. 287.
83. For discussion of Mensch's view, see G. Mensch (1974), *Stalemate in Technology* (New York: Ballinger).
84. C. Freeman *et al.* (1982), *Unemployment and Technical Change* (London: Frances Pinter), p. 65.
85. C. Perez (1985), 'Microelectronics, Long Waves and World Structural Change: New Perspectives for Developing Countries', *World Development*, **13** (3): 441–63.

Chapter 4
Conceptual Tools

Our argument up to this stage has been a critical one consisting of two broad strands. First, we have explained our view that most of the main economic traditions have great difficulty dealing with the 'long run', especially where technological change is concerned. The reasons for this vary depending upon the tradition in question, but arguably a cause common to all traditions is a view of social science which seeks to emulate the philosophical tenets of classical physics. Under this view 'time' becomes in effect reversible, thus enabling economic systems to be 'modelled' in terms of a small number of variables interacting according to simple behavioural postulates and always tending towards equilibrium positions. Thus even the Marxian grand schema, for example, sees the withering away of the state as the last fluctuation before the equilibrium of a genuine communist world order.

It is our argument that such a philosophical position leads naturally to a view of economic events in which technological change, as a social process involving 'irreversible time' (which is surely what it is in reality), is relegated to an exogenous status, brought about by, and to be analysed in terms of, other social forces. It is a very small jump from this position to one in which the only way technological changes enter into economic models is through their *effects upon* the system under investigation. And as we saw for example in Solow's empirical investigation of the aggregate production function, even where the model purports to be dealing with temporal change, in practice this is treated as a series of step jumps with little or nothing being said about precisely what goes on between them. There is a clear analogy here with a similar lack of causal explanation in modern quantum physics.[1]

However, and this has been the second strand to our argument, it should not be concluded that what we have labelled as the economistic tradition has been indifferent to evolutionary approaches to economic change. On the contrary, there have been many instances of economists being so influenced right from the middle of the nineteenth century, and today there is an important emergent tradition which seeks to use evolutionary ideas in the analysis of technological change and economic growth. Nevertheless, it is our view that this tradition is (possibly somewhat unconsciously) still influenced quite strongly by what Capra once labelled as 'Newtonian-Cartesian' assumptions, and often ends up building models which are rather similar in important respects to their more mechanistic predecessors.

This chapter, and the following one, seek to make a definite break in this respect building upon the organic/systemic line of thought sketched out in the second part of Chapter 2. In order to do so we have moved entirely outside conventional economic analysis adopting ideas from the natural sciences, particularly the molecular ones, from philosophy and from the sociology of knowledge, as conceptual 'building blocks' for a revised theory of technological change. Special emphasis is placed, however, on Prigogine's theory of dissipative structures since this very clearly presents a *physical paradigm* in direct contrast to that of classical physics. And in so far as contemporary economistic approaches to the analysis of technological change are based on an underlying metaphysical basis which is essentially that put forward by Newton and Descartes, then we have felt the importance of putting forward a physical alternative which argues the primacy of an evolutionary explanation of the behaviour of natural systems.

And this is what Jantsch has attempted to do, showing that what appears to be true at the level of the chemical compound is consistent with similar behaviour of all microscopic and macroscopic structures, ranging from the microbiological to those of modern political economy. In essence, what we have is a form of general systems theory in which nature may be viewed as a nested hierarchy of complex structures in co-evolution with each other. The 'macroscopic' boundary of this approach is dealt with by modern theories of evolutionary cosmology while at the microscopic level modern developments in subatomic physics are attempting to unravel the complexities of a domain where atomistic analogies are becoming ever more meaningless and where matter appears to consist of indistinct 'packets' of energy in relationships of symmetry to each other.

Our own interests lie at the level of social systems where 'systemic exchange' may be seen more in terms of flows of *information* than in terms of flows of energy/matter. Here it is possible to conceive of social systems and subsystems operating in non-equilibrium conditions and in co-evolution with each other through a process of information exchange which permits phylogenetic continuity on a number of hierarchical levels. And since 'information' may be viewed as the basic raw material for 'technology', it is also clear that technological change may be seen through similar metaphoric spectacles. Section 3 deals with these aspects through an examination of recent developments in evolutionary epistomology.

Section 4 explores some elements of our final 'building block' — that concerning the sociology of knowledge. We have included this in order to take account of a very important strand of contemporary science policy debate — namely, the degree to which technological changes achieve social validation by means of a process of 'expert review' embodying the 'interest' and 'goals' of powerful institutions. Here 'knowledge' about the world is not determined by means of a dialogue with an independent nature. Rather the search for and evaluation of knowledge is seen to be a social activity whose status is therefore at least a partial function of social authority, with associated political and moral dimensions.

4.1 The Theory of Dissipative Structures

Very recently there has emerged within the molecular sciences a new systemic paradigm of *self-organization* which possesses a number of properties of potential relevance to the study of technological change. At the root of Prigogine's theory of dissipative structures is a dissatisfaction with the influence of classical physics on much modern scientific research, a dissatisfaction, incidentally, which is not new but has been rumbling beneath the surface, so to speak, since the days of Newton and Descartes themselves and more obviously since the writings of A.N. Whitehead in the early parts of this century, as we noted in Chapter 1.

Prigogine takes issue specifically with conventional treatments of nature which attempt to model it exclusively as a 'clockwork' mechanism, obeying timeless functional laws which are independent of the observer and which are progressively subject to discovery using a reductionist experimental method. The concept of 'reductionism' is conventionally used to describe a philosophical approach to science which argues that the only way to understand the behaviour of natural systems is to split them down into their constituent components, subject each component to rigorous investigation and finally add the analysed pieces together again. The opposite, or 'holistic', position argues that the behaviour of systems is to a considerable degree evolutionary from that of their constituent components and, therefore, that scientific investigation should focus also on the whole independent of its parts.

Under a pure mechanistic world-view nature may be seen entirely as a complex of particles moving through space/time according to simple externally given laws of force, not capable of self-organization into larger more complex systems. Viewed in this way:

> classical dynamics becomes the idealized case of pure motion of a particle or wave packet, a mere thought model which nevertheless is useful for many considerations. But the 'dirty' reality includes encounters, collisions, exchanges, mutual stimulation, challenges and coercions of many kinds. The collective with all its complexity can hardly be denied anywhere.[2]

The development of thermodynamics in the nineteenth century heralded a significant change in so far as it postulated an explanation of the macroscopic behaviour of whole systems. The second law of thermodynamics states that the entropy (or energy unavailable for productive work) of any isolated system 'can only increase until the system has reached its thermodynamic equilibrium'.[3] This to classical thermodynamics meant that any chemical system would inevitably progress *irreversibly* towards an equilibrium state characterized by maximum disorder and the incapability of producing useful energy: 'If the world had appeared as a stationary machine in the mechanical view, it now seemed to be doomed to the "heat death", a notion which influenced profoundly the pessimistic philosophy and arts of the turn of the century up to our days'.[4]

It was (and is) Prigogine's view that there are many examples of physical and biological systems which contradict both these positions. Far from nature obeying laws of mechanism and disorganization, on the contrary, increasing entropy states appear to bring forth new forms of organization through a continuous energy exchange with the external environment. 'Irreversibility' becomes a positive, creative phenomenon of continuous 'self-organization' as microscopic and macroscopic structures evolve in ever new and unpredictable ways.

As its simplest this may be seen in chemical reactions involving autocatalysis where entirely new structures can be created provided the system in question is far from a thermodynamic equilibrium and is capable of energy or matter exchange with its environment. Such structures are called dissipative structures, the most frequently cited example of which is the Belonsov–Zhabotinsky reaction involving the oxidation of malonic acid by bromate in a sulphuric acid solution and the presence of catalytic ions (usually cerium). Dissipative structures which are beyond a certain instability threshold do not return to a thermodynamic equilibrium but in effect export their entropy into their environments, import useful energy and/or matter, which is then used in a reproductive way to renew and expand the original system. Such structures are sometimes referred to as 'self-referential' (or subject to 'autopoesis') in the sense that their metabolic behaviour is not brought about by an outside agency, as for example in Thom's catastrophe theory,[5] but rather is entirely self-generated.

Jantsch shows that such 'natural developments' are not simply confined to inorganic chemicals (though it is highly significant that such structures are able to exhibit this kind of behaviour) but are consistent with the behaviour of *all* natural systems from the pre-biotic, through the biological, sociological right through to sociocultural organizations. All may be viewed as complex systems in co-evolution with each other evolving through time in homologous ways and in a hierarchical pattern — a far cry indeed from the metaphor of raw undecomposable matter whirling through space/time in a random manner.

It is not our purpose to go into these matters in any sort of detail, fascinating though they are. However, Jantsch has extended Prigogine's ideas in a number of interesting ways and in particular has begun to model sociocultural evolution along similar lines but including 'information flows' along with energy exchanges as an important interactive medium. We shall see in Chapter 5 how this may have considerable significance for the study of technological change. Meanwhile, let us review Jantsch's tripartite view of communication. First, *genetic* communication operates over long time periods compared to the life-span of any individual species member, and gives rise to a coherent phylogeny for that species. Second, *metabolic* communication comprises energy (matter) exchange which permits any organism to regulate its own development and to damp down the consequences of environmental fluctuation, usually by hormonal interchange. Third, *neural* communication represents an extremely rapid energy exchange which first of all facilitates organismatic homeostasis and development (in much the same way as metabolic communication but some one thousand times faster) and, second, allows for what Jantsch labels the *self-organization of information*. All three forms of communication play an essential role in evolutionary processes, but it is the third, the neural form, which facilitates a new form of interchange which begins to have technological relevance, namely that involving information flows.

It is not clear from Jantsch's own exposition whether 'information' is to be viewed as a sort of 'energy packet' and therefore as ultimately reducible to a simpler energetic calculus, or as something qualitatively different. However, Singh has shown how information theory is based upon statistical laws which are analogous to those of molecular thermodynamics,[6] a point first noted by Szilard in his examination of Maxwell's *Theory of Heat*. In effect, '*entropy* is information in reverse gear', leading L. Brillouin to coin the term *negentropy* to describe the information content of any set of messages.

We shall expand on these ideas further in Chapter 5, but meanwhile it seems reasonable to treat information flows *sui generis* as entropic. At the neural level it occurs as a result of networks of nerve complexes (involving thousands of millions of neurons) called 'nerve felt' (Marthaler 1976),[7] which require much smaller electrical potentials but which are capable of storing and transmitting information systems of very great complexity. They also involve the selective transmission of chemical substances as well as of electrical energy. What is clear is that the very dense chemico-electrical micro-circuitry in the brains of higher forms of life is capable of behaving in ways very similar to the simpler dissipative structures discussed above — only this time with respect to information rather than just with energy *per se*:

> The brain is a communication mechanism which is used and directed by the self-organisation of information. It has no more to do with this information than does the computer with information it processes. Although the comparison between brain and computer should not be carried too far since, to some extent,

they represent very different principles, it may be useful to also distinguish between 'hardware' and 'software' in the brain. The network of neurons, then, represents the 'hardware' and its possible multilevel self-organisation dynamics the 'software'.[8]

Moreover, such an information-processing system exhibits a similar capacity for self-transformation and self-transcendence, for 'autopoesis' in Jantsch's original terminology:

The self-organisation of information is an aspect of the self-organisation of life and the gestalts it produces are the gestalts of life. They are autonomous, as are the gestalts of other autopoetic system dynamics. They form their own world of symbolic representation of reality and are capable of emancipating themselves from this reality. Thus they can change and redesign reality. Self-organising pragmatic information may interfere with and co-ordinate energetic and material processes outside of the system in which this information becomes structured. Usually, this is expressed in the phrase: mind over matter. But this is true only to the extent that the matter/energy system to which this kind of mind belongs, namely the brain, remains excluded. The mind of the human organism controls the inanimate and certain aspects of the animate world, but the mind of an ecosystem does not dominate its members — their dynamics *is* the mind of the ecosystem, just as the co-ordinated dynamics of ants is the mind of the ant colony. Control and domination are dualistic notions — there is always a controller and a controlled. But mind is a non-dualistic notion which is inseparable from the matter in whose dynamics it expresses itself.[9]

Finally, therefore, Jantsch uses his tripartite communications schema to formulate a theory of 'mind' as a dynamic principle of self-organisation. On this view, 'mind' is not a separate entity from the body located, say, somewhere in the brain and acting as the 'ultimate co-ordinator or dictator neuron'. On the contrary, 'mind' is immanent. It is an intrinsic quality of all self-organising systems and in the processes through which they organise and renew themselves. Thus all forms of natural systems may be thought of as possessing a 'mind' while the higher the life form, the greater the power of the 'mind' to influence the rate and direction of evolutionary change.

Jantsch postulates three such orders of mentation:

(1) the *organic* mind, the self-representation of the organism as a result of its genetic, metabolic and neural processes;
(2) the *reflexive* mind, the mind which is capable of forming alternative models of reality as a result of information exchange processes;
(3) the *self-reflexive* mind, which is capable of modelling a reality in which 'the original system itself is represented'.[10] Such a mind is capable of a historic sense and therefore of '*anticipation* — in a passive sense as expectation and anticipated experience, in an active or creative (goal-setting) sense as creative design of the future'.[11]

And it is this last mental order, characteristic of the more highly evolved mammals which permits a form of self-organization of direct relevance to technology and technological change. Information can now be stored in sociocultural systems, used to create more information and hence artifacts possessing socioeconomic value. It can also, as we shall see, impose selective cognitive patterns on the outer reality, thus moulding and ordering the world to preconceived subjective categories which are reinforced by social sanction but which are 'emancipated from the dictate of the environment to a very high degree'.[12] But whereas in the domain of technologically produced artifacts there is an important sense in which our mental structures may be seen as comprehending an outer reality, in the domain of mentations concerned with ideas, plans, world-views, ideologies and other values which are divorced from any direct tangibility, not only are such mentations subject only to an artificial social validation but the very institutions themselves which give them social form are an expression of a collective social subjectivity. Jantsch includes science itself in this category, seeing it essentially as a social process of interaction between the 'subjective' and the 'objective' mind.

Hence we see that Prigogine's concept of the dissipative structure, conceived of initially as representative in nature of a non-mechanistic physical reality, is capable of providing a metaphor of much wider generality. Let us now explore in more detail how it may have applicability in the study of technological change.

4.2 Evolutionary Epistemology

We have postulated a theory of the behaviour of complex systems which is based upon the exchange of both energy and information between any systemic component and its own immediate environment. We have shown also how it is the capacity to transmit, store and receive information which characterizes the higher forms of life and, especially within the sociocultural sphere, permits humankind to create and validate knowledge about the world and to use this knowledge in a technological manner — to build artifacts which satisfy economic needs and to improve the economic capacity of such artifacts over time. Hence, in a sense 'knowledge', or useful information, becomes, as it were, a fundamental currency for technological practice — the medium of exchange for economic progress through time.

But is such knowledge a purely abstract category or can we say more about it in a concrete sense? A relevant branch of epistemology is that of evolutionary epistemology, relevant in the sense that its proponents believe that knowledge itself follows evolutionary laws. Thus the production, validation and distribution of knowledge is never stationary but is always in a state of flux as organisms learn more about their environments and use this knowledge for ontogenetic purposes. The roots of evolutionary epistemology lie in biology for it is mostly biologists like Campbell, Lorenz, Williams and Lewontin who have developed this mode of enquiry. For example, Plotkin (himself a psychologist) points out that biological systems may be regarded as knowledge systems in so far as organisms, no matter how complex, have continually to exchange information with the environment if they are to survive.[13] How such knowledge is gleaned, sifted, stored, embodied genetically and transmitted environmentally plays a central role in contemporary theories of biology, particularly in notions of adaptation.

It is through adaptation that the organism is able to preserve its own integrity in a hostile environment, though there is considerable debate about the precise relationship that obtains between the genetic make-up of the organism and the environment of which it is a part. The dominant view within contemporary biology appears to be a neo-Darwinian one in which random genetic mutations are differentially selected by environments resulting in specific phenotypical growth through inheritance. The mutations are random and may be thought of as biological hypotheses put to a selectivity test and accepted or not depending upon the environmental 'fit'. It is in this sense that the organism 'knows' increasingly about the environment which conversely moulds the organism to itself. Plotkin puts this (Lorenzian) position as follows:

> the Lorenzian position expresses a powerful conception of any adaptation comprising some form of organisation that is congruent with the environmental order to which it is relative. Such congruence can only come about through the gaining and storing of information about the environment, including a programme for the translation of this information into appropriate phenotypic traits, and the subsequent propagation of the information and its re-expression in future organisms.[14]

Thus the evolution of the organism is seen to be a 'knowledge-intensive' process. Information or knowledge 'in biological terms describe a *relationship* between the order of the world, whatever that order is, and the answering and reciprocal organization of the phenotype whose end-directedness relates to those particular patterns of environmental order'.[15] Plotkin argues also that this relationship is a two-way one since 'the order of the world is only known by its reflection in the organization of the organism, and also because the order of the world may itself be modified by the organization of the organism — especially at higher levels where development and learning and imitative behaviour are permitted'.[16]

Finally, no form of knowledge is a simple copy of reality since the process whereby it is understood is a function of the categories within which it is sought. In modern philosophies of science this is now well understood but, of course, it is equally valid at the more fundamental level:

knowledge is a dynamic, dialectical interaction between information entering a biological system and thus changing that system, but in turn being changed by the pre-existing structure of the system. Any biological system as 'knower' acts upon the world that it knows and thus changes it. Knowledge is thereafter never static and neither is its attainment. It is a constant interplay between a changing world and a changing knower.[17]

It follows from this that information *per se* is of limited value even at the organismic level, since in order to be useful — to 'be knowledge' — it must resonate between systemic components in a continuous process of articulation until its value is perceived. Information only becomes valuable once it affects behaviour and this may take a process of interchange involving often considerable periods of time.

And again it follows also that specific quanta of information from the standpoint of one systemic component will not in general possess the same degree of value to another such component, simply because of ontogenetic and environmental differences. Since all organisms are unique at least to a degree, what is useful knowledge to one will require 'reprocessing' before it can have equal usefulness to another. If you like, the 'knowledge-intensive' properties of any given piece of information is only ever latent. It possesses a degree of variability and differentiability which is a function of the status and location of any organism which may wish to use it. We shall see later that this property is of particular importance to the study of technological change.

Our discussion so far, although by no means complete, would appear to indicate a *prima facie* case for regarding biological evolution as a process built upon continuous and interactive knowledge flows. How, then, may these insights be translated usefully into the wider frame of social behaviour concerned with economic production? In Chapter 2 we set out a framework of 'nested hierarchy' within which economic behaviour may reasonably be situated. Since the relationships are very complex we have used Koestler's notions of 'arborization' and reticulation' (based upon a hedge analogy) to simulate the kinds of multidimensional interconnectedness which obtained within any socioeconomic system and which can give us a first approximation to the biological processes outlined above. The basic unit of organization is the 'firm', defined initially as a legal/financial entity in economic space, whose function it is to transform resources according to an economic rationality. Firms have their own internal patterns of organization which are both cause and consequence of *how* transformation is carried on. At a higher level firms are additively members of wider groupings of 'industries' defined in terms of resource classification. Finally, industries are grouped into a unifying economic system which conducts relations with other economic systems according to given rules. At any level of the hierarchy the 'environment' is a function of relations between units at that and higher levels, while internal components of such units may be thought of in genetic or epigenetic terms.

The analogy with biological systems may then be seen as follows. In biological systems the 'objective' of the organism is first to survive, grow and reproduce, and second to economize on energy costs. With respect to economic systems, similar objectives may obtain as encapsulated in theories of the firm which stress growth maximization (say, of sales) subject to a minimum profit constraint. However, whereas 'knowledge' within the *biological* system concerns how *energy* transformation may be conducted, 'knowledge' within an economic system concerns transformation of 'values' of resources which are not congruent with quanta of energy contained in these resources. In this sense the 'technology' of an economic transformation, while still a knowledge-intensive process, differs from the 'technology' of energy transformation for an organism. Nevertheless, from the standpoint of an explanatory evolutionary theory this can be viewed as a function of the knowledge embodied within that technological process. Hence, at least at a first approximation, the systemic similarities are considerable.

From a dynamic point of view, however, we argue that the appropriate analogy is Lamarckian rather than Darwinian since firms 'learn' on the basis of techno-economic experience and thence proceed to incorporate such 'learning' into future behaviour. Thus we view firms as organisms constantly altering their own respective behaviours (through a wide range of different means) with their environment (and thus modifying it) but at the same time being buffeted by that environment in ways that are, at least to a degree, unpredictable. One very important means of bringing this about, though not by any means the only one, is that of getting access to new information which *might* improve performance (that is, technological change as it is conventionally defined in the economics literature).

It is this purposive set of activities which we shall set out in Chapter 5 as an interactive set of knowledge flows, mediated by past technological practice and fed by more fundamental scientific research. And it is here that we may begin to draw out a more fundamental difference with respect to biological systems — namely, the systemic behaviour of technology itself independent of its role within any one firm. For there is, as we shall see, evidence that the technological behaviour of firms is by no means random but on the contrary it is highly purposive, guided by a collective social assessment of how to commit resources to improving economic productivity, and although any given technological system (or paradigm) may eventually fail, and have to be replaced, it provides in the interim a socially accepted way of insuring against uncertainty. We shall argue also in Chapter 5 that such paradigms are sanctioned at least in part by the cognitive authority of a socially contexted basic science. However, it is useful at this stage to introduce some recent developments in the sociology of knowledge which relate both to the epistemological issues we have been exploring and to the more concrete science and technology policy issues to be tackled later in the book.

4.3 The Sociology of Knowledge

In recent years there has been a resurgence of interest in the sociology of knowledge. One reason behind this has been the growing realization that 'scientific research' can no longer be viewed as an unambiguous arbiter of the 'truth' about nature and, by extension, on the competing claims of those who would call in scientific expertise in support of their respective positions with regard to socially contentious issues. Instead, 'science' is coming to be seen more as a social activity, pursued under what are often rather rigid behavioural rules sanctioned by authority and conservative in terms of adherence to given tradition.

This being the case, the scene has apparently shifted from largely philosophical questions about how 'good' science *ought* to be conducted (in terms of rules of evidence and so on), to how scientists *actually behave*, both philosophically and individually, in pursuit of their goals. There are important policy aspects involved here which are both cause and consequence of such a trend. On the causal side it is at least arguable that an important factor is the need for a much more adequate understanding of a social institution which not only absorbs increasing resources (much of it public) but is also used extensively to legitimate social action (both private and public). More consequentially, 'science policy', in the sense of the disposition of public resources to this or that area of science, can no longer be held to be independent of how scientific institutions actually behave. Instead, what scientists do, how they organize themselves to do it *and*, very importantly, what reasons they put forward in justification, are very much matters for social concern and therefore social research.

With respect to the sociology of knowledge itself, a central issue has been concerned with 'interests' and 'goals' and the extent to which scientific activity is concerned as much with propping up existing institutional and cognitive structures as it is with extending the 'boundaries of knowledge' in some disinterested fashion. Of course, to the extent it is, it is no longer possible to view investment in science in starkly input–output terms — science being viewed, as it were, as a necessary intermediate ingredient in the pursuit of independently defined social goals. On the contrary, science itself, at least partially, defines its own goals and proceeds to persuade its patrons that these are what are socially necessary.

What lies behind this new approach is a view of the process of knowledge acquisition which emphasizes the social context within which knowledge is sought and given validation, as opposed to the traditional view which stresses the degree of 'correspondence' between scientific experiment and an independent external 'reality'. It is also consistent with the approach of evolutionary epistemology outlined above. One of the best short accounts of it is given by Barnes,[18] who makes use of the work of Mary Hesse, the Cambridge philosopher, which models the process of knowledge acquisition as a series of

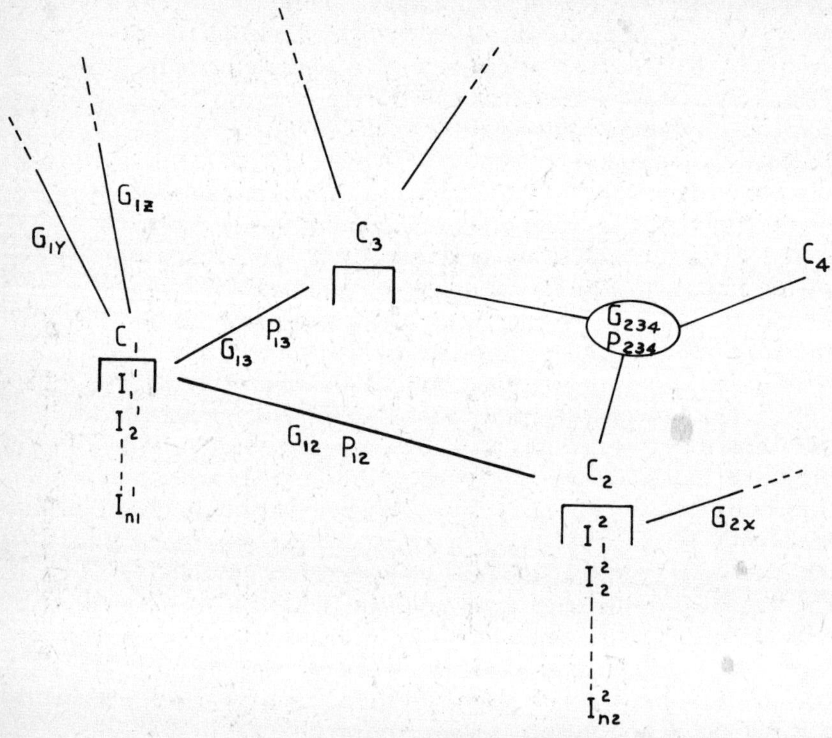

Notes: Subscripts and superscripts refer to specific concepts or instances.
C = Concepts
G = Generalization amongst concepts
I = Instances, or extensions, of concepts
P = Probability attached to generalizations

Figure 4.1 A Hesse 'net'. (*Source:* Barnes 1983)

associative, socially validated and revisable, inductive and conceptual networks. The argument, put simply, runs as follows.

From a very early age people learn things through a perceptual interaction with a complex environment under the authority of a parental figure (or figures). Learning takes place through two mechanisms: (1) *ostension*, that is having objects pointed out and labelled; (2) *generalization*, that is connecting such labelled objects together in classification schemes of increasing complexity. Generalizations are never absolute but are on the contrary revisable — they have a probability attached to them. A Hesse 'net' portrayed in Figure 4.1 is a graphical expression of this process.

Imagine a number of concepts (C_1, C_2, . . ., C_n) tied together with a number of generalizations (G_{12}, G_{13}, G_{23}, . . ., G_{xy}, . . ., etc.). Such a net is simply a small part of a very large three-dimensional 'whole' which comprises the entire conceptual resources possessed by any individual within a given culture. Under every concept stands a number of specific instances or *extensions*, some of which are given by ostension, some by verbal communication and some by personal inference. Thus 'the (ex)tensions of each net provide the connnections which attach the net to the physical environment',[19] and for any individual the process of knowledge acquisition may be seen as a widening of linguistic resources so as to encompass an ever-increasing understanding of reality.

And yet such an understanding is *never absolute*, but is on the contrary *revisable, judgemental* (we pass judgements as to what we see), *social* (we agree proper conceptual usage as a result of social intercourse) and *conservative* (once mental sets are established we are reluctant to change them). Moreover, knowledge thus acquired provides an important means of establishing *cultural coherence*, differentiating our own culture from other alien cultures, prescribing correct/moral behaviour and in other ways validating given social attributes. It follows, of course, under this view that there is no need to postulate an *independent* rationality, logic or reality to justify any given body of knowledge. Knowledge simply is what we as social beings declare it to be. Nature answers the questions we ask of it. In Hesse's terminology, all nets, or bodies of knowledge, are *equivalent* — they stand in the same relation to the physical environment and there is no need to postulate the existence of an underlying Kantian reality — 'things in themselves' — as the ultimate touchstone of natural truth.

From our standpoint the significance of this (relativist) position lies in its import for scientific research. We now know from the work of Thomas Kuhn that science can no longer be regarded as a simple confrontation between fact and theory according to the classical inductivist philosophers, like Mill. Nor can it be regarded as 'Whig history' — as the gradual unfolding of a pre-existent 'truth' by means of the experimental method. On the contrary, all 'facts' are theory dependent in the sense that their cognition depends to a degree on the scientific instrumentation used to perceive them, and their acceptance as valid by scientific communities depends very much on social factors:

Scientific investigation so often described wholly in terms of the 'reason' and perception of the isolated individual and his experience, is presented as a complex interaction between a research community, with its received culture, and its environment. According to Kuhn, knowledge and competence in a mature science are transmitted in the course of a dogmatic and highly structured training, which inculcates an intense commitment to existing modes of perception, beliefs, paradigms or problem-solutions, and procedures. Such commitment is the prerequisite for *normal science*, the typical form of research in a developed field, which amounts to 'a strenuous and devoted attempt to force nature into the conceptual boxes supplied by professional education' (Kuhn, 1970, p. 5). At no point is cognition intelligible as a manifestation of 'reason' or 'logic' alone; at no point does an addition to knowledge correspond purely and simply to a further aspect of reality itself. What it is possible to think and to know are to an extent prestructured. Whatever attains general credibility does so through processes involving cognitive commitments, acquired through socialisation and maintained by the application of authority and forms of social control.[20]

Thus according to Kuhn what is classed as normal science is very much a routine affair where scientists, knowing what they want to find, duly find it. It is only during periods of 'revolutionary science', that is where the scientific community demonstrates widespread unease about the viability of the existing 'paradigm', that problems begin to arise:

Kuhn's account of normal science is a fascinating and insightful description of a conventional activity. Yet he himself occasionally encourages us to forget this. His discussion of the insufficiency of logic and experience at a time of paradigm change can create the impression that at other times they are sufficient. He even occasionally refers to normal research as 'cumulative', which as a common-sense description is reasonable enough, but which evokes all the wrong associations for those philosophers who deeply desire to make out as much as possible of the history of science as 'rational progress'. Thus encouraged, some of these have argued that the meaning of concepts is stable and unproblematic in periods of normal science, so that 'rational evaluation' is possible therein; only the discontinuities in meaning at times of revolution create problems for orthodox philosophical accounts of scientific judgement.[21]

Hence the conclusion is sometimes reached that however irrational periods of revolutionary science are, during the more common periods of normal science it is possible to evaluate scientific activity according to independent logical criteria.

Barnes disagrees. To him *all* science (revolutionary, normal or whatever) is socially contexted and cognitively contingent:

Normal scientists are not rational automata, using words according to their inherent meanings or extensions. Existing usage always leaves future usage to be developed by users themselves. It is precisely because of this that the continuing role of authority and social control is of ineradicable significance in normal science. Normal scientists cannot be impressed with the similarity relations of a scientific specialty by authority, and then left to themselves as individuals, to be looked after, as it were, by the implications of those similarity relations. A similarity relation cannot function as an instruction which tells a rational automaton how to behave; on the contrary, it is a resource which must be sustained and developed by collective human agency. This is the profound sense in which normal science is a social activity. And this is why Kuhn's matter-of-fact account of routine scientific activity threatens epistemological orthodoxy more radically even than his explicitly philosophical discussion of revolutionary states of affairs.[22]

So what then brings about a scientific revolution? After all, revolutions of this kind have, we all agree, taken place, and Kuhn identifies them as such, giving careful documentation of the scientific developments that can be so considered (e.g. Lavoisier/Oxygen, Dalton/Chemical Compounds, Einstein/Relativity). Barnes points out that Kuhn is rather vague on this point, making reference to *gestalt switches* or *continuous refutation of paradigm-induced expectations* as being in some sense prime movers behind revolutionary expectations, but there is no account given of precisely how this happens. What, for example, determines whether an apparent set of counter-instances is seen as a puzzle to be solved by the usual routine methodological denials (further '*ad hoc*' assumptions, reclassifications, ignoring the evidence, etc.) as opposed to an anomaly, which requires a fundamental paradigm shift?

The answer must be, Barnes aruges, in the invocation of social goals and interests. Science is a *social* activity wherein knowledge about the world is pursued and validated according to *social* norms. Such norms are of two broad types. First, those associated with *technical prediction and control* refer to the overt direct interests of the scientific community in carrying out its customary tasks in any field — for example, verifying experimentally a set of known physical constants. Here the rules of the game are well established, as to what counts as 'good science', and the social institutions through which the rules are effected are habit and peer authority. However, a second and concealed set of interests are those associated with *social persuasion and legitimation*, and such interests are complex, subtle and often relate to deeply held beliefs about the way the world simply is. In this sense such interests should not simply be construed as referring to crude vested interests of the obvious type (such as those associated with job protection for particular scientific groups) but should be seen also in more starkly metaphysical terms. A good example of this might be the modern reductionist predisposition in bio-medical research, where a great deal of effort and resources are spent on microbiological research in order to identify 'agents' of human disease (such as viruses, bacteria and the like), charting their behaviour and developing 'magic bullets' (usually drugs) to wipe them out. It is clear, as Inglis has pointed out, that there are a variety of beliefs which provide a powerful metaphysical context for such research and of which most practising scientists are largely unaware.[23] There are, for example:

(1) the belief that nature is such that fragmented research on the 'parts' of any system can, when aggregated, inform us meaningfully about the total behaviour of the whole system;
(2) the belief that it is the virus that is the problem rather than the cellular environment within which the virus lives;
(3) the belief that the virus is the primary cause of the disease rather than merely the carrier of it;
(4) the belief that killing the virus is therefore the best way of getting rid of the disease;
(5) the belief that chemotherapy (drugs) is the best way to do this — and so on.

Now, beliefs of this kind, usually shared by the patients themselves, since they have no other independent source of knowledge validation, perform a vital social function. They permit the scientist to carry out his work with the security of academic validity behind him. Were he constantly beset by doubts as to whether, for example, the environment itself was the prime cause, it is very unlikely that he would have the motivation necessary to carry out his research well, in terms of the methodological norms laid down by his peers. And yet we must surely agree at the same time that this research is cognitively contingent. It is predicted upon a particular set of beliefs about the nature of reality which is given social validation by the scientific peer group. And if this is so, then appeals to 'good scientific practice' to support the validity of this kind of research must be seen as impressively circular.

Thus two sets of interests are continuously and simultaneously operating, and what Barnes appears to be arguing is that the decision by a group of scientists to regard a set of counter-instances as anomalous can only be explained in terms of these interests, what they consist of and how they interact. What these are in any given context is therefore a proper subject for social research the outcome of which is itself to be seen as socially contingent, and so on in an infinite regress.

4.4 Re-cap and Evaluation

Let us now pause so as to summarize the argument of this chapter. Our overall objective has been to establish a metaphorical structure for the analysis of technological change in a socioeconomic context, and to do so in a way which may help to avoid the pitfalls arguably associated with the economistic paradigm, variations of which are conventionally used for this purpose. What we have done is to venture outside that paradigm and to engage directly with evolutionary ideas which are avowedly antithetical to the Cartesian mechanics of classical physics.

Our first 'building block', Prigogine's theory of dissipative structures, developed later by Jantsch into a more general dynamic systems theory, was chosen at least partly for this very reason — that it provides an account of natural processes which is evolutionary in its very essence. On this approach, nature is to be viewed mainly as a hierarchical network of organic systems 'co-evolving' through time in the direction of increasing differentiation and complexity. The mechanism through which such developments occur is one of energy (matter) exchange with the local environment under conditions in which the systemic components under consideration exhibit behaviour of a 'far from equilibrium' type. Jantsch has shown how for the higher forms of life, including social systems themselves, such exchanges also take the form of information flows. And hence it is not unreasonable to suppose that where the *technological development* of social systems is concerned, such information flows may be seen as the basic raw material out of which technological transformation is to be fashioned, at least as a necessary condition.

Certainly, such a hypothetical position is consistent with recent epistemological work which starts by viewing biological systems as knowledge systems, exchanging 'information' with their environment so as to fulfil evolutionary goals, and goes on to view the acquisition of knowledge itself as an evolutionary process. We have used this as our second building block and have noted that one property of 'information exchange' between organismic units which may have significance for the economic analysis of technological changes is its essentially *resonating* character. In order for *information* to achieve the status of *useful knowledge* it needs to undergo a process of evolutionary articulation between 'supplier' and 'recipient'. It follows also that the 'value' of any given piece of information is highly variable depending not only upon its evolutionary articulation but also upon how it is combined with other pieces of information in specific instances. We shall use these properties to develop the notion of the 'technological paradigm' in Chapter 5.

Finally, as our third building block, we reviewed some recent work in the sociology of knowledge which stresses both its pragmatic and revisable nature as well as its socially contexted character. This has significance in so far as technological changes in modern society achieve acceptance not only in terms of their economic power, their capacity to satisfy economic need, but also in terms of their congruence with institutional goals and interests, including importantly that of the scientific community itself. We shall see in Chapter 5 and also later in the text that an area of concern in modern complex societies is the use of scientific expertise to give validation to specific techno-economic practices, thus arguably building a degree of circularity into the making of science and technology policy.

Notes and References

1. See D. Bohm (1980), *Wholeness and the Implicate Order* (London: Routledge).
2. E. Jantsch (1980), *The Self-Organizing Universe* (Oxford: Pergamon), p. 25.
3. Ibid., p. 25.
4. Ibid., p. 26.
5. R. Thom (1975), *Structural Stability and Morphogenesis* (Reading: Benjamin).
6. See J. Singh (1966), *Information Theory, Language and Cybernetics* (London: Constable), p. 77 et seq. See also this passage and Chapters I–III for a demonstration of the statistical equivalence of information theory and thermodynamics, and D. Brooks and E. Wiley (1984), 'Evolution as an Entropic Phenomenon' in J. Pollard (ed.), *Evolutionary Theory* (Chichester: Wiley), pp. 141–69.
7. D. Marthaler (1976), 'Geheimmsvoller Nervenfilz', *Neue Zurcher Zeituing* 2, Nov. Summary of an article by F. Schmitt *et al.*, *Science*, **192**: 114–20.
8. Jantsch, op. cit., p. 161.
9. Ibid., pp. 161, 162 (emphasis in original).
10. Ibid., p. 163.
11. Ibid., p. 164.
12. Ibid., p. 177.
13. See H. Plotkin (ed.) (1982), *Learning, Development and Culture* (Chichester: Wiley).
14. Ibid., p. 6.
15. Ibid., p. 6.
16. Ibid., p. 7.
17. Ibid., p. 7.
18. See B. Barnes (1983), 'On the Conventional Character of Knowledge and Cognition', in K.D. Knorr-Cetina and M. Mulkay (eds), *Science Observed* (London: Sage), pp. 19–51. See also B. Barnes (1982), *T.S. Kuhn and Social Science* (London: Routledge & Kegan Paul); B. Barnes (1977), *Interests and the Growth of Knowledge* (London: Routledge & Kegan Paul); D.C. Bloor (1976), *Knowledge and Social Imagery* (London: Routledge & Kegan Paul); and J. Law and P. Lodge (1984), *Science for Social Scientists* (London: Macmillan), especially Section IV. All exponents of these views owe a great debt to Mary Hesse's 'network' theory of knowledge. See, for example, M. Hesse (1974), *The Structure of Scientific Inference* (London: Macmillan).
19. Barnes, 'On the Conventional Character of Knowledge and Cognition', op. cit., p. 25.
20. Barnes, *T.S. Kuhn and Social Science*, op. cit., pp. 10, 11 (emphasis in original). The reference to Kuhn is to the *Structure of Scientific Revolutions* (Chicago: Chicago University Press).
21. Barnes, ibid., p. 83.

22. Ibid., p. 5.
23. See B. Inglis (1982), *The Diseases of Civilization* (London: Hodder & Stoughton).

Chapter 5

Towards an Evolutionary Theory of Economic Change

In this chapter we intend to build upon the critical foundations outlined in the previous chapters so as to provide something approaching an interpretive framework for the case material in the following section. You will recall our argument that an important defect of the traditional economistic approach is its essentially deductive and mechanistic character. We argued in Chapter 2 that such an approach is bound both to oversimplify and misrepresent the true nature of a process which is inherently a complex one of continuous flux and interaction. And indeed in Chapter 3 we have seen also that at various points well-known economists and social commentators have attempted to apply the organic/evolutionary metaphor to the economic process without ever taking matters as far as they might have.

We shall start our own evolutionary model by exploring in some more detail the arguments raised in the previous chapter concerning the role of information flows in systemic communication. Existing treatments in economic analysis tend to be weak since economic actors are assumed either to be perfectly informed about all choice possibilities or are able to use prices to provide all necessary information for the resource allocation decision. Our own view, however, is that the flow of information plays a much more central role in the process of economic change, which is inherently an uncertain activity. Lack of information introduces uncertainty into the investment decision and to that extent renders it 'innovative' or 'entrepreneurial'. Essentially, it is how well the entrepreneur is able to orchestrate and guide an innovation within such a context of very great complexity, that determines his eventual success.

We then take these ideas further in the following ways. First, we define information flows in terms of formal information theory — and thus distinguish logically between 'information' and 'knowledge' as conceptual categories. Second, we define the 'science/technology system' as the institutional setting for the generation of new information about nature which will later become contextualized in the form of new economic knowledge. Third, we show how such a view of relations between information and knowledge is consistent with recent research by Lundvall and others which emphasizes user–supplier interaction in the innovative process. Finally, we shall shift focus in a more explicitly dynamic (or diachronic) direction through a further development of the concept of the technological system, or paradigm, which has been the focus of considerable research in recent years. An important conclusion which we reach is that it may be useful to regard the science/technology system as at root one of interactive knowledge flows punctuated by socioeconomic discontinuities. The 'technological paradigm' then becomes, as it were, a socioeconomic 'device' to deal with resultant uncertainties and lack of appropriability. Without it, technological changes simply would not take place at all, or at least they would appear with much less frequency.

Returning to the discussion in the previous chapter, it may then be seen that innovation is itself an entropic process. Just as biological systems, viewed as dissipative structures, evolve through the metabolism of matter/energy introduced from the immediate environment, so productive units evolve in a similar way. Information is imported into the system, combined with pre-existent competences so as to generate 'new knowledge' which may then be used to transform economic resources at higher levels of techno-economic efficiency. Notice that parallel 'far-from equilibrium' and autocatalytic conditions will normally also prevail in the sense that such an innovation process often takes place under circumstances characterized by external threat (e.g. competition) and internal turbulence (the disruption of firm-specific routines). In addition, it is clear that the appropriate metaphor is not the conventional neo-Darwinian one, since innovations build upon previously acquired knowledge and competence, but should be seen as Lamarckian, or purposive, with a certain chance element thrown in.

Finally, we bring all the ideas developed in this chapter within an overall framework of diachronic change which emphasizes the primary role of the science/technology system gradually articulating innovations in interactive resonance with markets for goods and services. Such a framework (or model), we argue, enables a clearer perspective to be obtained on how to make and implement appropriate policies for science and technology. In particular, for the socioeconomic system as a whole, it requires the formulation of an appropriate institutional framework.

5.1 Information and Knowledge

Central to our analysis of the technical-change process is the role played by the generation and diffusion of 'information' and its integration into economic systems. For our purposes there are probably three separate senses in which the word may be used, so that to begin with at least it is useful to try to define the concept both in itself and as distinguished from its close relative 'knowledge'.

5.1.1. *Neoclassical Information*

To the neoclassical economist information is an important category in so far as it bears upon the arguments of constrained maximization theory, and a slight digression into this is necessary at this point. The basic aim of neoclassical economics is to explain how scarce resources get allocated amongst competing ends (the positive allocation problem) and how such resources may be reallocated so as to improve social welfare (the normative efficiency problem). This is done by means of an axiomatic procedure wherein ideal boundary conditions are postulated with regard to human and institutional behaviour and technical conditions, followed by an assessment of how far actual experience deviates from such an ideal. Thus in terms of behaviour, for example, consumers are generally assumed to be 'utility maximizers' and producers 'profit maximizers'.

An important difficulty is that in order to achieve determinant solutions to the ideal state, it is necessary to make fairly heroic assumptions about the boundary conditions. For example, in order for a state of general equilibrium in product and factor markets to obtain, institutional conditions have to remain constant, technology does not change, consumers and producers have perfect knowledge of all relevant information regarding production and consumption, there are no 'externalities' which cannot be 'internalized', and so on. Under such conditions unique product and factor prices may be established for all goods and services from which standpoint suboptimal deviations may be deduced.

Kay has argued that theorizing in this manner produces the 'economics of Nirvana', the ideal conditions being totally unrealistic for useful analysis.[1] In particular, he argues against the assumption of perfect knowledge since ultimately all 'economic problems are reducible to problems in information' and that in 'the absence of information problems there is no economic problem'.[2] For example, many of the functions that are routinely handled by firms (finance, marketing, R&D) would become unnecessary, no uncertainty would minimize the level of transactions costs incurred by relying on the market to provide resources, the removal of bounded rationality (the limited cognitive capacity of individuals to assimilate and process information) would remove the need for hierarchy within firms and hence ultimately, Kay argues, the firm would reduce to the small single-product enterprise and we should have 'converted' our 'real world' firm into a passable imitation of a standard neoclassical firm having an omniscient entrepreneur controlling capital and homogeneous labour'.[3]

Of course, defenders of the neoclassical tradition argue that the price system itself conveys all the necessary information for economic decision making and that the idealized neoclassical firm is merely a device introduced to simplify analysis. However, both positions are difficult to defend. The former argument is manifestly not the case given the enormous complexity, speciality and sophistication of modern products, while the latter presupposes the analytical usefulness of this particular form of neoclassical abstraction. Above all, economics represents a set of tools with which to achieve a better understanding of how economic systems work, but the tools are only as good as the reality they are intended to represent. The general equilibrium paradigm, to the extent that it models anything, may be seen as a card-board cut-out of the type of economic system which obtained during the early phases of the Industrial Revolution — atomistic producers, single-product firms, simple technology, limited range of products, and so on. For a world of large firms, conglomerates, state production, rapid technical and institutional change, and complex products we need something different.

5.1.2. *Information Theory*

Neoclassical information in the above sense does not make any distinction between 'information' and 'knowledge'. The concepts are interchangeable and are used loosely to describe a category of boundary conditions which prevent economic actors from behaving as they ought to so as to achieve some putative optimum in terms of the allocation of resources. What the formal theory of information does is to define the concept in a way which is logically independent of 'meaning' and in so doing provides the basis for a more general theory of systemic communication — something we shall require in the argument ahead. In particular, it allows us to relate the flow of information to that of energy/entropy and thence to develop a model of the technical change process which has the property of systemic generality.

Information theory conceptualizes 'information' in terms of a flow of 'messages' which have 'news value'; that is, they cause surprise to recipients. In the 'communication engineer's purification of the term the stress is on the quantitative aspects of the *flow* in a *network* of an *intangible* attribute called *information*'.[4] Such a network consists of three main parts:

(1) a transmitter;
(2) a receiver;
(3) a communications channel.

Since the medium of communication is not in general similar to that of the transmitter or receiver, there needs to be a means of translating signals at the beginning and at the end of the process, so that any typical communication system may be represented as shown in Figure 5.1. For example, a radio system operates by converting sequences of voice production into electromagnetic waves which are beamed through the atmosphere to be received and understood by listeners.

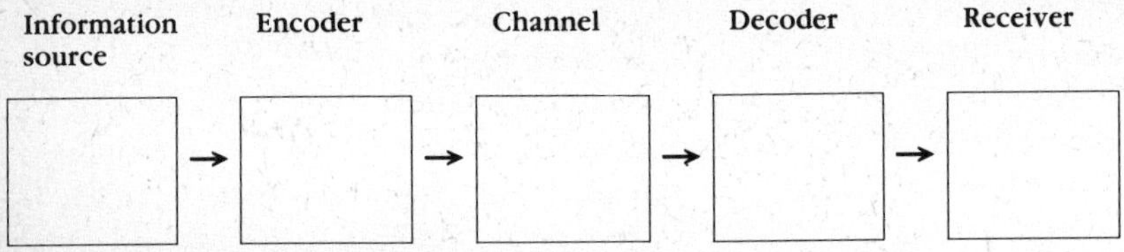

Figure 5.1

Thus 'information' turns out to be closely related to energy. Its flows are conventionally quantified in statistical terms, that is by means of a multiplicand of probabilities attached to 'bits' of information where the total information content of any message, in a given 'ensemble' of possible messages, may be measured by the logarithm of the probability of its occurrence. Logarithms are used so as to convert combinations of discrete probability measures to a summation. Hence the information content in any complex of messages is then simply the sum of its individual components. Thus:

$$M = - \sum_{i=1}^{n} P_i \log_2 P_i \qquad (1)$$

where M = amount of information
P_i = probability of the ith message being selected
n = number of possible messages

A logarithmic base of two is chosen conventionally to define a standard binary unit of information (a 'bit') where there are two possible messages which may be communicated— the simplest system. Where such messages are equally probable the information content of the system becomes

$$\log_2 = 1 \quad \text{i.e. 1 'bit'} \qquad (2)$$

If there were twenty-seven possible messages, the information content of that system would be

$$\log_2 27 = 4.76 \text{ bits} \qquad (3)$$

Singh shows that no information system has this freedom of information content because of practical limitations. The English language, for example, is such that not all of its letters are equally likely to be chosen. It has the property of 'redundancy' and it is this redundancy that gives it 'intelligibility'. The amount of redundancy in any given system using the above notation is measured by the fraction

$$R = 1 - \frac{\sum_{i=1}^{n} P_i \log_2 P_i}{\log_2 n} \tag{4}$$

Notice, finally, that we have defined the information content of any system in a way which is completely independent of semantic meaning. It is merely 'a measure of one's freedom of choice when one selects a message from the available set, many of which may well be devoid of meaning'.[5] It is thus used logically in computer science. From our point of view it has the additional property of being similar to an energetic measure, because since our measure of information is statistical it is therefore directly analogous to the statistical mechanics of molecular systems where the degree of freedom of any closed system (its entropy), or its *thermodynamic probability*, is a measure of the deviation of molecular (or micro) 'states' from the average (or macro) 'state' of the whole system:

> when the state of motions of the molecules in the body is highly *disorganized* or anarchic, with each molecule in the chaotic whirl of a law unto itself, the number of microstates leading to one and the same macrostate is much more numerous so that its thermodynamic probability becomes exceedingly great. This state of great thermodynamic probability obviously yields much less information about the actual structure of the internal motions simply because there are now so many more alternatives to choose from. Thermodynamic probability of a body thus provides us a measure of information about the state of its internal motions even if it does so in a negative way.[6]

Thus the greater the amount of information in any given system, the smaller will be its entropy, or the greater will be its 'negentropy', and equally the greater the flow of information into any system, the greater the degree of organization such a system will exhibit.

We shall see later that it is this property of information which has direct relevance to the process of economic production since it is precisely such *organizational* features which permit the conversion of information into useful knowledge and thence technical change.

5.1.3 *Scientific Information: The Science/Technology System*

A third type of information is that which is directly concerned with the productive process itself. It is the information which is necessary to enable the producer to transform resources into products and to sell them. Of course, not all such information is scientific knowledge in the conventional sense. Machlup in his investigation of the 'knowledge industry' postulated five classes of knowledge, only two of which ('practical' and 'intellectual') could be regarded as being directly concerned with economic production, but the former category clearly includes the wide range of tacit, informal information without which no production would be possible.[7]

Nevertheless, it is clear that modern economic production is increasingly dependent upon information, the generation of which is a highly organized professional endeavour. It is useful to conceive of purposive activity of this kind as being generated within a *scientific infrastructure*, or a *science/technology (S/T) system* and communicated to the productive system by means of a complex process of iterative feedback. Typical institutional components of the S/T system are the R&D departments of firms, government research establishments, universities and specialist consultancy companies, and so on. Hence the S/T system cuts across the publicly/privately owned sectors of the modern economy and may be thought of as a multi-tiered set of institutional sources of information many of which are in communication with each other, although not necessarily as part of the normal process of economic production.

A very simple outline of the S/T system is provided by Freeman, who provides a 'map' with R&D activity as the heartland relating out to various institutional categories of relevance such as academia, industry, government, and so on.[8] Clark (1985) has shown how it is possible to enumerate such a map at least in principle as an informational 'input-output table' precisely analogous to that used in conventional social accounting, the 'inputs' of resources (finance, equipment, materials and skilled manpower) giving rise to inventive 'output' of various kinds which may be accounted for in proxy ways, for example through patent counts.[9]

While an important advantage of this sort of exercise is that it allows one to gain a clearer picture of the disposition of economic resources to the S/T sector and its component parts, there are a number of limitations as to how it may be used analytically. For example, existing measures of 'inventive output' (licences, patents, R&D expenditures) are notoriously inaccurate, there are complex intersectoral effects (including non-requited financial flows from the government to the private sector) and it is difficult to normalize heterogeneous data. For these and other reasons the value of much analytical work has been compromised and no doubt will continue to be so until better data are developed.

A further problem is conceptual and arises because of the necessity to treat the S/T system analogously to economic sectors, that is as a set of productive activities which may be normalized by attaching money values to inputs and outputs. Although there may well be some usefulness in such a procedure as a rough guide, it suffers from the attempt to convert the intangible (information) into a concrete economic quantity. Thus we have seen above that information *per se* can really only be understood in energetic terms, defined independently of whatever meaning may be attached to it. Indeed, we have argued that the value of any quantum of energetic information is purely *contextual* — it is entirely a function of the economic context in which it is to be used. Nor should this be surprising. To the tribesman of Papua New Guinea the fluctuations of the Dow-Jones index have no relevance. To the Wall Street speculator they are, often literally, a matter of life or death. But if information itself has no inherent value *sui generis*, how can we subject it to economic calculation? What does it mean to establish statistical relationships between informational activities like R&D and measures of economic performance?

Here we are close to the ultimate paradox of the social evaluation of science and technology. By definition the creation of information is the creation of novelty whose value is indeterminate through economic space and time. Even if we could measure apparent past relationships with accuracy, this can tell us very little about what to do in the future. The allocation problem from the point of view of the informational investment decision is insoluble — at least to a considerable degree. We argue that in fact economists have not come to terms with a basic weakness of their tools — namely, that they cannot be applied to the process of technological change itself and hence the continued attempts to do so merely produce more artificiality and confusion.

It is in this sense that we take issue with writers like Machlup who insist that the concept of 'information' be equated with that of 'knowledge'. Despite acknowledging that there are important technical differences between them, he chooses to treat them as interchangeable on grounds of common usage: 'Hence, in [the] ordinary uses of the word, all information is knowledge.'[10] Although this enables Machlup to investigate the 'knowledge industry' in an economistic way, we believe that it serves merely to obscure the important issues of time, uncertainty and indeterminateness. Conversely, by treating the technical change process as an 'open system' of linked and resonating information flows, we may be getting much closer to a model which is realistic.

Thus we shall make a clear distinction between information and knowledge in our analysis. The former is a dimensionless energetic category whose production and movement throughout economic systems is pervasive and is accomplished in a variety of different ways, but it only becomes 'knowledge' having economic value to the extent that a particular context allows it to do so. It follows that both 'information' and 'knowledge' are indeterminate as economic categories, the former because no *'a priori'* value can be set upon it, the latter because its value derives only from its context at a particular configuration of economic space/time. We are back once more to the irreversibility of economic time. It is certainly possible to derive *ex post* rates of return to investment in 'knowledge-generating activities' with the benefit of hindsight. However, it is equally impossible to perform similar calculations *ex ante*. Conversely, it may be more reasonable to view the flux of information as occurring *alongside* that of economic quantities, providing 'knowledge' regarding *how* production and consumption may be carried on efficiently and *how* new production and consumption possibilities may be developed through time.

Certainly, this view is consistent with recent research into the nature of innovation where user–supplier interaction is seen to be of central importance to success, while much of such interaction is essentially informational. Lundvall, for example, argues that innovations arise out of 'interactions', or 'collisions', between technical opportunity and user need.[11] Innovators, therefore, need information about both. But the acquisition and interpretation of such information involves costs which can be quite high since producers and users are always separate even where they co-exist within the same organization.

Looked at in this light, production and innovation are part and parcel of the same exchange process since every act of *economic* exchange is at the same time an act of *informational* exchange which allows both producer and user the opportunity to conceive of ways whereby production and consumption may be carried out more efficiently: 'Production and innovation are interdependent. Information obtained in relation to production and in relation to the regular flow of products, feed the innovational process. Innovations reshape production and the regular flows'.[12] Information *flows* take place through information *channels* in the form of specific *codes*. The establishment of such channels/codes may be regarded as an act of investment, but once established, of course, they tend to lose flexibility to the extent that they are programmed to receive, process, store and disseminate only particular kinds of information.

Lundvall uses these ideas along with some empirical case material to argue that innovations succeed best in 'organized markets' — that is, where user–producer relations are partly market-related in the conventional sense but partly also hierarchical with producers and users establishing 'codes of conduct' to ensure mutually beneficial relationships. Here he disagrees with Williamson, who views hierarchies as brought about in order to economize on transactions costs.[13] On the contrary, hierarchies are a response to the need for information flows between buyer and seller in the process of technical change. If *all* resource flows are market-mediated, there will tend to be a great deal of *information-impactedness* (lack of essential information flow), while if such resources are mediated by hierarchy, then one reaches the conventional monopoly position where there is little incentive to innovate. Only where an intermediate set of relations exists will effective innovation be possible.

5.2 Scientific and Technological Paradigms

How, then, can we extend these ideas on information into a coherent framework for the analysis of technological change? You will recall that in a sense what 'drives' a socioeconomic system through time is the readiness of its constituent elements to absorb and develop new technology. And it is from this standpoint that the concept of the technological 'paradigm' takes on a particular conceptual importance as an operant vehicle for technical change. In what follows we shall develop the notion in relation to its intellectual parent, the scientific paradigm, so as to show that both notions may be subsumed under the concept of socially contexted and bounded knowledge flows. Viewed in this way, it is possible also to view technological changes as the resultant of two kinds of socioeconomic pressures: (1) the institutional 'push' associated with developments within the S/T system itself; (2) the influence of market demands. The interesting policy questions may then lie in how exactly the state should intervene so as to achieve its stated aims in the most efficient manner.

A useful starting point is Kuhn's influential book *The Structure of Scientific Revolutions*, which we introduced earlier and which has been the mainspring of much influential work in the sociology of knowledge over the past twenty or so years. In particular, Kuhn's view that the growth of scientific knowledge is not a linear but a cyclical process strongly influenced by the professional authority of scientific communities, has raised again a wide range of interesting questions about the intrinsic nature of knowledge, its relation to external reality (assuming such a reality to exist) and how such knowledge is validated and promulgated in a social context. What gives particular immediacy to this resurgence of interest in themes that have a considerable intellectual history is, of course, a range of developments in the power of modern technology to process information at speeds and accuracies which are several orders greater than anything known before, with consequential influences on economic production that are liable to be very dramatic indeed.

A particularly important aspect of these post-Kuhnian developments was raised at the end of Chapter 4. Under this 'pragmatic' or 'utilitarian' view *all* knowledge is sought for practical reasons and should be understood therefore in utilitarian terms. Furthermore, 'utility' has to be seen not only as a strictly economic phenomenon — that is, in terms of the satisfaction of consumption needs — but also as a function of the social interests of the scientific community itself. Sometimes (indeed very often) such 'interests' are the conventional ones of *technical prediction and control*, which are those we have been brought up to believe are the absolute values which pervade all scientific endeavour. However, underlying these overtly scientific aims are deeper goals of *social persuasion and legitimation*, which are clearly much more intrusive than conventional wisdom would allow.

We may view both forms of 'interest' not in starkly differentiated terms, however, but rather in terms of a hierarchy of interests which determine conventional practice. At the highest metaphysical/cerebral level there are values which stress experimentalism, reductionism and the slow painstaking activity of 'science' as a 'craft', gradually unfolding the secrets of nature. At a rather more mundane level there are the professionalized interests of the resultant disciplines, involving access to the state for research funding, job security and the like. At this level, too, there are a variety of bureaucratic interests relating to 'client' groups which may require scientific 'expertise' to legitimate their own activities. Such interests usually take a variety of different forms ranging from those of the civil service itself, through para-statal organizations to consumer organizations. Often such organizations employ their own 'scientific-experts' whose job includes the maintenance of close links with the relevant disciplines within the scientific sector and who thus act as technological 'gatekeepers' with an important legitimatory role. Finally, there are of course the direct economic interests of social groups (mainly business firms and trade unions) which require 'expertise' in order also to validate their respective social functions.

Here we have an intriguing 'symbiosis of power' through which the scientific community both collectively and with respect to its component subsystems achieves self-validation by virtue of attaching itself to powerful client groups, which themselves seek to consolidate and expand their own power basis through this same process of expert validation. Under such circumstances, 'objective truth' appears a very imperfect touchstone; it is what serves the practical interests of those individuals and groups who happen to possess the most tenacious hold on the means of wealth and power at any point in time. Both in terms of the orientation of scientific research by topic and in terms of its 'success', there may well be gross inefficiency in the scientific quest which never reaches public awareness. At least to some extent, science is a closed system.

Notice, finally, that the existence of 'objective reality' out there, so to speak, is to a large extent independent of this argument. If knowledge is simply sought for practical/utilitarian reasons and, therefore, is what people say it is, there is still no necessary contradiction with the postulate of an external reality. On the contrary, 'reality' may be viewed as placing boundary conditions, as it were, on what scientists are able to claim. Thus it will presumably never be possible to persuade more than a handful of people that the moon is made of green cheese. Conversely, the issue between reductionist and holistic approaches in modern biology is not so clear cut. Returning to the example mentioned in Chapter 4, the endeavours of biochemists and geneticists to develop a 'magic bullet' to destroy a postulated 'cancer virus' may continue to receive social and economic sanction for decades to come regardless of how little success they have had in the interim. In this sense the existence or non-existence of an ultimate reality is largely irrelevant to most modern science policy issues.

This is a subtle but important argument. Our position is not *necessarily* antithetical to the existence of an objective reality. Rather it argues that since all observation is theory-dependent, there is no independent sense in which nature can act as a neutral arbiter in scientific disputes — which are thus decided by the interactions of social interests. A useful metaphor is to view 'nature' as being separated from the observer by an opaque cloud. What science does is to provide clues about the dimly perceived reality behind the cloud, but such clues are continuously open to question and debate. There are some areas where the cloud is relatively thin, general agreement prevails and the resultant 'facts' achieve practical validation in the form of social artifacts. Conversely, in other areas the cloud is very dense and we have only the vaguest idea of the true descriptions of the shadowy forms which we perceive very dimly in outline.

5.3 Technological Change

Can we then make the same inferences about 'technology' and 'technical practices'? Is it possible, if you like, to apply the 'interests' model of science to technological developments and thus draw similar conclusions? Clearly, there are important similarities which may be outlined as follows.

First, there is now a lot of evidence that dominant technologies hold sway at any point of time in most industrial sectors. Such technologies — technological systems/paradigms — provide the *heuristic* for everything that we understand as technologial change.[14] For example, Gardiner and Rothwell have shown how industries as diverse as aerospace and agricultural machinery can provide examples of how dominant designs get established and 'stretched' over long periods of time through continuous interaction with customer application.[15] Indeed, they argue, a key determinant of any given design's 'robustness' (very roughly, its capacity to act as a technological paradigm), is the degree to which producers are confronted by demanding users — 'tough customers' in the authors' terminology. Similarly, Constant, in his account of the jet engine revolution, shows how aircraft engine designers were for long periods strongly wedded to propellor-driven/piston engine power, and were very reluctant to take seriously any rival technological system.[16] And more recently, Sahal has attempted to model technological systems in terms of dimensionless physical proportionalities.[17]

A second parallel relates to the way given technological practice is enshrined socially. For example, in a later paper Constant postulates the importance of 'communities' of practitioners which represent 'well-defined, well-winnowed traditions of technological practice. These communities and traditions are in the central locus of technological cognition'[18] and they represent powerful agents of social validation. Induction into a community is by means of an apprenticeship system through which novitiates are taught to master and demonstrate certain skills while entry into the profession is determined by a system of examinations. Engineering Councils issue 'codes of conduct' which help to ensure high professional standards. And of couse, like all such institutions which seek to monopolize the provision of a particular set of services, they are liable to fall victim to the corruption that often attaches to the holders of absolute power — bureaucratization of control, undue proscription of practitioners who deviate from normal procedures, unwillingness to consider novel approaches, and so on.

Thus, just as within the scientific community proper practice is validated, controlled and sanctioned by the major scientific 'disciplines', so similar mechanisms of social control may be discerned within technological communities. Examples in Britain might be engineering institutes like the Institute of Electrical Engineers; or the British Medical Council, which is given the social responsibility of ensuring 'good medical practice', or the British Association for Adoption and Fostering in the case of statutory child care. In all cases, where 'knowledge' and 'technique' are used to determine how goods and services are provided to the public and where such knowledge is seen to be complex and esoteric, it is normal for its provision to be validated in ways very similar to those used by scientific communities.[19]

A third similarity lies within the realm of 'interests'. It is almost a truism to suggest that precisely the same types of interests identified by Barnes as dominating the scientific sphere, also appertain strongly in the case of technological communities. A well-known example from early industrial history is that of the destruction of communities based upon hand-loom weaving by the advent of more modern power-driven machinery.[20] Nowadays, 'economic' interests of this type are probably more communally diffuse (except for coal-mining and some textiles manufacture), but they are still clearly an important factor in the genesis (or not) of technological change. In somewhat identical fashion, bureaucratic interests are often similarly present. For example, in a series of case studies on technological decisions, Braun, Collingridge and Hinton show how once large projects (like Concorde) get established, the associated momentum becomes virtually unstoppable.[21]

Finally, in both cases, for any given paradigm to be defeated, there has to be an alternative candidate which shows promise of dealing with the pitfalls and puzzles experienced in the operation of existing technological practice, since in the absence of such a candidate it is likely that attempts will continue to be made to prop up the status quo — to regard 'anomalies' as 'puzzles'. Indeed, just as with many examples in science, revolutionary change with respect to any given technological paradigm often arises from a source or sources *outside* that community.[22]

Hence we can see that in a number of important respects scientific and technological paradigms exhibit striking elements of similarity. However, there are also important differences, and it is in the examination of these differences that we may begin to grasp the inner nature of technical change. In the first place, although both technical and scientific knowledge is enshrined in established community practice the *technological* community is normally much more complex and differentiated. For example, Constant shows how aircraft engine technology is linked with a variety of other 'communities' (airframe manufacturers, airlines, government bodies, ancillary industries) in a hierarchical structure with overlapping interests and functions. Such a structure has an inertia of a different sort compared to a scientific community which normally enjoys a much greater measure of autonomy: 'the process of radical change in any one system requires the translation of its consequences into the interest frame of each of many relevant communities and the persuasion of each of them that the overall gains to be had from the new system outweighs its costs to them'.[23]

Here the resistance to change lies in the composition of the paradigm itself, since the successful genesis of a new technological sytem requires also a series of concomitant changes at other levels. Indeed, Cutting has pointed out that unlike in science, where the agreed success of a rival paradigm can fairly quickly drive out the older one, technological paradigms can often remain in apparent competition over fairly long periods.[24] A good example of this is nineteenth-century alkali production in Britain where the newer Solvay process, although apparently more economically efficient than the older Leblanc industry, continued to be challenged by the latter until well into the twentieth century.[25]

Yet at the same time, Simon has shown how the high degree of differentiation exhibited by technological paradigms is by the same token a source of continuous incipient instability.[26] This occurs due to the vulnerability associated with lack of overall control, since changes in any one part of the system create conditions for corresponding change in other parts. Such tensions do not normally obtain within scientific communities, which are often well 'cemented in' to established functional and bureaucratic practice.

Ultimately, however, the essential difference relates to market influences. Technology is enshrined in artifacts which are bought and sold as part of an economic system. To the extent that economic relations are mediated by markets, no technological paradigm can regard itself as 'safe'.[27] Conversely, the more any given technological system is protected from the market, the more it is likely to operate in a manner similar to that of a scientific paradigm — that is, established and developed with producer and bureaucratic interests primarily in view. Such technologies are not hard to find, since very often they are developed and operated through the public sector either as public goods (e.g. defence), or as a state monopoly (nuclear power generation), or as inputs into either of these. Here 'science' plays the role of legitimator and validator of established practice, a practice which may continue for long periods even where on many criteria the technologies themselves are manifestly not working.

Nevertheless, Constant, for example, shows that science *can* play an altogether different role,[28] but only when conditions are appropriate. In the case of the turbo-jet, its paradigmatic success was not due so much to the failure of the old paradigm (even as late as 1942 propeller-driven aircraft were cheaper, safer and more reliable) as to predictions about what *would happen* as technical performance improved (in the case of the propellor, malfunction at high speeds). He labels this phenomenon 'presumptive anomaly' and argues that it has a catalytic role similar to that conceptually postulated by Kuhn. Notice, however, that it only becomes anomalous because of competitive forces, because of the possibilities of market failure. In the absence of such an independent constraint, the existing paradigm might well have continued over a much longer period, as for example in the case of nuclear energy, where British experience suggests an inertia which can only be explained through the influence of powerful ideological and institutional commitments, combined with lack of critical market constraints.

5.4 Science and Technology Systems

What, then, can we conclude from this juxtaposition of scientific and technological paradigms? It certainly seems clear that technological paradigms, to the extent that they can be identified, are much closer in many respects to their scientific counterparts than a lot of the extant literature would appear to suggest. This is true in organizational terms, in terms of their respective heuristic natures and in terms of the very close contemporary links between scientific and technological changes. Where the analogy breaks down lies in the greater complexity and market vulnerability of technological paradigms, but even here the differences are more a matter of degree than of kind.

But does this not suggest that what we are witnessing is not some radical split between 'science' and 'technology' of the kind suggested by writers like de Solla Price,[29] but is rather a continuum of 'knowledge flows' produced under two competing forces — 'cognitive and related interests' on the one hand, and 'market forces' on the other? A traditional metaphor which is often used to describe the relations between science and technology is that of 'science' as a reservoir of 'knowledge' from which 'technology' draws the necessary quantum as and when needed.[30] The reservoir is continuously expanded through the 'knowledge-seeking activities of scientists while 'technology' as a separate social system satisfies social demands for goods and services, at the same time (occasionally) providing some interesting problems for 'science' to seek solutions for.

Figure 5.2 depicts just such a crude system. The *S* sector continuously replenishes its 'knowledge' through interaction with, and uncovering the secrets of, an objective and independent 'nature', while the *T* sector (in this case contiguous with productive units $T_1, T_2, \ldots, T_5$) uses what 'knowledge' it needs to provide increasing amounts of economic 'output' to the general public (*M*). To some extent also, the *T* sector 'advises' the *S* sector on precisely what bits of 'knowledge' to seek from nature, although it cannot be too directive here since disinterested research will often be just as fruitful. Nature continuously springs surprises. There is a lot of evidence that a social division of labour of the above kind is perceived by many members of scientific and technological communities (and by the general public) as being a rough but reasonably correct description of the way scientific information is produced and applied to social production.

Our argument is essentially that this is not so and that a rather different metaphor is more accurate. Figure 5.3 represents a stylized view of a set of relations which are at once both more complex and more continuous. To begin with science (*S*) and technology (*T*) overlap to a marked degree. While it is true that certain parts of *S* are relatively autonomous, their autonomy is never absolute (even a relatively 'pure' subject like low-temperature physics requires complex instrumentation) while other areas are almost completely contiguous with clients in the *T* sector (e.g. publicly funded research establishments). The technology sector is at once larger and more complex. It is larger simply because it is much more directly involved in economic production. It is more complex by virtue of the systemic factors outlined above, each $T_{xyx\ldots}$ 'pole'[31] relating to a number of its fellows in a shifting sequence of

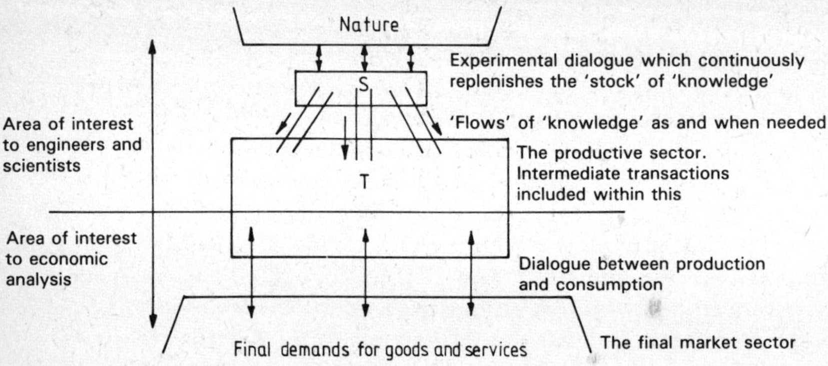

Figure 5.2 The pipeline model

Characteristics

1. Discrete division of labour between isolated 'sectors' each of which may be regarded as a closed system for analytical purposes. Hence 'black box' nature of associated analyses.
2. Investment in 'science' seen as separable from investment in 'technology'. The former is the province of government, the latter that of productive enterprise.
3. Analytical emphasis upon the socioeconomic consequences of technological changes to the relative exclusion of the process of technological change itself.
4. Intermediate transactions within the *T*-sector viewed as part of the 'roundaboutness' of economic production and thus treated in terms of markets rather than in terms of technological flows.
5. We use the word 'knowledge' rather than that of 'information' since in normal usage the latter embraces the former from the viewpoint of 'social usefulness' in both 'market' and 'interests' senses. Put another way, information by itself only possesses social value to the extent that it may be usefully employed when it becomes 'knowledge' under our definition.

information linkages often embodied in hardware but not necessarily so. It follows also that the flows between any *T* and any *S* are never simple but are often mediated by other *T*'s and *S*'s so that the necessary communications flows are difficult to achieve. Finally, the flows should be seen in terms of a 'resonance' between any two poles. Information is only useful to the extent that it fulfils the goals of the user, and in order to achieve this it has effectively to flow in both directions. One implication of this is clearly to place even greater potential obstacles to the flow of information between the various component parts of the science/technology system.

Hence it should be clear that the notion of clear, unobstructed information flows between differentiated *S* and *T* systems is a chimera. On the contrary, the interrelations are so complex and the uncertainty so great that ways have to be found of ensuring an adequate rate of technological

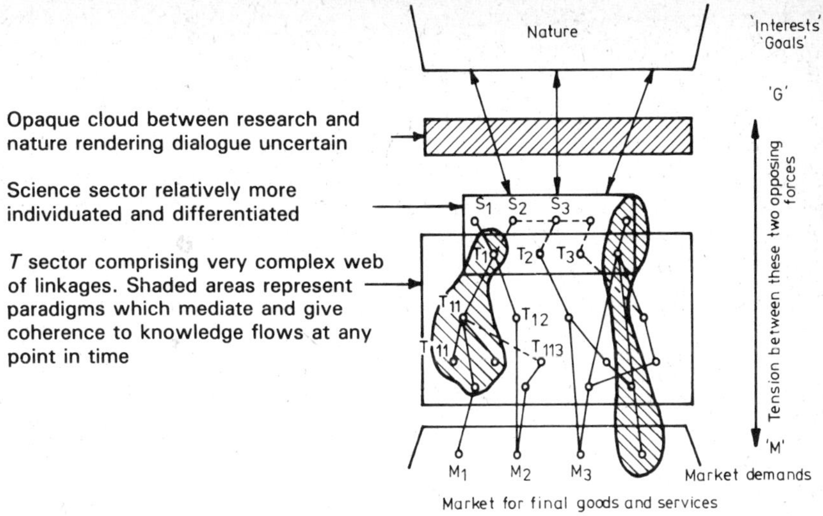

Figure 5.3 The interactive model

Characteristics

1. Overlapping activities of *T* and *S* sectors (R & D departments of firms do some basic or strategic science, while many basic science labs are to an extent directly concerned with markets).
2. Not all connections are drawn in but one can imagine a multidimensional network of very great complexity.
3. Dotted lines represent weak linkages. Solid lines represent strong linkages.
4. Linkages are 'two-way' or 'resonating' flows of information. Often these will be embodied to a degree in economic commodities, but of course information flows take many other forms (see point 5 under Figure 5.2 above).
5. The *T* poles are continuous with production units and hence may be thought of as akin to junctions in electronic circuitry. Often they act as blockages to the free flow of information (resistors), but they act also as information 'stores' (capacitors) and as information progenitors (amplifiers) where the circumstances are appropriate.
6. The shaded areas represent technological paradigms which mediate and give coherence to information flows at any point in time with respect to any given product type. They should be conceived of also as shifting through time in response to the *G* and *M* forces portrayed on the right-hand side of the diagram. Technology is thus in a state of continuous flux. There is no equilibrium of the kinds postulated by conventional economic analysis.

change, and the technological 'paradigm' is precisely such a social device since its heuristic properties provide, as it were, a pathway of relative certainty in the midst of considerable ignorance. Not only does it provide, for any given range of products, a set of broad design parameters which are accepted as datum for firms' R & D activities, thus in effect short-circuiting at least some of the 'blocks' to information flow mentioned above, it provides also a reference point for relations with the science system itself, which is then able to gear its applied strategic research in directions which show some promise of success.

Indeed, it is difficult to see how in the real world of constant shifts and uncertainties, technological changes could take place in the absence of paradigms. To quote a well-known aphorism out of context: if technological paradigms did not exist, they would have to be invented.

The technological paradigm defined in this way (i.e. as both a cognitive and an institutional 'standard case' for technological practice) acts as a fundamental propellant of economic growth, either in itself with respect to any given productive sector or in combination with other paradigms so as to produce more radical innovations — what Sahal classes as 'meta-evolutionary' processes like the microprocessor or biotechnology.[32] The amoeba-like structures portrayed in Figure 5.3 are thus potentially unstable, vulnerable both to market shifts and to the innovative behaviour of firms in competition with one another. However, Nelson and Winter's 'search routines' (the intracellular DNA through which their productive units modify firm behaviour) are not random, but on the contrary are highly purposive, guided in a fundamental sense by the ruling technological paradigm. And notice that this essentially Lamarckian analogy operates not only with respect to *current* practice, but in addition allows for the anticipation of *future* paradigmatic breakdown. Constant's 'presumptive anomalies' are only recognizable within the context of paradigmatic behaviour. The future is determined *both* by the present *and* by those who have the capacity to use the present to anticipate what is to come. In Prigogine's terms, we are living in an economic world which is no longer static, mechanistic and reversible but in one characterized rather by irreversible flux, where dynamic change is the order of the day and where attempts to model in terms of equilibrium states are at best futile and, at worst, misleading.

Hence it is much more realistic to view the innovation process as an essentially evolutionary one rather than in terms of the conventional comparative static schema through which innovations occur (by magic) and are thence diffused throughout economic space in essentially unchanged form until some postulated pre-existent economic equilibrium is re-established. Just as the physical world does not behave in this way, neither does socioeconomic reality. Innovations do not just happen. They have their own life-cycles of birth, growth, maturity and death during which they themselves are transformed, often in unpredictable and unrecognizable ways, in co-evolution with their socioeconomic environment. They occur under permanently non-equilibrium conditions driven by the actual or perceived threat of present and future competitors, by other environmental changes such as action on the part of political authorities, and by factors internal to productive units themselves — factors which may be best imagined in terms of intrasystemic fluctuation. They occur under conditions of uncertainty, even of 'ignorance' in the technical meaning of the term. And they depend in a fundamental sense upon an information exchange with components of the science/technology system which has many of the characteristics of an entropic process, useful information (or knowledge) being formulated with the aid of economic resources and thence itself being used to transform conditions of economic production.

5.5 Towards an Evolutionary Perspective on Long-Run Economic Change

Let us now attempt to pull the various strands of our argument together. Erich Jantsch has argued that one advantage of general systems theory is that it incorporates static structures and the dynamic evolution of such structures under one conceptual umbrella. In this chapter we have in effect put forward a similar perspective on the evolution of an economic system which may be viewed as a complex hierarchical structure subject to continuous perturbation. A very important source of perturbation are the possibilities for technological change which continuously impinge on economic systems through the influence of Schumpeterian competition, and the ultimate sources of such possibilities occur within the science/technology system itself.

Returning to our schematic diagram (Fig. 5.3), we postulate the process operating as follows. Within the science sector itself (Box *S*) new ideas are continuously being tested out in a complex cybernetic process of trial and error. The precise form this takes is indeterminate but can be likened to the embryonic development of the fertilized egg as described by Waddington.[33] Just as the DNA-encoded genes drive the evolving cellular structure in precisely the correct pattern to produce the eventual creature (i.e. through a complex process of biochemical signals and feedback at the surface membranes of the dividing cells), so the technological paradigm provides the DNA which allows the dominant technology with respect to any given product, to 'realize itself' in economic practice. Similarly, just as a cell finding itself in the wrong environment will die, so there will be some product/process ideas or designs which will simply not be commercially viable and hence will be discontinued (or in some cases even suppressed) by R&D management as part of the normal vetting process. And when eventually the technology has, so to speak, played itself out in relation to the market environment, it will be superseded by a new 'phenotype' in a continuous process of punctuated evolution.

Figure 5.4 shows schematically how the process works. At the macro level the science system produces a major invention, like photovoltaic power, for example, which is recognized immediately for its likely commercial implications. However, at this early stage all activity stays mainly within the science sector since there will normally be much

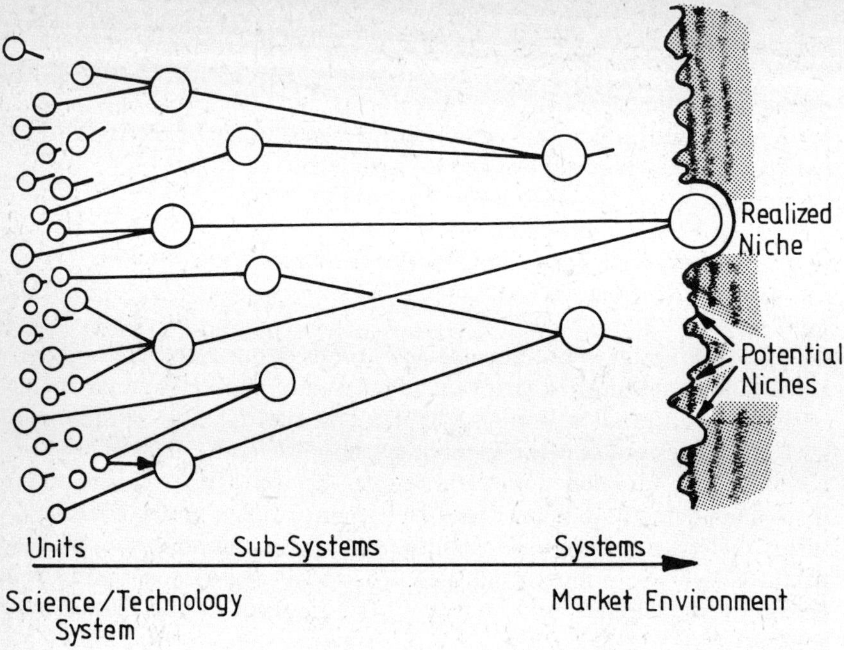

Figure 5.4 Technological articulation

exploratory research taking place as to exactly *how* the basic idea (or knowledge) may be embodied (this is so despite whatever links may exist with outside bodies — such as sponsors, government, etc.). Hence it may be better to characterize this stage as one of *articulation* of the invention rather than its *diffusion*, so as to portray the potential innovation as an evolving system rather than as a fixed entity moving through economic space.

Many of the ideas become embodied in analytical designs whose 'feasibilities' are investigated at an early stage, usually in an engineering sense rather than in a commercial sense, although some commentators like Salter, for example, have suggested that economic considerations are often introduced early on in the development stage.[34] Eventually, some specific devices are much more successful than others — the environment begins to make a preliminary selection either on technical or on market grounds or both. Those that show particular promise now begin to appropriate more resources, including very probably resources from outside the science sector itself. Thus firms may agree to sponsor further experimental development with a view to acquiring future property rights, or governmental institutions may commit resources to more rigorous and expensive development work, for example by financing prototype production or in other ways underwriting the associated risks of product development. Finally, the technology moves out into the economic environment where it is articulated in markets, establishing itself in 'market niches' through a parallel cybernetic process of continuous feedback and product development with particular sets of consumers. In this way the process of innovation may be seen as one where the science/technology system acts as an 'embryonic factory' constantly producing new technological variants which are subsequently tested out in the market place.

What are the advantages inherent in such an evolutionary model of the technical change process? First, it appears to encompass both the science push and the market pull theories of innovation in an integrated and realistic manner. Instead of postulating innovations as discrete happenings *either* mainly elicited by pre-existing markets *or* driven by technological determinism and in both cases in conditions of complete certainty, they are seen rather in terms of process and flux, influenced *both* by technology push *and* by market pull, evolving through time in ways that cannot be completely predicted and taking on substantive forms which are heterogeneous through economic space and time. Innovations do not *diffuse*. They *become*.

Our own position, however, is that the science/technology system is dominant. Thus, while it is certainly true to say that many innovations in the early periods of industrialization probably did not stem directly from scientific research, there is a powerful sense in which this has become progressively less true as we move into the twentieth century. And in so far as we are considering *revolutionary* technologies — that is technologies which have a massive impact upon the whole economic system — it is difficult to conceive of a modern example which has not originated (or at least has not been developed to a considerable degree) within the science/technology system, often with the aid of considerable expenditures. Thus, in so far as we are considering the development of industrial capitalism, a social system which depends for its survival on the continuation of economic production, there will remain a primary role for the science/technology system to continue to develop revolutionary/radical technologies which will act as a propellant to long-run economic growth. To the extent that any economic system is able/willing to opt out of international competition in this sense, of course, the science system will not play the same key role. Innovation may then begin to concentrate on institutional changes in a post-industry society.

A second point concerns the *power* of inventions in terms of how significant they are likely to be in an economic sense once they have become fully articulated. Here it is useful to highlight Freeman's three categories of technological system: (1) incremental; (2) radical; (3) revolutionary.[35] A system is incremental if each new innovation tends to be a fairly minor variant of existing products/processes. It is 'radical' if it results in an entirely new product or process. It is 'revolutionary', however, if it has a major impact on the wider economic system. Freeman postulates four broad characteristics which a revolutionary technology should have. These are:

(1) the capacity to engender widespread cost reductions;
(2) the capacity to engender significant improvements in product/process quality (e.g. performance characteristics);
(3) the capacity to engender wide intersectoral linkage;
(4) social acceptability.

According to Freeman, while there may be very many innovations occurring through time, only a small proportion are likely to have great socioeconomic significance (they are radical or revolutionary), and of these only a tiny fraction will be genuinely revolutionary in the senses described above. It follows that one necessary feature of technology policy-making within any given economic system will be the capacity to *identify ex ante* precisely these technologies, and the better countries are at this, the greater the technological lead they will be able to enjoy and the faster the long-run rate of economic growth. In this sense, long-run competitiveness at an international level is a function of *absolute advantage* derived from technology rather than one of *comparative advantage* derived from a particular configuration of factor endowments. Indeed, one of the major drawbacks of traditional international trade theory (which prescribes policy on the basis of the law of comparative advantage) is that it is using an essentially short-run mechanism describing how markets reach a static equilibrium, to describe how any economic system might move through time.

A third advantage of viewing long-run change in this way relates to intersectoral complexity. If you remember, Koestler emphasizes, using the hedge analogy, two aspects of any complex system, that of its 'arborization' (the process by which any given system evolves from different roots or *stems*) and its 'reticulation', the pattern of interlocking between different stems to create associative systemic nets at various points. Looked at from an evolutionary standpoint it is clear that new ideas within the science system often (if not usually) derive from a variety of different intellectual roots with different disciplinary skills coming together on likely looking projects. Thus often the internal organization of firms allows for complementary skills being brought together in R&D divisions to permit the effective solution of problems.

A final point concerns *policy*. At an early stage in the development of a new technology — that is, before it has earned the right to call itself a 'paradigm' — Brooks has pointed out that there may be many competitors (e.g. nuclear power, where LWRs only won out after a period of competition with other designs), but gradually the field narrows to a much more defined trajectory which sets the agenda for commercial articulation.[36] Productive units and other associated social institutions begin to concentrate (and compete) on a much narrower range of products and processes, and economic factors such as cost reduction, product quality and market penetration play an increasingly important role.

Where such technologies are revolutionary, they act as a fundamental propellant to the economic system, requiring far-reaching institutional changes which, however, may be difficult to bring about since older vested interests will be threatened. In this sense, the new technology sets up a turbulent environment for socioeconomic units. Those which can adapt and respond, survive. Those which cannot, become redundant, die or are encapsulated by those which can. There is a continuous 'flux' on the socioeconomic plane such that the whole system is propelled at a given rate through time, and what we have is a diachronic side to the organic metaphor. Whereas the static, or synchronic, aspect portrays the organizational stucture at a point in time, the dynamic, or diachronic, aspect portrays how the whole system evolves through time. The two aspects however, cannot be separated, since they are both parts of an inherent interrelatedness and any attempt to do so will distort both understanding and policy prescription.

Given this we can now highlight the essential public policy problem for any system. How can this evolutionary whole be controlled (or steered) in such a way as to meet socioeconomic goals? For example, if the primary goal is to be rapid growth of international competitiveness in traded goods and services, how should governments attempt to promote conditions which will foster appropriate behaviour on the part of productive units? Notice that this is not as straightforward as it might appear since it involves the identification *ex ante* of revolutionary technologies — a difficult task! Also a number of writers (e.g. Collingridge 1980)[37] have stressed the institutional rigidities associated with technological 'monocultures' (Brooks 1985)[38] and hence the need to build mechanisms for 'surprise' into the institutional policy process (e.g. sponsoring competing technologies even where there are high short-run costs in so doing).

Of course, there are other goals many of which will alter policy configurations. A major commitment to defence/warfare, for example, may hinder progress towards a socioeconomic goal and similarly with attempts to create a 'non-market' society (Ramos 1981).[39] It will be our contention that policies of this *strategic* type which relate essentially to long-term structural change must of necessity be closely connected to science and technology, since it is science and technology which together create the ultimate propellant to long-term developments. They will also have to pay close attention to the establishment of appropriate institutional structures which can act, as it were, as 'midwives' to the innovation process. Thus 'institutions' are not to be regarded (as they are in much of the conventional economics literature) as a sort of nuisance factor preventing the free working of 'natural' economic forces. On the contrary, they are a necessary feature of successful innovation. We shall develop this point further in the ensuing chapters.

Notes and References

1. N. Kay (1986), *The Emergent Firm* (London: Macmillan).
2. Ibid., p. 40.
3. Ibid., p. 38.
4. J. Singh (1966), *Information Theory, Language and Cybernetics* (London: Constable), p. 9 (emphasis added).
5. Ibid., p. 13.
6. Ibid., p. 75 (emphasis added).
7. F. Machlup (1962), *The Production and Distribution of Knowledge in the United States* (Princeton, NJ: Princeton University Press).
8. C. Freeman (1974), *The Economics of Industrial Innovation* (Harmondsworth: Penguin), see p. 325.
9. N. Clark (1985), *The Political Economy of Science and Technology* (Oxford: Blackwell), pp. 62–74.
10. Machlup, op. cit., p. 8.
11. B. Lundvall (1985), *Product Innovation and User–Product Interaction* (Aalborg: Aalborg University Press).
12. Ibid., p. 5.
13. O. Williamson (1985), *The Economic Institutions of Capitalism* (London: The Free Press).
14. There are a number of writers who have attempted to develop this picture of technological change. The first that we are aware of was E.W. Constant (1973), 'A Model for Radical Technological Change Applied to the Turbojet Revolution', *Technology and Culture*, **14** (4): 553–72. See also, however, R. Nelson and S. Winter (1977), 'In Search of a Useful Theory of Innovation', *Research Policy*, **6**: 36–77; D. Sahal (1979), *Recent Advances in a Theory of Technological Change* (Berlin: International Institute of Management); and G. Dosi (1982), 'Technological Paradigms and Technological Trajectories: A Suggested Interpretation of Determinants and Directions of Technical Change', *Research Policy*, **11** (3): 147–62.
15. P. Gardiner and R. Rothwell (1985), 'Tough Customers: Good Designs', *Design Studies*, **6** (1): 7–17.
16. E.W. Constant (1980), *The Origins of the Turbojet Revolution* (Baltimore: John Hopkins University Press), see Ch. 1, pp. 1–32.
17. Sahal, op. cit.
18. E.W. Constant (1984), 'Communities and Hierarchies: Structure in the Practice of Science and Technology' in R. Laudan (ed.), *The Nature of Technological Knowledge: Are Models of Scientific Change Relevant?* (Dordrecht. D. Reidel), p. 29.
19. Although such attempts to give the apparent seal of scientific approval to established technological practice are often abused. For an account of this and related issues, see I. Illich (1975), *Tools for Conviviality* (London: Fontana).
20. See E.P. Thompson (1973), *The Making of the English Working Class*

(Harmondsworth: Penguin).

21. E. Braun, D. Collingridge and K. Hinton (1979), *Assessment of Technical Decisions*, (London: Butterworth, SISCON). See also D. Collingridge (1980), *The Social Control of Technology* (Oxford: Oxford University Press), for a more rigorous treatment of this point.
22. Constant, possibly somewhat strongly, puts the point as follows: 'Old communities and traditions virtually never [give birth to] radically new technologies. No manufacturer of piston aircraft engines invented or independently developed a steam turbine. No manufacturer of steam locomotives independently developed diesel engines. In the case of both firms and individuals, community practice defines a cognitive universe that inhibits recognition of a radical alternative to conventional practice. When abrupt transitions in technological practice do occur, as happens from time to time, they almost always are the work of people outside, or at least on the margins of, the conventional community' (Constant, 'Communities and Hierarchies', op. cit., p. 30. See also W.R. Maclaurin (1949), *Invention and Innovation in the Radio Industry* (London: Macmillan).
23. Constant, op. cit., p. 12.
24. G. Cutting, 'Paradigms, Revolutions and Technology', in Laudan (ed.) op. cit., pp. 47–65. Cutting raises also the interesting point, first noted by Wojick, that comparisons of paradigms in technology presuppose a common evaluation standard (or policy). Changes in this will also produce paradigm shifts, as for example where government regulations raise ecological standards and therefore place new restrictions on what firms may produce, and how they may produce it.
25. See K. Pavitt and M. Worboys (1977), *Science, Technology and the Modern Industrial State* (London: Butterworth, SISCON), see pp. 14–16.
26. H. Simon (1969), *The Sciences of the Artificial* (Cambridge, Mass.: MIT Press).
27. Burton Klein (1977) expands on this point in his book, *Dynamic Economics* (Cambridge, Mass.: Harvard University Press).
28. Constant, op. cit., Chapter 1.
29. D. de Solla Price (1965), 'Is Technology Historically Independent of Science?', *Technology and Culture*, **VI** (4): 553–68.
30. A good example of this approach is the prevailing attitude to the role of agricultural science in helping to improve yields/hectare in rural areas of developing countries. This attitude holds that the proper role of such science is to develop basic principles in research laboratories and experimental farms but that the business of transferring these principles to poor farmers is the province of another part of government bureaucracies, that concerned with agricultural extension. There is now a lot of evidence that this social division of labour often does not work very well. See N. Clark (1985), *The Political Economy of Science and Technology* (Oxford: Blackwell), pp. 196–207, for some further discussion of this point.
31. The use of the term 'pole' here is akin to its use by economic geographers like François Perroux. Indeed, C. de Bresson has suggested precisely such a usage for empirical research into the locus of innovations within a complex industrial system using input/output analysis. See C. de Bresson (1985), *Technological Development Poles: An Operational Concept for Policy Analysis* (mimeo, SPRU, University of Sussex, 13 June). Notice, however, that such operational 'poles' are also analogous to electronic components and junctions on an integrated circuit; and it is arguable that in this sense the metaphor is more complete. Information may be likened to electricity to the extent that its effective flow from pole to pole (and thus

throughout large sections of an economic system, however defined) depends upon a two-way resonating interaction by which each pole communicates what information it needs as well as what information it can provide. The imaginative reader will readily perceive social analogies to resistors, capacitors and the like.

32. D. Sahal (1985), 'Technological Guideposts and Innovation Avenues', *Research Policy*, **14** (2). See also Rosenberg's account of incremental technical change in machine tool production in the nineteenth century: N. Rosenberg (1976), *Perspectives on Technology* (Cambridge: Cambridge University Press), pp. 1–38.
33. See, for example, C. Waddington (1957), *The Strategy of the Genes* (London: Allen & Unwin).
34. W. Salter (1960), *Productivity and Technical Change* (Cambridge: Cambridge University Press).
35. See C. Freeman (1986), 'Induced Innovation, Diffusion of Innovations and Business Cycles', paper presented at Centre of Canadian Studies Conference on 'Technology and Social Change', June 12–13, pp. 26–32.
36. H. Brooks (1985), 'The Typology of Surprises in Technology, Institutions and Development', mimeo, Harvard University, 4th Sept.
37. D. Collingridge, op. cit.
38. Brooks, op. cit., p. 2.
39. A. Ramos (1981), *The New Science of Organizations* (Toronto: Toronto University Press).

Part III

Case Studies of Technological Systems

In this section we set out details on the emergence of two technological 'systems' which show economic promise, fuel ethanol and photovoltaics. In each case it is clear that the technologies do not arrive ready made, as it were, for economic application but on the contrary emerge as a result of a very complex evolutionary process, in one case going back many centuries. A number of features may be seen. First, both technological systems may best be thought of as amalgams of various technical 'units' or 'sub-systems', which have themselves their own unique histories often relating to quite different industrial products. Second, the pattern of evolution is governed by the interaction of environmental forces (economic and regulatory) and scientific knowledge. Third, institutional structures play an important 'enabling' role at various stages in a technology's economic development. Fourth, evolution is both purposive and uncertain with firms and other agencies often committing resources to keep abreast with likely developments, but at the same time not really knowing what the outcomes will be. Finally, the technologies are not homogeneous, but change their respective structures in different economic contexts.

Chapter 6 identifies the major features of the evolutionary path followed by ethanol technological systems. These systems first originated in the beverage sector and were later relocated in the energy market. It shows that the initial development of ethanol systems proceeded with minor incremental changes. However, changes in the energy environment created new conditions to which ethanol technology could not effectively adapt without further changes. The process of innovation, supported by the private and the public sector, has generated a wide range of conjectural technological variants while at the same time improving the ability of existing systems to adapt to changed market conditions. We use mainly the cases of recent Brazilian and US experience as specific examples.

Chapter 7 deals with a more modern technology and one which stems more directly from a base in experimental science — photovoltaics. It tells the (as yet unfinished) story of a source of renewable energy which in the initial stages are commercially unviable, but which has more recently become less so in respect of specific market niches and as a result of a number of state-supported R&D programmes. Although publicly financed support has been crucial in all cases, different countries have produced quite different strategies for developing the technology, and it is still uncertain which will be most likely to pay off, although the most promising technological directions are now becoming clearer. As in the case of ethanol technology, the pattern of institutional support plays a key enabling role.

Chapter 6

Development of Ethanol Technological Systems*

6.1 Ethanol as a Fuel Option

Ethanol, also known as ethyl alcohol, has been on mankind's list of beverages from time immemorial. Babylonian records reveal a 6,000-year history; and historians have pushed the European record back to the period after the third ice age, some 10,000 years ago. The commercialization of the liquid was started in Europe by monks around AD 800, but it was not until the nineteenth and twentieth centuries that alcohol was produced on a large commercial scale. Ethanol is conventionally obtained by breaking down simple sugars with an enzyme (zymase) contained in yeast (usually *Saccharomyces cerevisiae*). The process also releases carbon dioxide and heat.

The type and complexity of the production process depends on the feedstock used. In the case of sugarcane or molasses, the process is shown in Figure 6.1.The cane is cleaned and crushed and the juice is extracted. This may be done through conventional crushing or by diffuser technology. The juice or molasses resulting from sugar production is then pre-treated for fermentation and the resulting beer is distilled and dehydrated (if anhydrous ethanol is required). The fermentation is done using yeast grown for separate batches or recovered from fermented beer depending on the type of process used. The process therefore goes through stages of feedstock preparation, fermentation, distillation and dehydration.

The use of ethanol as a fuel is as old as the internal combustion engine itself. When Nikolas Otto designed his first internal combustion engine, he tried it on ethanol not gasoline, and numerous studies were conducted on the use of fuel ethanol at the turn of the twentieth century. Henry Ford described ethanol as the 'fuel of the future' and designed his Model A to run on ethanol, gasoline or a combination thereof. Its physical characteristics make it a suitable fuel for use in internal combustion engines, and various countries have used fuel ethanol at one stage or another. It was the discovery of oil and its spread, however, that blocked the development and application of ethanol as a fuel.

One of the most important features of any liquid fuel is the amount of energy it contains by volume or weight. This is important because the weight and space occupied by various components of mobile systems such as vehicles is a significant determinant of their overall efficiency.

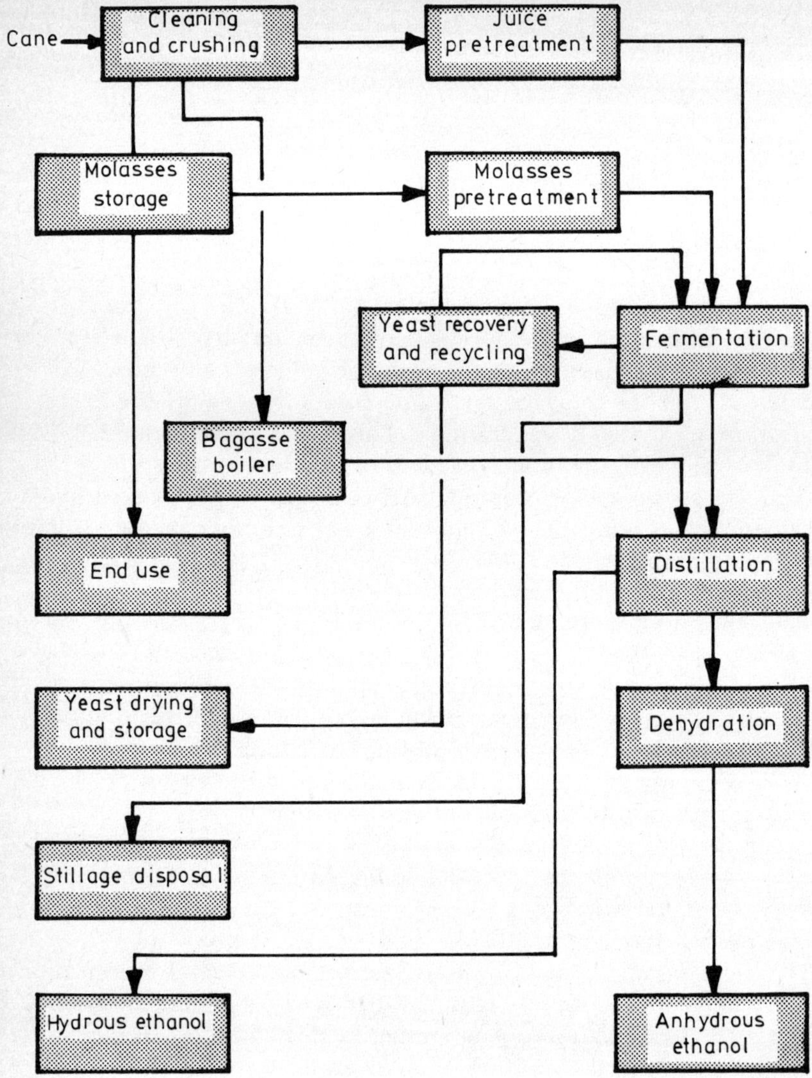

Source: Juma (1986)

Figure 6.1 Fuel ethanol from cane juice and molasses

As Table 6.1 shows, a kilogram of ethanol contains 26.6 megajoules (MJ) as compared with 43.8 MJ in gasoline and 42.8 MJ in diesel. Although it would apear that there is a large differential between ethanol and the other fuels, the gap narrows when the fuels are compared by volume. Nevertheless, these difficulties show that fuel ethanol has a lower energy content than the other fuels.

Table 6.1 Physical properties of selected fuels

Property	Ethanol	Gasoline	Diesel
Formula	CH_3CH_2OH	C_4 to C_{12}	C_{14} to C_{19}
Energy content (MJ/kg)	26.60	43.80	42.80
Energy content (MJ/l)	21.00	32.00	36.40
Specific gravity	0.79	0.73	0.85
Research octane number	106–11	79–98	—
Motor octane number	89–100	71–90	—
Cetane number	0–5	5–10	45–55
Molecular weight	46.10	100–5	240.00
Auto-ignition temperature	423.00	257.00	—
Flash point °C	13.00	−43.00	38.00

Source: World Bank (1980)

Although, because of its low calorific value, ethanol has an unfavourable fuel economy compared to diesel and gasoline, it burns with a slightly higher thermal efficiency which partially off-sets the calorific differential. Moreover, its higher octane value can help in improving fuel economy. At normal compression ratios, ethanol delivers about 5.0 per cent more power than gasoline. This can be raised to 15 per cent by increasing compression ratios from 8 : 1 to 4 :1. Such engines have already been designed and are operating in Brazil where over 2.2 million cars now run on neat hydrous ethanol. Ethanol can be used also in blended fuels partly to boost the octane rating and partly to replace the lead that is conventionally used to eliminate engine knocking.

It is completely soluble in these fuels so long as there is no water in the system thus enabling blending to take place with varying degrees of ignitability and combustibility. But if water is present, the blend separates into two phases, one rich in gasoline and the other mainly an ethanol–water mixture, and since ethanol has an infinite miscibility with water the ethanol–water phase will stall the engine and can cause considerable corrosion to engine parts. Phase separation is therefore a critical problem in case of engine mismanagement. Another important feature of the technology is that ethanol requires more heat for vapourization than gasoline, making starting difficult, especially in temperatures below 10°C. The Brazilian ethanol cars are fitted with small gasoline tanks which are used for cold starts while, for additional preheating, the exhaust manifold of the engine is placed in contact with the intake manifold. This ensures that the intake air is preheated by the exhaust air without any additional fuel cost.

One of the significant advantages of the technology is that it is based on biological materials which are renewable, and hence it relies on global energy flows as opposed to energy stocks. Moreover, the entropic implications of using renewable biomass resources are lower

Table 6.2 Ethanol yield from biomass resources

Crop	Yield (tonne/ha/yr)	Ethanol	
		Litres/tonne	Litres/ha/yr
Sugarcane	50–90	70–90	3,500–8,000
Sweet sorghum	45–80	60–80	1,750–5,300
Sugar beet	15–50	90–100	1,350–5,500
Fodder beet	100–200	90–100	4,400–9,350
Wheat	1.5–2.1	340	510–714
Barley	1.2–2.5	250	300–625
Rice	2.5	430	1,075–2,150
Maize	1.7–5.4	360	600–1,944
Sorghum	1.0–3.7	350	350–1,295
Irish potatoes	10–25	110	1,110–2,750
Cassava	10–65	170	1,700–11,050
Sweet potatoes	8–50	167	1,336–8,350
Grapes	10–25	130	1,300–8,000
Molasses	—	245	—

Source: National Academy of Sciences, Washington, DC

than those of relying on non-renewable resources. Table 6.2 shows that simple sugars can be obtained directly or indirectly from a wide range of biological materials, and where simple sugars are not readily available, starch can be converted to simple sugars and then fermented to produce ethanol.

6.2 The Origins of Ethanol Technological Systems

The significant functional units of the ethanol technological system used in the field of energy originated in the beverage environment where development was marked by a series of incremental innovations, largely in response to external selecting pressures such as competition, regulation, taxation and other institutional interventions.[1] The external pressures on brewing not only constituted quantifiable market variables such as price but also included factors such as taste and habit among consumers. Often such factors tended to slow down the tempo of technical change where the system had been allowed to settle into particular design configurations and practices. In addition, significant developments in brewing occurred long before organized scientific research became a major input into industrial production. In a detailed study of the industry in England over the 1700–1830 period, Mathias concludes that the industrial transformation of brewing relied on traditional techniques and 'occurred in a generation unhelped by a major invention'.[2] Fermentation, the most important biochemical process in brewing, was extensively used, but its scientific aspects remained unexplored for a long time.

Ironically, the growth of fermentation knowledge was partly retarded by institutional rigidity in the scientific community. For example, the leading German chemist, Liebig, believed that fermentation was caused by the motion set up in the liquid by some decomposing substance. The theory of the Frenchman Cagniard de la Tour and the German chemists Knetzing and Turpin in the late 1830s, that yeast was a vegetable organism which caused fermentation by its own development, was strongly opposed by Liebig for over twenty years. It was Louis Pasteur who, in 1860, showed that yeast was indeed a living organism whose natural changes led to alcoholic fermentation. Nevertheless, brewing continued without much scientific input, although British chemists were beginning to call on brewers to take advantage of the systematic knowledge that was accumulating among chemists.[3]

Eventually, however, the increased availability of technological knowledge along with changing economic as well as legal pressures, gradually led to the systematic application of scientific knowledge to brewing, although it is worth noting that while scientific knowledge relevant to some aspects of brewing was available, it was not actually applied until changes in the external environment generated pressures which required the use of available innovations. This is consistent with our adaptive landscape approach, in that changes in the external environment created suitable conditions for the application of particular innovations which had originated in other sectors of the techno-economic field and which were then relocated within the brewing sector. The first significant innovations were the introduction of the thermometer and the saccharometer, which were associated with quality control and regulation. Both innovations were adopted by the industry from other fields. The saccharometer was merely a hydrometer which had been calibrated to measure the specific gravity of beer while the thermometer enabled brewers to determine exact process temperatures.

The application of scientific knowledge to brewing did not occur in a smooth way but advanced unevenly in association with changes in external pressures which led to competition among different scientific instruments. This process of instrument selection was bound up with institutional issues, especially in relation to the legitimation of particular instruments through legal endorsement. Legalisation became important because most of the pressures on brewers originated from the government, and indeed the innovation process became largely a series of attempts by brewers to find technical ways to circumvent regulation. The dynamic was co-evolutionary.

The user of the hydrometer in the gauging of spirits in England, especially for excise duty collection, was itself an interesting case in point. Following its adoption by the authorities in the late 1750s, disputes arose over the accuracy of two particular types. Modifications to improve accuracy were introduced in one of the instruments, but it took up to 1803 for a selection to be made and efforts continued to challenge the selected instrument for another fifteen years when the choice was legally confirmed by the Hydrometer Act of 1818. Subsequent inventions in Scotland were more accurate and challenged those used in England. The degree of accuracy in hydrometers was important because minor deviations could lead to loss of profit among producers.

The instrument also provided valuable information which was later applied to the costing of various inputs and the setting of product prices. Since the operative unit in feedstocks was the amount of fermentable substances, as expressed in the form of sugar, the saccharometer became useful in establishing the value of the raw material. With the thermometer, it became possible to control brewing temperatures and therefore keep the industry going in summer as well. The proposal for this sort of innovation first went to the naval brewhouses, which often faced unexpected fleet arrivals in summer, forcing them to brew under unfavourable temperature regimes. With the piped circulation of water at controlled temperatures, it became possible to brew beer in summer. Hence while the instruments allowed for quality control and enabled production efficiencies to improve, they also freed the industry from dependence on suitable weather and climatic conditions. Moreover, instrumentation increased the ability to control fermentation and consequently reduce losses arising from contamination.

Major advances also occurred in the industry as a result of state fiscal policies, many of which were aimed at reducing the export of Scottish alcohol to England.[4] For example, increased taxation in the 1780s based on the quantity of malt forced Scottish distillers to increase the amount of raw grain. However, this showed a lack of scientific knowledge in the field of enzymatic hydrolysis on the part of the authorities, who did not know that the amount of diastase in the malt (even if it accounted for only 20 per cent of the entire feedstock) was enough to turn the starch in the raw grain into fermentable sugars. On discovering this innovative response among distillers, the authorities moved to impose duty on the wash since it was assumed that each unit of the wash yielded the same amount of alcohol. In response, the distillers raised the concentration of fermentables in the feedstocks by adding sugar and treacle. Subsequently, duty was determined by hydrometers as in England.

Another example of this co-evolutionary interaction between technology and regulation was a 1788 piece of legislation in Scotland which led to significant improvements in distillation since it restricted, and based the levy on, the size of the stills used. Distillers responded by raising the pace of distillation and consequently increasing throughput. An alternative method was to make the stills shallower and thereby increase the rate of distillation. James Watt, after finding out that liquids boiled at lower temperatures under reduced pressure, tried the technique on stills but there was no widespread use at the time. Shallow distillation led to new problems — such as saturated carbon dioxide, which caused froth in the still. Soap was added to the still to eliminate this problem.

As suggested earlier, scientific details on fermentation remained unknown until Pasteur's work, and even then it took twenty-three years before the knowledge was turned into technological practice. The cultivation of pure yeast was first successfully applied by Hansen at the Carlsberg brewery in Copenhagen. This was a significant advance because artificial selection was applied to yeast for the first time, thus introducing into brewing a technique which was being widely used in agriculture. The introduction not only eliminated the wild yeast varieties, which caused contamination, but also guaranteed that a robust strain could be propagated and used on a large scale, resulting in increased culture uniformity and higher possibilities for controlled fermentation. But the technique required lower fermentation temperatures, preferably achieved by artificial refrigeration, a factor which was partly used to explain the initial resistance among British brewers, where plants operated at higher temperatures (12°–13°C) than on the Continent (5–6°C).[5] Lower temperatures were also required for storage, but the elimination of wild yeasts would also have removed the distinct flavours of the British beers, on which part of the demand was based. In those ways the Hansen approach may be seen as an innovative response to problems arising from brewing practice. The approach constituted a recombination of existing pieces of knowledge from brewing and agriculture. On the one hand, the fact that fermentation was caused by a wide variety of living organisms was central to the innovation. On the other, the fact that these organisms could be isolated and propagated on a large scale enabled him to suggest a way of eliminating the contamination problem.

Thus much of what constitutes ethanol production is based on the convergence of different functional units introduced over a hundred years ago. The changes which have since been introduced into the system have been adaptive and incremental. Most of them did not originate in the sector itself but were adapted from other uses. The system is built around fermentation and distillation processes. The feedstock phase of the process has drawn technological inputs from the agricultural sector while chemical engineering has enriched the distillation and purification phase. But the convergence of these different technical units is governed by the inner logic of the structure of the ethanol production system viewed as a whole. These developments, which firmly established ethanol production technology in the beverage environment also prepared the ground for its relocation to the energy environment, since the technical characteristics of ethanol made it a candidate source of liquid fuel. However, whereas the ethanol technological system was relatively well established in its beverage environment, a shift to the energy environment would mean a whole new process of niche realization under which both the technological system and the environment would be transformed in unpredictable ways.

6.3 Technological Relocation

Ethanol as a source of energy tended originally to be used in isolated niches protected from market competition. It is important, however, to identify the specific reasons for producing fuel ethanol. Its production (and use) in Brazil in the 1920s and 1930s was largely aimed at reducing surplus sugar and stabilizing the international sugar market. These operations were not conducted with any competitive considerations in mind, such as, for example, the cost of ethanol in relation to alternative sources of liquid fuels, and as a result there were no major external pressures on the manufacturers to improve the efficiency of ethanol production. Moreover, production was conducted by the government. Since the purpose of the technological system was to reduce surplus sugar, the directors of the programme argued that the efficiency of plants be assessed in those terms and not in terms of economic efficiency.[6] This could be achieved without any technological improvements. As a result, there were no strong internal or external pressures influencing the internal evolution of the system which remained uncompetitive with gasoline and relied on the same techniques applied in the beverage environment, namely, a batch process with long fermentation periods which relied on conventional sources of raw materials. Furthermore, the use of the technology was not associated with a lobby of scientists and technologists who wanted it institutionalized. For such a development, we turn to the historical and institutional efforts to establish a more permanent ethanol niche in the United States in the 1930s as an illustrative case.

These efforts were associated with the Farm Chemurgic Council, which flourished between 1935 and 1939, sponsored by the Chemical Foundation. The Council believed in the efficacy of scientific knowledge, especially chemistry, to revolutionize agricultural production and raise the US economy from depression. It believed that 'modern science has placed new tools in the hands of man which enabled a variety of surplus products of the soil to be transformed through organic chemistry into raw materials usable in industry',[7] a view that may have been influenced by the success of chemists following the extensive use of chemical products in the First World War. The Chemical Foundation obtained finance from nearly 5,000 German chemical patents seized by the US federal government from Germany during the First World War, many of which belonged to the I.G. Farben complex.[8] The patents were sold to the Chemical Foundation by the Alien Property Custodian, who later resigned from the government and became the president of the Foundation. Government action subsequently brought against the Foundation in the Supreme Court was defeated. In fact, not only did the US chemical industry exploit the patents, but the government in 1922 also imposed a protective tariff against the products of a reviving German chemical trust, a tariff which remained intact until the 1964 Kennedy round of tariff negotiations.[9]

The Farm Chemurgic Council provided a framework for the application of the existing stock of scientific and technical knowledge to the generation of a permanent source of energy. This stock of knowledge had accumulated during the First World War when fuel shortages stimulated interest in this source. The fear of further shortages in the post-war period served as an impetus in both innovation and institutional reform. Legislation was introduced which distinguished industrial alcohols from alcoholic beverages, although efforts to expand the use of ethanol in the 1920s failed because of technical problems (such as corrosion) as well as the discovery of more oil fields, technical advances in petrol refining and the use of tetra-ethyl lead as an octane booster. Thus attempts to enlist institutional support for fuel ethanol were overwhelmed by counteracting advances in the petroleum sector.

Most of the ethanol produced in the United States after the First World War was obtained from fermenting blackstrap molasses, which was relatively easy because molasses contains readily fermentable sugars. But the 1930s were associated with surplus corn, which was not readily fermentable, thus requiring changes in the molasses-based ethanol technological system to incorporate a section for the hydrolysis of starch into simple sugars. However, we have seen that the technology for doing so was already available and had been used in the beverage environment for a long time. What was needed was recombinant innovation to adapt a hydrolysing unit for the existing molasses-based technological system. This process represented a departure from previous *ad hoc* projects to a more systematic approach to ethanol production which required institutional reform to legitimate the realization of ethanol niches in the corn-growing states such as Illinois, Iowa, Indiana and Nebraska.

The introduction of such reforms required changes in the criteria used to evaluate fuel ethanol. It was no longer an issue of reducing farm surpluses but rather one of technological intervention whose economic viability had to be judged against other options, and since the production of corn had already incurred high costs, legislative reform efforts were defeated. Here it is important to note that the Department of Agriculture was not in favour of using the agricultural surplus for industrial products but preferred restrictions on acreage,[10] despite the fact that studies had identified a wide range of raw materials which could be used for producing ethanol.[11] Deprived of any support, the Chemical Foundation then decided to go it alone, setting up the first ethanol plant at Atchison, Kansas, in 1936.

The plant was based on a variety of raw materials obtained in the region but it encountered enormous legal and raw material supply problems in its first six months. It came on stream in 1937 and produced ethanol at a cost five times higher than the refinery price of gasoline so that although ethanol from the plant was widely marketed, the Council had to subsidize its production. Eventually, the Foundation withdrew its support for the Council in 1937 due to the running out of its German patents and thereby signalling the end of the project. The plant was finally shut down in 1938 after the Foundation had invested US$600,000. Subsequent efforts to revive it failed because the management could not raise the US$125,000 needed to match a loan from the Reconstruction Finance Corporation. Subsequently, the failure of the project became an issue of political conflict in the state, involving claims and counterclaims against the oil industry.

The collapse of the Atchison plant was linked to a wider conflict between government policies (as enshrined in the New Deal) and the appeal to the role of science in reducing agricultural surpluses and increasing farm incomes. Thus, while the government favoured financial payments to farmers, the chemurgic movement advocated the use of chemical knowledge to turn agricultural surpluses into industrial products and the issue became a political conflict between the government and the Council, on whose board well-known critics of the New Deal served. The government defused these conflicts by establishing four research laboratories devoted to the utilization of farm surpluses in 1938, implicitly recognizing that the project had demonstrated the technical feasibility of fuel ethanol application and at the same time agreeing to pursue the ethanol option as an experimental project rather than as a commercial venture.

The US Department of Agriculture decided to build a small ethanol plant at its Peoria laboratory producing between 300 and 500 gallons a day for experimental purposes under the 1938 Agricultural Adjustment Act, and later the government subsidized ethanol production during the Second World War. The Atchison plant went into production again during this period, but for the energy market, not as an industrial feedstock. The ethanol was used for munitions manufacture and synthetic rubber production. Again the Second World War period demonstrates that ethanol was drawn into the industrial sphere to solve problems generated in other economic sectors. These conditions, however, did not provide major incentives for the internal evolution of ethanol technology. The Atchison plant had shown that a technological system was available which could provide an alternative energy source but which could not compete with conventional sources of liquid fuel. Later the rise of nuclear power, based on physics, made the chemurgic movement and related innovations less relevant. Indeed, the innovations that came later to be applied in ethanol technological systems emerged in other disciplines. Many of these applications had to await the market opportunities created by the 1973 oil crisis. Hence, over the 1930–73 period the basic technological system changed only marginally. There were no major environmental pressures that could have facilitated technical advances or induced system-specific innovations. The main feature of the system remained its batch configuration.

6.4 Technical Change and Corporate Restructuring

In recent years the structure of the technology market has remained heterogeneous with established suppliers of traditional batch systems still playing a large role. Most of the large engineering firms possess the capacity to design and build ethanol plants but there is no distinct ethanol technology market except for some specialist firms that have for a long time supplied distilleries to the beverage sector. Some of these firms are subsidiaries of large engineering corporations, but none of them played a significant role in the supply of technology to the developing countries in the 1970s. This was largely because the main market for ethanol technology was Brazil and hence the supply of ethanol technology to the energy sector was dominated by Brazilian firms such as Codistil (a subsidiary of Dedini), Zanini and Conger.

At the time of the oil crisis, these Brazilian firms had established themselves as major suppliers of ethanol technology for the beverage sector, and relocation to a different market did not need any major changes in technological capacity or management techniques. The largest five ethanol technology suppliers in Brazil had the capacity to produce more than 128 distilleries per year, producing up to 120,000 litres each in the early 1980s. Codistil alone could supply about 60 per cent of this output. This meant that the real market structure of ethanol technology was dominated by Brazilian firms, which increased their production capacity by large margins (measured in ethanol output per day) over the post-1973 decade. Codistil, for example, increased the average capacity of its output from 86,000 litres per day in 1974 to 109,000 litres a day in 1984 reaching a peak of 123,000 litres per day in 1980. Much of the recent decline is accounted for by the diversification into smaller distilleries as well as by the sale of experimental plants

Table 6.3 Change in Codistil's plant and capacity production

Year	Plants sold	Average capacity (litres per day)
1973	2	50,000
1974	16	86,000
1975	24	68,000
1976	33	87,000
1977	46	89,000
1978	58	85,000
1979	33	105,000
1980	47	123,000
1981	46	117,000
1982	25	97,000
1983	37	117,000
1984	30	109,000

Source: Juma (1986)

producing 5,000 litres a day. Over the period as a whole, design configurations changed only marginally to incorporate scale expansion. Codistil started selling 120,000-litres-a-day plants in 1974 for the first time. Plants with the capacity of 220,000 litres a day were sold in 1976 and those producing 240,000 litres a day were first supplied in 1981. By 1983 Codistil had started supplying plants with the capacity to produce 300,000 litres a day (Table 6.3).

Based on the experience gained in the supply of technology to the diverse Brazilian conditions, Brazilian firms also increased their capacity to export ethanol plants. Whereas Codistil exported only one plant (to Bolivia) in the 1960s, its exports in the 1970s and 1980s increased to include destinations such as Venezuela, Costa Rica, Paraguay, Bolivia, Cuba, Peru, Haiti and Pakistan. In addition, Conger and Zanini also exported plants to Peru, Venezuela and Kenya. The size of the Brazilian market and the export potential led a number of firms in the industrialized countries to establish offices in Brazil. Without such linkages, the technological potential among industrialized-country firms to manufacture ethanol technology would not have been adequately fulfilled. Brazilian firms also established links with firms in the industrialized countries with the aims of getting access to emerging technologies as well as of supplying technologies to these countries. For example, Zanini entered joint ventures and technical co-operation agreements with Zahnraederfabrik Renk A.G. of West Germany and Foster-Wheeler of the United States. The Foster-Wheeler deal included the supply of distilleries to the US market. Conger, on the other hand, took up a 5 per cent shareholding in Vogelbusch of Austria in order to have access to stillage-reducing technology. Conger acquired the know-how but did not market the process as widely as had been expected.

It is worth noting that suppliers of ethanol technology such as Codistil also have the capacity within their industrial complex to supply other technologies related to sugarcane production. The complex design configuration of the various technical units and the scientific knowledge associated with ethanol technological systems make it relatively difficult for new small firms to emerge in this sector since much of the relevant know-how in the early stages has already been embodied in capital goods and operating skills associated with batch processes. But the new design configurations with potentially higher performances embodies knowledge that is possessed by firms that already exist in different sectors. Moreover, some of the established firms support university research, especially in the United States, by allowing researchers to patent their innovations while the financiers retained the right to license the technology.

The post-1973 trends did not see major market restructuring with any significant concentrations like those witnessed in photovoltaics.[12] This is partly because no large markets were envisaged and radical innovations could not easily be brought to commercial application. Moreover, ethanol technological systems constituted a large number of distinct units whose design control was distributed over a relatively large number of firms. Even more important was the fact that no major market niches were perceived outside the Brazilian energy environment. It was expected that the Brazilian market would be an open terrain in which new technological systems would be tested and adopted. However, the country relied on locally produced batch processes as part of its policy to protect local industry.[13]

The firms that brought their expertise to ethanol R&D or initiated new R&D efforts included chemical and pharmaceutical firms, engineering companies, food and drink corporations, biotechnology-dedicated companies and oil corporations. Firms such as Novo Industri (Denmark) and Gist-Brocades (Netherlands), which had long-standing capabilities in enzyme production, could bring their expertise to the ethanol sector, especially in the prospective area of enzymatic hydrolysis. With capability in enzymology and process engineering, Novo Industri designed a continuous fermentation process but did not find a market for it. Diamond Shamrock entered the ethanol market by building an experimental plant in the United States while at the same time funding research at the University of Arizona. Its entry into the market was clearly to acquire competence in the field while at the same time passing on some of the necessary R&D work to university scientists. Again this illustrates the fact that corporate strategies were not built on instant enthusiasm for the immediate expansion of ethanol niches. The support for university research was mainly aimed at widening the range of potential technological variants in ethanol production systems. Other chemical firms involved in ethanol production include W.R. Grace and Union Carbide.

Market restructuring also resulted in interesting corporate recombinations. The engineering firm UHDE GmbH joined expertise with the chemical firm Hoechst to develop an innovative continuous process based on tower fermentation, one of the simplest advanced ethanol technological systems unveiled in the post-1973 era. Pilot plants are operating in West Germany, Brazil and an imitation of it has been developed by the Brazilian firm Zanini with additional scientific input, especially in dense yeast selection done at a Brazilian agricultural university. This process had been designed for the US market but was later transferred to Brazil. Another form of corporate restructuring has involved the formation of Swedish AC Biotechnics by Alfa-Laval and Cardo of Sweden. AC Biotechnics is responsible for marketing the Biostil process along with other biotechnology processes. It obtained resources and expertise on genetic engineering, fermentation and other bioprocessing techniques from Alfa-Laval and Cardo. It also inherited experience in process design, engineering, equipment and plant construction and has now turned to marketing the process outside Brazil. Other engineering firms have bought out small traditional ethanol technology suppliers. For example, the German firm Krupp has acquired Hermann Buckau/Wolf, which established the first ethanol plant in Africa.

Oil firms also registered their interest in ethanol technology by funding university research. Atlantic Richfield Company (ARCO), for example, supported the research at Arkansas University on enzymatic fermentation. The involvement of ARCO and Texaco was largely to acquire expertise in the field while at the same time funding university research. This strategy has enabled them to stay on the forefront of scientific advance without necessarily committing massive financial resources and building in-house capabilities in technological systems whose prospects are still uncertain. Nevertheless, the corporate restructuring that followed the 1973 oil crisis has not resulted so far in many major increases in the use of ethanol technology. Furthermore, technological innovations have been restricted to process optimization and there are no major departures from the already established functional units. Competition is largely over the marketing strategies of various firms and their links in countries where potential niches exist.

6.5 Technological Diversity and Complexity

However, the oil crisis represented a significant turning point in the evolution of ethanol technological systems since it opened up opportunities for their extended diffusion into the energy environment. As rising oil prices changed the relative competitiveness of fuel, ethanol production costs, which had been previously considered too high, were brought into a reasonably competitive range with imported gasoline. But even more significant was the possible emergence of ethanol niche opportunities in areas that had been dominated by oil. This had four main effects. First, it stimulated recombinant innovations to improve the performance of ethanol technological systems using existing know-how. Second, it set in motion new R&D efforts. Third, new institutional arrangements were made in various countries to support such efforts. Finally, the shifts led to a restructuring of the international market for ethanol technology. All these changes were underpinned by two main features. First, innovation was directed at improving the performance of ethanol technological systems in a relatively new environment (with added selection criteria such as ecological and energetic considerations). Second, the process of technological evolution was marked by increased diversity in technological variants. Given the uncertainties surrounding the technology and the lack of a favourable track record in niche realization, this diversity tended to widen the scope for selection and adaptive prospects for technological systems.

One of the most significant parameters in the energy sector was the cost of fuel ethanol. As indicated earlier, ethanol had been used in niches which were protected from competition with gasoline or with other alternative liquid fuels such as methanol. But for it to operate within acceptable competitive limits, ways of reducing the production costs of ethanol had to be identified. This set in motion a wide range of efforts to rationalize the efficiencies of the various functional units which constituted the overall technological systems. One of the areas which received much R&D interest was improving fermentation. Whereas the history of the ethanol system had been dominated by batch fermentation systems, the post-1973 efforts were directed at generating technological variants using continuous processes with higher volumetric efficiencies. Research was also directed at improving conventional batch processes. The variants that have so far been operated or tested fall into three broad categories: improved batch, semi-continuous (or cascade) and continuous fermentation processes.

The *batch process* involves the repeated emptying, cleaning, sterilizing and refilling of the tank. The fermentation cycle in this process takes 36–48 hours under temperatures held at 20–30°C with an initial pH of 4.5. The conversion efficiency falls in the 90–95 per cent range and yields ethanol concentrations of 10–16 per cent (weight/volume). The yeast used in batch processes is grown separately and innoculated into every tank. Batch processes are easy to use and require little highly skilled labour. Moreover, the risks of yield loss are low because the fermentation process is distributed among several tanks. However, the low fermentation productivity due to long down times represents an obstacle to improved process efficiency. One of the first improvements on this process involved the recycling of yeast. This does not increase fermentation efficiency as such but it reduces the time needed to grow yeast for each batch.

Cascade systems embody improvements over the batch process. Tanks similar to the ones used in batch processes are connected in series allowing the substrate to be fed into the first tank constantly while at the same rate being withdrawn from the last tank. The process uses the same number of tanks as in batch systems but takes less fermentation time because of the cascading flow of the substrate. Not only does it save down time, but it also reduces the chances of infection through air contact between ambient and internal fermenter surfaces. Such systems may also use yeast recycle units. Substrate flow in the process is done either with the use of gravity or pumping. The cascade process was developed by making modifications to the batch process on the basis of available engineering concepts on volume-control and flow regulation.

Improvements on the cascade design have led to the concept of *continuous fermentation* in which both the substrate and yeast are recycled. This process has resulted also in a large number of variants which have reached different stages of development. The change from batch to continuous fermentation has been mainly to reduce down-time and increase volumetric efficiency. It has also contributed to savings in the time and substrate needed for growing fresh yeast for every batch per unit of output. Because of higher volumetric efficiency, these systems employ less capital equipment and space per unit of output. On the other hand, they are more sophisticated and require skilled operators.

In addition to questions of production efficiency, issues related to feedstock availability have generated new pressures. Raw material costs and availability have always played a significant role in the viability of fuel ethanol, and indeed most of the early ethanol programmes were aimed at reducing surplus agricultural products such as sugarcane or corn. The latter resource led to the introduction of starch-based fermentation processes in the energy field. But for the technological system to establish a long-term niche, raw material supply had to be guaranteed. The use of corn, or any other grain, raised questions related to possible competition between food and energy despite the fact that many of the early projects were based on surplus agricultural yield or residues. Guaranteeing long-term raw material availability required either intensified agricultural yield in traditional supplies or diversification into new areas, especially where resource conflicts are minimal. One such area is the use of starch or cellulosic material such as agricultural residue or municipal solid waste (MSW) for ethanol production. These resources often have a low opportunity cost and might therefore be economically turned into ethanol. But this has required improvements and modifications in technological systems to enable them to convert cellulosic material to fermentable sugars. The field of cellulosic fermentation thus generated a range of novel technological variants.

Concern over other uses for surplus grain led to research on cellulosic materials as another ethanol feedstock. Although cellulose is the most abundant renewable resource available for conversion to fuel, it is also one of the most difficult to break down into fermentable constituents. Cellulose occurs as a crystalline form that is reinforced by a lignin-hemicellulose complex. Various ways of degrading it include biological, chemical, mechanical and thermal methods. Any of these methods will lead to a slightly different system configuration whose techno-economic performance at any stage can only be established through testing. The use of weak acid to degrade cellulose is not a new technique. Dilute and concentrated acids were used in cellulose degradation during the First World War. The conjectural technological variants that were being developed at various US universities included the application of new scientific knowledge and technical advances to this established concept. The key problems in the acid hydrolysis include low sugar recovery, corrosion and poor economic returns. As a result, R&D efforts have not been able to bring pilot plants to commercial application, although research still continues.

Starch-based plants have been attractive in the industrialized countries because they provide a way of getting rid of surplus grain. One of the main problems in starch-based plants has been the low energy balance because of the absence of fibrous residues such as bagasse for steam generation. This problem has been overcome by advances in process energy optimization and recent plants now operate at positive energy ratios. Firms such as Buckau-Wolf (formerly Gebr. Hermman Buckau Walther) are now supplying energy-efficent starch-based plants. Similarly, energy-efficient plants are now operating in the United States. For example, the Staley Manufacturing Company plant at Loudon (Tennessee) uses only 21,000 BTUs for a gallon of ethanol produced, more than 20 per cent less than in conventional plants. The plant produces 40 million gallons of anhydrous ethanol a year from corn, making it the second largest ethanol plant in the United States.[14]

A significant achievement in continuous fermentation was made by Alfa-Laval engineers, who designed a process which utilizes concentrated feedstock. This system was designed to reduce the amount of stillage released during ethanol production. Instead of the 11–15 litres of stillage normally released for every litre of ethanol produced in batch processes, the Biostil process releases between 0.8 litres and 4 litres, depending on the concentration of the substrate. The process was designed to deal with the environmental problems associated with

Table 6.4 Comparison of Biostil and conventional plants in Brazil

Parameter	Biostil	Conventional
Yield (% of theoretical limit)	94.5	87.0
Stillage (litre/litre of ethanol)	0.8	11.0
Personnel requirement	3.0	7.0
Space requirements (cubic meters)	350.0	1,350.0

Note: The figures are based on plants producting 150,000 litres a day
Source: Alfa-Laval, Sao Paulo, Brazil

ethanol production and differs considerably from other techniques since the ethanol is continuously stripped from the fermenter broth at low concentrations thereby eliminating the need to dilute the substrate with massive amounts of water. Dilution is required to protect the yeast from poisoning. The Biostil process has another adaptive parameter which most other continuous processes do not have. While most other continuous processes run the risk of ethanol loss through contamination, the Biostil process has been designed specifically to reduce the risk of concentration. First, its internal design allows the yeast to undergo pasteurization, thereby killing off the bacteria. Second, the feedstock is subjected to high osmotic pressure, low sugar concentration, between 4.5 and 5.0 per cent ethanol, and high yeast concentration in the fermenter. These conditions do not favour the growth of bacteria (Table 6.4).[15]

The technology was targeted for the Brazilian market, but several factors hindered its widespread use. First, the process was about 20 per cent more expensive than the conventional batch processes. Second, the process required carefully controlled operating conditions, relied on skilled personnel and therefore had high labour costs. Third, the Brazilians gradually increased the use of stillage as fertilizer and therefore undermined one of the most important attributes of the Biostil process. As a result, the process has not had the expected rate of commercial application in Brazil. According to Alfa-Laval officials, the firm has turned down offers from Brazilians who it suspected would replicate the plant and introduce cheaper versions on to the market. Alternatively, some Brazilian distillery manufacturers contend that the Biostil process is too sophisticated for Brazil and there is no need for replication. It is interesting to note that the Brazilian government, through the Secretaria de Tecnologia Industrial (STI) funded the development of the Flashfern process to a pilot scale. The core concepts of the Flashfern are similar to Biostil's.[16] The development of local versions of the Biostil process could also have retarded its diffusion as potential adopters waited for the new variants which were likely to be cheaper and more appropriate to Brazilian conditions.

One of the most innovative variants in ethanol production has been the application of genetic engineering to cellulose degradation. Studies on cellulosic degradation in the United States originated in the military, especially in trying to reduce rotting of military supplies in the tropics during the Second World War. A research programme at the US Army Natick Development Centre set out to investigate 'the causal organisms, their mechanism of action, and the development of methods of control not requiring the use of pesticides'.[17] This led to major advances in enzymatic hydrolysis, which were later applied to ethanol production, especially using the soil fungus *Trichoderma*. This area has also attracted the use of carefully selected and genetically engineered organisms to produce energy, an approach which not only represents a change in the source of raw materials but also in the methods and disciplines applied to ethanol production. However, many of these innovations have remained at laboratory level. The main obstacle to their commercial adoption has been high capital costs. By 1981 the capital cost estimates were in the range of between US$3.5 and US$2.5 million. A large share of the cost was accounted for by high feedstock prices. There is still the possibility however, that feedstock costs could be reduced by further research into more efficent means of cellulose transformation.

Apart from the development of new variants, research efforts have also been directed at reducing the energy used in the production of ethanol since ethanol production typically shows positive energy balances. Innovations in this field have concentrated on distillation (or separation), which accounts for 25–50 per cent of the energy used in ethanol production. Innovation in separation units has taken three routes. First, existing technology has been improved through incremental modifications. Second, technical advances made in other engineering fields have been introduced into ethanol technological systems.[18] Third, radically new technological variants have been proposed. These fall into two main categories: distillation and non-distillation. The non-distillation variants represent a departure from conventional distillation techniques in that they use solvent extraction, adsorption/absorption, membrane and diffusion techniques.[19] Although their energy requirements are less than those of conventional distillation, the installed capital equipment costs remain relatively higher. However, some of these systems, especially solvent extraction and grain adsorption, have reached competitive levels and additional improvements would enable them to displace conventional techniques.

Finally, the increasing complexity of ethanol technological units and pressures for systems control have led to the increased application of information technology in fermentation. As pointed out earlier, a technological system functions as a whole under the pressure of functional imperatives and its rationalization requires the ability to process, transmit and control various pieces of operative information. This requirement has led to the increased used of computers in ethanol technological systems. This use is largely a continuation of the instrumentation and control process that started with the introduction of saccharometers and hydrometers, but while such instruments measure isolated variables, computers can handle combinations of variables and system performances. With computers, advanced system configurations can be designed and the fermentation process closely monitored, controlled and adjusted to maintain optimal performance. Many of the computer-aided fermentation (CAF) techniques have been relocated from the pharmaceutical environment, which, for example, has applied the approach in the production of penicillin. The early applications of CAF were at experimental- and pilot-plant levels.[20]

6.6 Technological Imperatives and Institutional Reform

We have seen that the introduction of a new technological system is usually associated with a process of socializing knowledge, thus providing a framework within which options can be generated, selected and retained. Furthermore, such an institutional framework provides also a forum for the continued assessment of the external environment so as to give direction to the evolutionary process. This makes institutions *endogenous* to the process of technological change. In this way the demands, or imperatives, of ethanol technological systems required reform to existing institutions or the creation of new ones. The early stages of renewed generation for ethanol technological variants are characterized by considerable institutional support, partly to underwrite the high costs of variant generation and the losses that might result due to the uncertainties inherent in new technological systems. Public sector support varied from direct support for increasing production capacity, as in the case of Brazil, to support for R&D programmes, such as in the case of the United States and other industrialized countries. These differences, however, were not mutually exclusive. Brazil, for example, mobilized R&D in its civilian and military research institutes, especially on the end-use side. New engines that utilized hydrated ethanol were designed and marketed largely through the collaboration of local research institutes (mainly the air force) and the private sector.[21] The United States, on the other hand, concentrated its support on the generation of new ethanol production systems.

The US biomass fuels programme had long-term objectives with specific targets to the year 2000. These targets embodied the need to raise the performance of conjectural technological variants and also specified the desired size of the ethanol niche. For example, the cost target for 1 million BTUs was set at no more than US$3.5 (at 1977) prices for the year 2000. To achieve these objectives, the plan emphasized the technological co-evolution of different units. It was envisaged that this approach, coupled with the extensive generation of conjectural variants, would offer a higher chance of bringing some of the emerging technological systems to the commercial stage. The approach was aimed at raising total system performance, recognizing that the subsystems, or units, were only significant in relation to the whole system. Notice also that the support for ethanol technological systems was not an isolated development but part of a large programme aimed at increasing the role of biomass in general in the energy environment.[22] Support for fuel ethanol was given by both federal and state governments, leading to significant R&D advances.

These technological advances did not immediately reach the market and as a result most of the technological systems used in ethanol production before and after 1973 were predominantly of the batch process type. The largest market for such technologies was Brazil, which launched its national ethanol programme in 1975 using traditional batch systems manufactured in the country. The prospects for extended market niches brought on to the scene a new form of market restructuring in which firms with relevant scientific and technological know-how increased their R&D on generating technological variants.

The development of ethanol technological systems in the United States in the 1980s has also been influenced by fluctuations in the institutional climate. Much of the R&D and other tax incentives to stimulate the application of the technology were started during the Carter administration, which was favourable to alternative energy options. But government support under Reagan has dwindled and many of the new research routes that had been earlier perceived as fruitful have now been abandoned (Table 6.5). This change in the institutional climate was not directly related to changes in oil prices but to perceptions about the role of government in the development of alternative energy sources.

On the whole, the evolution of ethanol technological systems has been marked by increased complexity, adaptive flexibility and system diversity. The drift towards complexity and flexibility has been helped or retarded by the public sector and other institutions. Although efforts were undertaken to introduce radically new process recombinations, the international market was still dominated by batch processes in the late 1970s and early 1980s. Some of the new R&D routes that had been initiated in the 1970s were abandoned or curtailed as oil prices started to fall in the 1980s.

Table 6.5 DoE's renewable energy budget, 1981–5 (US$ millions)

	Carter request 1/1981	Reagan request 9/1981	Budget authority 1982	Budget authority 1983	Budget authority 1984	Reagan request 1985
Photovoltaics	161.60	54.1	75.0	58.0	50.4	47.5
Solar thermal	149.80	57.5	76.0	61.10	60.3	46.3
Biomass energy systems	55.50	18.0	20.5	16.00	—	28.1*
Alcohol fuels	32.60	8.8	10.0	5.00	28.4	—
Wind energy systems	73.60	18.3	34.4	31.40	26.5	23.3
Ocean energy systems	36.80	—	20.8	10.50	5.5	3.5
Renewable energy infor.	12.70	3.5	6.7	3.00	3.3	6.0
Renewable energy inter.	13.00	8.8	4.0	10.00	0.5	0.5
Programme support	—	—	3.5	1.00	0.8	0.5
Solar research A/C	—	—	12.3	—	—	—
Programme direction	6.90	4.0	4.0	5.80	6.0	4.9
Total	558.96	170.1	268.2	201.94	181.7	163.6

* Amount includes funds for alcohol fuels
Source: Kraft *et al.* (1984)

Notes and References

1. To illustrate this point we shall limit our analysis to the fermentation stage of the process. This analytical boundary is based on various factors. First, fermentation is the stage that has seen most innovations. Second, it is the core part of the whole process; it is at this stage that ethanol is actually produced. The process of ethanol production stretches from agricultural production to waste treatment (with the intermediate stages of feedstock production, fermentation, distillation and dehydration).
2. P. Mathias (1959), *The Brewing Industry 1700–1830* (Cambridge: Cambridge University Press), p. 63. He goes on: 'But industrial success of this order itself induced the search for, and application of, new techniques. When conditions are propitious, the virus of economy and efficiency is an infectious one, as much as the sickness of inertia when they are not; and men touched with the hope of gain by reorganising their breweries had their wits sharpened in the search for profit by other means. Moreover, the problems of success, as well as its opportunities, stimulated activity towards preserving the conditions which allowed it, making the role of innovation a cumulative one.
3. Ibid., pp. 64–65.
4. See Al Clow *et al.* (1952), *The Chemical Revolution: A Contribution to Social Technology* (London: Batchworth Press).
5. See M. Teich (1983), 'Fermentation Theory and Practice: The Beginning of Pure Yeast Cultivation and English Brewing, 1883–1913', *History of Technology*, Eighth Annual Review, p. 130. See also E. Sigsworth (1965), 'Science and the Brewing Industry 1850–1900', *Economic History Review* 17: 536–50, for a rejection of the notion that scientific advance had any revolutionary impact on British brewing; and T. Cochran (1948), *The Fabst Brewing Company: The History of an American Business* (New York: New York University Press), pp. 102–28, on the role of science in American brewing. Glamann gives an account of the role of science in the rise of the modern brewing industry. See K. Glamann (1984), 'The Scientific Brewer: Founders and Successors During the Rise of the Modern Brewing Industry' in D. Coleman *et al.* (eds), *Enterprise and History: Essays in Honour of Charles Wilson* (Cambridge: Cambridge University Press), pp. 186–98.
6. B. Nunberg (1978), 'State Intervention in the Sugar Sector in Brazil: A Study of the Institute of Sugar and Alcohol', unpublished PhD, Stanford University, Palo Alto. Nunberg provides a detailed review of ethanol production in Brazil over this period and the institutional forces that shaped the utilization of ethanol.
7. See Chemical Foundation (1935), *Proceedings of the Dearborn Conference of Agriculture, Industry and Science*, Dearborn, Michigan, May 7 and 8 (New York: Chemical Foundation), p. 32.
8. J. Borkin (1978), *The Crime and Punishment of I G Farben* (New York: The Free Press), pp. 150–3.
9. C. Pursell (1969), 'The Farm Chemurgic Council and United States Department of Agriculture 1935–1939, *Isis*, **60** (203): 308.
10. Ibid., pp. 309, 310.
11. The decision was largely influenced by political differences between government officials and the promoters of fuel ethanol, especially on agricultural policy. It appears that while the government was unwilling to move immediately into large-scale agro-industrial projects such as fuel ethanol, it considered them as an option that needed to be pursued more

carefully. In the meantime, the New Deal supporters managed to have their approach accepted more readily. The choice of technological options was therefore influenced by broader political issues pertaining to the direction of socioeconomic evolution.

12. See the discussion in the following chapter.
13. Efforts to open up the Brazilian market for foreign technology under a World Bank project failed as local firms won most of the bids. This happened because the competition was based largely on capital costs, a factor which gave the Brazilian firm a competitive edge over foreign suppliers.
14. See C. Morris (1983), 'Huge Plant for Ethanol and HFCS', *Food Engineering*, June.
15. See L. Garlick (1983), 'Fermentation of Molasses Cane Juice Using Continuous Fermentation', *The Sugar Journal*, **46** (4): 15.
16. Another version of the Biostil concept, the Engenho Novo process, was supported by the Financiadora de Estudos e Projetos (FINEP), which also co-sponsored the Biostil plant at Sao Luiz.
17. See E. Reese (1976), 'History of Cellulose Program at the US Army Natick Development Center', *Biotechnology and Bioengineering*, Symposium No. 6, p. 9.
18. D. Essien *et al.* (1983) 'Energy Conservation in Ethanol Production by Fermentation', *Process Biochemistry*, **18** (4), p. 31.
19. For a detailed review of these techniques, see L. Douglas *et al.* (1983), *Evaluation of Nondistillation Ethanol Separation Processes* (Boulder, Colo.: Solar Energy Research Institute), pp. 11–27.
20. See C. Cooney (1979), 'Computer Application in Fermentation Technology: A Perspective', *Biotechnology and Bioengineering Symposium*, No. 9, pp. 1–11.
21. Brazil established a most elaborate institutional network on fuel ethanol. For a description of the network, see World Bank (1981), *Brazil: Alcohol and Biomass Energy Development Project* (Washington, DC: World Bank).
22. See US ERDA (1977), *Program Plans*, Fuel from Biomass Branch, Division of Solar Energy, US Energy Research and Development Administration, Washington, DC, pp. 1–3.

Chapter 7

The Evolution of Photovoltaic Technology

7.1 Photovoltaics in History

The historical development of photovoltaics may be seen in terms of the convergence of scientific advances in fields such as light, electromagnetism, quantum mechanics and electronics. Major theories in these fields sought to explain phenomena such as energy forms, light diffraction, polarization, velocity and the interaction of radiation and matter. In 1839 Becquerel discovered the photoelectric effect — the capacity of materials to convert light energy to electrical energy — and the subsequent history of photovoltaics technology has been mainly associated with new discoveries of photosensitive effects in specific materials.

In 1873 Willoughby Smith demonstrated photoconductivity in selenium. This discovery induced further research which led to the discovery of spectral sensitivity of selenium photoconductors, to the development of the light meter and later to activities such as the simulation of human eye response by a combination of selenium cells and colour filters.[1] Further developments were the discovery of photosensitivity in copper and copper oxide by Hallwacho (1904), the connection of the photovoltaic effect to a barrier layer (1914) and the discovery of silicon by Berzelius (1917).

Copper and copper oxide photovoltaics were subsequently applied in photometry until they were replaced by selenium cells, which had achieved the then considerable conversion efficiency of 1.0 per cent. This value was also reached by the thallium sulphide photovoltaic devices developed in 1941. Concurrent research in electronics led to the development of the single-crystal silicon photovoltaic device in the same year, although it took another six years of research on impurity diffusion to turn this into a practical device. The initial conversion efficiency was 6.0 per cent. With technical performance firmly established, Bell Telephone Laboratories installed a photovoltaic array on a telephone in Georgia to power a repeater amplifier which worked for a year, although the generated power could not compete commercially with conventional sources. Despite this, two semiconductor firms started photovoltaic production, hoping to enter the communications market.

The first major photovoltaic application was in generating energy for satellites. This was a significant application because the life of the early satellites was limited to some 3–4 months, depending on the discharge rate of installed electrochemical batteries. Photovoltaics prolonged this period to over a year and because of the military importance of the space programme and US–USSR space competition, photovoltaics R&D took on considerable significance. The US military supported the initial diversification into other materials,[2] while reducing photovoltaic costs became a major preoccupation of US industry and the R&D establishment. The 1973 oil crisis created a new impetus for terrestrial applications and led to further R&D activity, especially in the United States and Japan. It also indicated that the extensive application of photovoltaics was a possibility through the creation of Schumpeterian economic space or market niches in which photovoltaics could penetrate and establish their contribution to the overall energy mix. But shifts in the energy environment alone did not guarantee the realization of market niches. Realizing the niches was largely dependent on the technical evolution of photovoltaics systems themselves.

Thus the evolution of photovoltaic technology was guided by entrepreneurial vision amid high levels of risk and uncertainty. Kelly noted in the initial stages of the US photovoltaic programme that they probably knew only slightly more about photoelectric generation than James Watt had known about producing mechanical energy from steam: 'Like Watt, we know that the technology works, we know something about the principles which govern it, and we can dare to speculate about a promising future.'[3] It is this promising future that has since maintained interest in photovoltaics among many scientific and entrepreneurial communities.

7.2 Technical Change in Functional Units

7.2.1. *Single-Crystal Materials*

The use of photovoltaics in satellites was a major turning point in the history of solar electricity. The first firms that emerged in the 1950s to meet the demands of the space industry relied on single-crystal silicon cells as the most important functional unit for the manufacture of photovoltaic modules. Single-crystal silicon was a primary candidate partly because it was already being produced for the semiconductor industry but more important because the material has the ability to convert a large section of the light spectrum to electricity with a maximum theoretical efficiency of 23 per cent.[4] Hence, since the value of silicon is in its photovoltaic effect, much of the research is related to how much of the light spectrum can be converted to electricity.

Silicon is conventionally produced in the electronics industry by adding carbon to silica in a batch process. The added carbon reacts to remove the oxygen in the form of carbon dioxide, leaving silicon with a very low level of impurities and hence suitable for semiconductor use. This stage is followed by the growth of polycrystalline ingots using the Siemens process. Here the silicon is reacted with an electronically heated seed rod. The silicon is slowly deposited on a red hot rod, which then grows into an ingot weighing some 100 kg. The polycrystalline is then treated in the Czochralski process under carefully regulated temperature regimes to yield a single-crystal silicon ingot which is finally sawed into thin wafers (0.025 cm).

During the fabrication process, wafers are doped with different materials making one side negative and the other positive. The two sides are separated by a junction of static electricity which forms spontaneously during the doping process. Metal contacts are then attached on both sides as electrical connections. Although the process appears simple, it is a complicated microfabrication technique carried out under highly controlled conditions, showing that a particular material, even at the level of functional units, is bound up in an extended innovation hierarchy which involves system performance and techno-economic viability. Also, since the ultimate goal is to adapt a product to market conditions, the production process becomes a crucial aspect of the choice of materials at the level of functional units.

The initial concern was to reduce the production costs of producing single-crystal silicon, which accounted in the early stages of the technology's evolution for more than 50 per cent of total module costs. In the late 1970s, for example, ingots grown in the Czochralski process cost US$200–400/kg (cf. the US$50–70 for polycrystalline blocks cost). The process of wafering resulted in some 50 per cent silicon loss in the form of sawdust (kerf). The Czochralski process has since undergone several incremental technical changes as part of the efforts to reduce silicon costs. These include pulling more than one ingot per crucible, producing thinner wafers with lower kerf loss, and increasing the diameter of the ingot. Wafering has also benefited from a variety of new thinner saws, multi-bladed circular saws, and wire saws — some of which cut more than 1,000 wafers at a time. Over the 1978–80 period alone, kerf losses were reduced by 25 per cent and blade life was raised from 2,500 to 3,100 slices.[5] However, industrial projections show that single-crystal wafers may have trouble getting down to the less than US$1-per-peak-watt needed to make photovoltaics competitive with other sources of electricity.

Radical innovations have also been introduced in the development of functional units, especially in growing crystalline silicon. These innovations are radical because they introduce or eliminate significant steps in the silicon production process. Alternative techniques being developed include producing sheets from molten silicon through ribbon or dendrite processes. A typical ingot-wafer throughput is about 0.15 square metres (m^2) per hour while that of a ribbon machine is 0.5 m^2

per hour. At pilot plant level for example, Mobil Solar (United States) has made ribbons with 12–14 per cent efficiency and Westinghouse Electric (United States) has produced ribbons with 16 per cent efficiency. In ribbon production, a die is immersed in molten silicon and the silicon is drawn up the split by capillary action. The formation of the crystals is then effected by attaching a seed crystal at the top of the melt. This yields a rectangular ribbon of 10–13 cm which is cut into appropriate sizes and doped like wafers. The dendrite process does not use a die which shapes the ribbon but uses instead two specially made seed crystals called dendrites which are simply dipped into the melt side by side and a ribbon is slowly pulled.

A third option in the search for alternative ways to produce solar grade silicon has been a casting process under which molten silicon (1,100°C) is poured into a special pot and allowed to solidify under conditions that would allow a single crystal to form. This is then sliced and doped. A final option is the coating of molten silicon on a ceramic substrate thereby forming a thin silicon film. The process takes only 25 per cent of the silicon that would otherwise be used in the conventional Czochralski method. It is indicative that all four approaches not only cut down on energy and time consumption but are also 'rectangular'. This is an important requirement not for functional unit efficiency but for module and system efficiency.

Hence it is clear that even at the level of innovation in functional units, variability and selection play a significant role. Different conjectural approaches whose long-term competitiveness is uncertain have emerged in the area of single-crystal silicon production alone. Photovoltaic materials must obey certain functional imperatives which determine design configurations, which in turn give the resultant photovoltaic systems particular forms. For example, devices that capture sunlight must take certain forms which optimize the process like the need to face the sun. This and other design imperatives provide the morphological context for photovoltaic devices. Because the morphological context forces conversion materials to take particular shapes, process techniques developed for one material require modifications before being transferred to other materials. These design imperatives and morphological considerations change as the innovation process rises up the evolutionary hierarchy, as portrayed in Figure 7.1.

But even the individual functional units, design imperatives and morphological considerations generate significant functional subsystems. For example, while conventional photovoltaic panels are flat-plate systems, conversion efficiency may be increased through the concentration of light and considerable variations have been generated in the development of concentrators. These subsystems result largely from the recombination of two known functional concepts: conversion materials and light concentrators. Conjectural subsystems that have

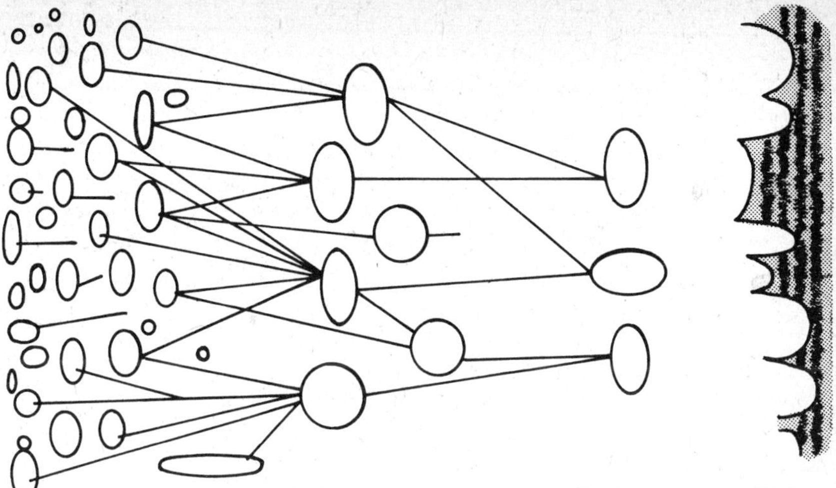

Figure 7.1 Articulation path

emerged include the use of Fresnel lenses, parabolic troughs, cylindrical troughs and point focusing. In turn, such recombinant innovations tend to generate further problems whose solutions often require new research in the basic functional units. For example, light concentration tends to increase the generation of heat. This becomes a selector for heat-tolerant materials such as gallium arsenide. Alternatively, thermo-photovoltaic systems may be devised which capture heat or incorporate coolants.

Other new ways of increasing conversion efficiency include *tandem cells* under which different materials are used in stacks to capture the different sections of the solar spectrum. But these approaches involve the rearrangement of the various physical materials. Alternative techniques are being developed which involve the rearrangement of the solar spectrum itself. An example is the *luminescent solar collector* (LSC), which comprises a flat box with a reflective mirror base and a top cover doped with luminescent dyes. The dyes absorb the light and reradiate it at wavelengths that can be converted by a specific material at one of the inner edges of the collector. The system has a maximum theoretical efficiency of 75 per cent. Many of these technologies are still in their early stages of development and are thus still far away from commercial application. Nevertheless, such divergences then follow slightly different design imperatives and introduce 'functional polymorphism' into the range of final photovoltaic systems.

We have seen that bringing down the costs to levels where photovoltaics could compete with conventional sources of electricity has required massive reductions in the cost of single-crystal production as well as improvements in conversion efficiency. The cost of 1.0 pW from photovoltaics was some US$1,000 in the early 1960s when the average cost using conventional sources was less than US$1.0. Incremental technical changes have since involved reductions in the production costs of ingots, raising efficiency through better material processing and fabrication, as well as reducing energy consumption in the whole process. However, there contributions have remained fairly limited and the future of pholovoltaics will depend on major changes in the material base as well as on production techniques.

The existence of variability in photovoltaic materials has been part of the historical development of the technology. While silicon was treated as the most promising material, the US military was already working on alternative materials, especially cadmium sulphide (CdS).[6] This material was not discovered in an organized search for photovoltaics materials but was identified during semiconductor research into the properties of various rectifying contacts to CdS crystals in 1954. Research on this material was conducted by the US Air Force Aerospace Research Laboratory jointly with the private sector in the laboratories of Harshaw Chemical, Shiozawa and Eagle-Picher. Many of the research findings were not published.

This research was not a result of perceived limitations of the silicon cells but resulted from the fact that a material was available whose potential could only be established through R&D. This would tend to suggest that variability in R&D may not necessarily be due to the performance of the dominant technology, as much as to the need to pursue other options under conditions of great commercial uncertainty. It appears also that scientific advance is partially self-propelling and does not necessarily require external inducements. The process of matching phenomena to application is part of the technological tradition.[7] The view that advances result from the search for solutions to specific problems is complemented by the random emergence of technical possibilities that have to be matched to hitherto unexplored problems: the photovoltaic effect was initially a solution looking for a problem. But the emergence of such technical possibilities often occurs within the limits of existing zones of scientific enquiry.

7.2.2. *Polycrystalline Materials*

While work on improving single-crystal efficiency has continued, major shifts have been made into polycrystalline materials. This represents a quantum shift from crystalline materials to alternative new ones which are structurally different and pose different challenges and options. Put another way, the shift marks a 'punctuation' in photovoltaic technology since not only does it represent a major divergence, it also opens up a new range of variations in raw materials for functional units. Polycrystalline silicon, for example, requires less stringent growth conditions, uses less material if prepared as ribbons rather than ingots, and can be deposited on less expensive substrates. Added to these advantages is the fact that the material has comparable efficiencies to single-crystal silicon. Indeed, polycrystalline cell efficiency has risen from 2.0 per cent in 1975 to 13.8 per cent in 1984. Firms such as Solarex Corporation (United States) and AEG-Telefunken (West Germany) are active in this area.

Although polycrystalline cells are made from silicon, alternative materials with higher efficiency are now being developed. These include cadmium telluride (CdTe) and indium diselenide ($CuInSe_2$). A pilot plant has been built by Sovolvo (United States), a joint venture of Boeing Aerospace and Reading and Bates to develop indium diselenide polycrystalline cells, and Boeing has demonstrated a $CuInSe_2$ cell with more than 11.0 per cent efficiency. The cells are produced through a thin-film technique, using the industrial methods of high-speed coating perfected by the paper and steel industry.

The shift to polycrystalline materials was not a sudden move but represented a more elaborate exercise in searching the materials base and making a selection of suitable candidates on the basis of efficiency, life expectancy and easy fabrication. In the early stages the search was conducted among materials known to have photovoltaic properties. This is a very wide category but it is reduced in practice to binary compounds because of their ease of fabrication. Even more important is the fact that the materials have to be selected on the basis of their ability to be doped as negative- or positive-type semiconductors (Fig. 7.2).

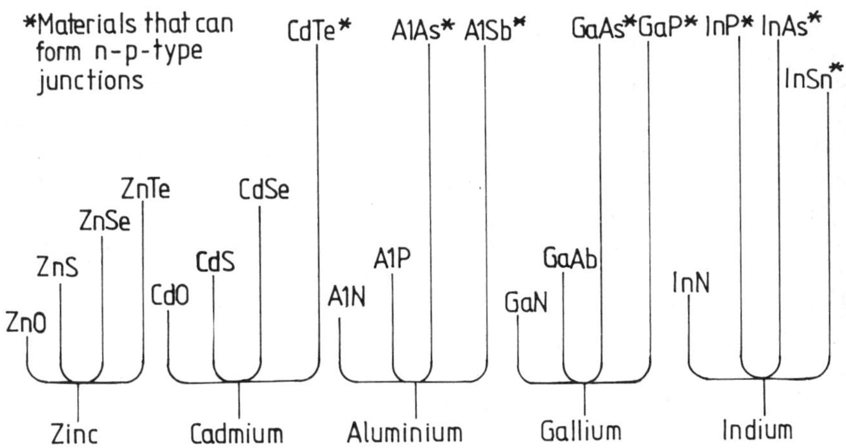

Figure 7.2 Material search trees (*Source:* Juma (1983))

Currently, selection has narrowed down the range of possible options to less than a dozen with varying maximum theoretical efficiencies. These include germanium (13 per cent), cadmium sulphide (18 per cent), cadmium telluride (25 per cent), indium phosphide (26 per cent), gallium arsenide (27 per cent) and aluminium antimonide (27 per cent). The selection process continues among these conjectural options on the basis of costs of production, life expectancy and amenability to fabrication, but it appears that cadmium sulphide and gallium arsenide are the most likely to succeed. The latter converts a wide section of the solar spectrum and is therefore inherently more efficient than other materials (Table 7.1). Moreover, it does not lose efficiency when exposed to heat as much as other material, a property that makes it ideal for use in concentrators.

Table 7.1 Highest proven cell efficiency (CM^2)

Type	Efficiency	Structure	Area (cm^2)	Developer
Crystalline silicon	19.10	Single crystal float zone	4.00	University of New South Wales
Crystalline silicon	18.00	Single crystal	4.00	Spire Corporation
Polycrystalline	11.00	$(CdZn)s/CulnSe_2$	1.00	Boeing Aerospace
Polycrystalline	10.90	CdS/CdTe	1.00	Eastman Kodak
Amorphous silicon	10.10	Glass/TCO/p-i-n	1.90	RCA Corporation
Amorphous silicon	08.50	Glass/TCO/p-i-n	1.00	Fuji Electric
Gallium arsenide	20.34	CVD heteroface	1.00	Spire Corporation
Gallium arsenide	19.00	CVD heteroface	4.00	Hughes Research Labs

Source: Fischetti (1984)

7.2.3. *Amorphous Materials*

The shift towards polycrystalline materials has taken place almost concurrently with the development of amorphous materials which are distinguished by their lack of crystal properties — the atoms are randomly distributed. Such materials have a high absorptive capacity and therefore very small amounts are required in the form of thin films. Moreover, since the crystallization process is eliminated, their production costs are much lower than the single-crystal or polycrystalline materials. Japan, under the 'Sunshine Project', opted for this material while the United States was investing in single-crystal and polycrystalline materials. The Japanese choice was based on different considerations with regard to raw material costs, production possibilities and market niches.

Amorphous cells were first fabricated in 1974 and though at that time they recorded low efficiencies (of about 1.0 per cent), they have since shown major improvements. For example, by 1982, RCA Corporation had produced a cell with 10.01 per cent efficiency and this process has subsequently been acquired by Solarex for attempted mass production. By 1983, amorphous cells accounted for 25 per cent of the world photovoltaic electricity, and the state-of-the-art efficiency reached over 11.00 per cent in 1985. The cells are easy to manufacture and handle, and Japanese firms have been dominant in this field, largely because producing such cells lends itself more easily to automated mass production. Most of the world's US$150 million devoted to photovoltaics R&D is now directed at amorphous cells, while some of the funding is directed at advanced concepts which include new materials and alloys as well as new system configurations.

The shift to amorphous materials is characterized by R&D to improve cell efficiency, prolong life expectancy and search for alternative fabrication techniques. The intensive R&D on fabrication techniques has included the introduction of silicon-carbon alloys and the glow discharge fabrication method which is being improved by US firms such as Chronar and 3M. Other techniques which are being developed include chemical vapour deposition (CVD), used by IBM and Chronar; low-pressure chemical vapour deposition (LPCVD), used by the Institution of Energy Conversion (United States); and Exxon's sputter method. To achieve high efficiencies with amorphous cells, new techniques are being investigated which include the production of cascade or multi-junction cells. In such functional units, amorphous cells matched to different sections of the light spectrum are stacked together enabling a large section of the solar spectrum to be converted to electricity. Spire (United States) is working jointly with the US government to produce such cells, and efficiencies of over 20 per cent are anticipated. Harvard and North Carolina universities are involved in similar work. Given fabrication limitations, it is currently thought that only two or three layers of silicon cells can be included in cascade functional units. However, research is being extended into the prospects of increasing the number of cells.

Thus so far there are three technologies competing for market penetration: single-crystal, polycrystalline and amorphous cells. It appears that single-crystal cells are approaching their conversion limits. The avenues for raising conversion efficiency while at the same time reducing unit energy costs have led, through a process of selection, to amorphous materials. Since every conversion material has its inherent limits, the search for and selection of alternative materials will continue. Amorphous materials will remain conjectural until they are displaced by other competing materials. As R&D continues at the level of functional units, accompanying process techniques also start to take shape. The ultimate goal of producing technologies that compete with conventional sources of electricity will thus continue to act as a major selector of the match between product and process innovation. But these changes have to be accompanied by innovations in other functional units which constitute the photovoltaic system. This is essentially a co-evolutionary process.

7.3 Co-evolution and System Configuration

A photovoltaic system is a configuration of various functional units which include cell modules; array structure and foundations; voltage regulators and other controls; storage batteries; instruments; power cables, buses and switchgear; electrical grounding network; and security enclosures. The module is the building block of the system; it consists of solar cells interconnected in both series and parallel and encapsulated within a supporting structure. A set of modules constitutes a panel, and an assembly of panels is called an array. Electrical loads in themselves are not part of the photovoltaic system, although the interaction between loads and photovoltaic systems may influence the direction of innovation. All the components except the cells are collectively called the 'balance-of-system' (BOS). Photovoltaic systems are classified either as flat-plate or concentrator. This classification is both functional and morphogenetic.

System performance is conventionally rated on the basis of the partial efficiencies of the functional units, modules, battery and other components, but the market environment selects more directly at system level suggesting a form of co-evolution in the BOS components. Co-evolutionary pressures may result from the imbalances generated by innovation in cells, and efforts to reduce the cost of conversion cells have tended to shift the share of total unit energy cost to the balance-of-system (BOS). This accounts for about 50 per cent of the total system costs. About 33 per cent of BOS costs are for electrical components (wiring, interconnects, control circuits, load management and voltage regulating devices), about 20 per cent for power storage, about 20 per cent for installation and checkout, and the rest for array, structure and site preparation. Unlike the cell, BOS components are usually made up of stable technologies which are not likely to undergo any major cost reductions and, as a result, the effects of BOS innovation on total costs has tended to be smaller than that accruing from conversion material improvement. BOS cost reductions can also be effected through innovation at cell level. For example, the use of larger cells reduces the need for interconnections and therefore cuts down on BOS costs.

However, BOS-specific innovations are required both to reduce overall system costs and to match the reliability of the components with that of the cells. Some of these problems cannot be solved until the system is operating and the feedback data is incorporated into subsequent

R&D. This is largely why the initial stages of photovoltaic penetration were devoted to testing. But co-evolution may occur without direct pressures. Parallel innovations in other sectors may become relevant. The case of energy storage illustrates the point. The conventional lead-acid and nickel-cadmium batteries are expensive, inefficient, prone to rapid discharges, relatively short-lived and require substantial maintenance. Alternative, advanced batteries being developed are more powerful, long lasting, reliable and easier to handle. The options being developed include zinc–chlorine, zinc–bromide, sodium–sulphur, hydrogen–halogen and iron–chromium redox batteries. Unlike the conventional batch batteries, the advanced alternatives operate on continuous flows.[8] All-solid-state storage systems such as the flywheel are also being developed as alternatives. For example, the flywheeel being developed at the Massachusetts Institute of Technology's Lincoln Laboratory can spin in a vacuum at a high speed (7,500–15,000 revolutions per minute) during the day and release enough energy for household use at night.

In this way system configurations represent complex interactions between various functional units which can only be understood in detail through the practical application of photovoltaic systems. However, it is possible to test approximately using computer simulations. The United States, for example, has extensively used the Solar Array Manufacturing Industry Costing Standards (SAMICS) computer programme developed by the Jet Propulsion Laboratories (JPL) at Pasadena, California. The programme has been operative since 1977 and firms simply phone in with preliminary cost estimates and get a comprehensive analysis of the price of the finished array. SAMICS has also been used to model factories. These estimates help in the identification of what parts of the systems need cost-reducing innovations.

7.4 Institutional Linkages

The development of photovoltaic technology in the major producing countries has relied heavily on public sector support at three main levels: support for R&D, provision of markets and raising public awareness about the technology. Indeed, it was largely through the support of the public sector that photovoltaic technology was developed to become potentially viable for terrestrial applications. Generally, support for R&D has been conducted as national programmes, but the expansion of the market has also involved international agencies and led to application of photovoltaic technology in the developing countries. While the R&D programmes set price goals and levels of efficiency to be achieved over specific time scales, the expansion of markets provided both finance as well as operating experience that were subsequently used to upgrade the technology. Most of the R&D in the United States, Western Europe and Japan has been done through complex government–industry, industry–university and government–university interlinkages. It is clear that these linkages are important in the early development of science-based innovations such as photovoltaics.

7.4.1. *The United States*

The United States initiated a two-component photovoltaic programme under the Carter administration. One of these was the Federal Photovoltaics Utilization Programme (FPUP) under which the government authorized some US$98 million for the 1979–82 period. The funds were spent on encouraging government agencies to incorporate photovoltaic systems into their activities, and providing marketing support for sale of modules. This was largely a procurement programme which aimed at setting up small remote-type systems. The programme guaranteed a market for those technologies that were ready for application but could not compete favourably with conventional sources of electricity. Moreover, such a programme ensured that the government would meet installation and monitoring costs. The 1978 US National Photovoltaics Act authorized the expenditure of US$1.5 billion over a ten-year period on photovoltaic research, development and commercialization.

The programme was aimed at providing the private sector with an incentive to invest in mass-production techniques for photovoltaics, and with this level of funding it had been estimated that photovoltaic technology would provide up to 20 per cent of US electricity needs by the year 2000, raising photovoltaic output from 1 MW of installed capacity in the late 1970s to 5,000 MW by the turn of the century. This was obviously a highly optimistic scenario which did not anticipate some of the institutional and technical problems that were later to arise. Initial funding was geared towards R&D with supporting experiments and involved universities, research institutes and the private sector. However, the government also actively supported the design, construction and operation of intermediate-type photovoltaic power systems ranging from 15 kW to 1,000 kW. By 1985 some seventeen systems had been completed and were operating as planned. Similar plants are now being installed by the private sector under subsidy and with the help of tax benefits schemes. Moreover, US laws require electrical utilities to interconnect small (renewable energy) generators (less than 80 MW) to their grids and to pay a fair price for any energy produced by the renewable energy system and fed into the grid. Such factors have led to increased private sector involvement in photovoltaic plant installation.

The US photovoltaics programme suffered from the budget cuts initiated by the Reagan administration, which argued that much of the R&D in systems that are near commercialization should be done by the private sector. As a result, in recent years federal funding for photovoltaics has been declining. For example, in 1979 the United States had the largest government budget on photovoltaic R&D, amounting to US$103.5 million. It rose to US$147 million in 1980. In 1981 the Carter administration requested some US$161.6 million to be spent on photovoltaics, but when the Reagan administration came to power the request was cut to US$72 million in 1982, to US$58 million in 1983 and US$50.4 million in 1984. Despite these cuts, however, the photovoltaic budget was second only to solar thermal and much higher than that for other renewable energy systems.

The reduction in federal funding for photovoltaics has had three main effects. First, the Department of Energy (DoE) through the Solar Energy Research Institute (SERI) has concentrated on funding advanced R&D. Second, large corporations, especially oil firms, have moved into R&D to fill the gap created by reductions in federal funding. Finally, private manufacturers have started to market their current systems without waiting for further major cost-reducing innovations. One of the effects of this latter development has been the construction of intermediate-size plants, some of which feed into the grid. The DoE (through SERI) has also begun to establish strong industry as well as university links to ensure that viable technologies are commercialized. SERI's target is to help in the production of modules that will produce electricity at US$0.20 per kWh by 1988. This is a short-term target that will hopefully see costs eventually reduced to US$0.15 per kWh, a figure that will have to be reached if photovoltaics technology is to compete favourably with electricity derived from oil. DoE's strategy is to solve some of the key obstacles to the industrial production of the most advanced photovoltaic technologies. The tasks have been distributed to three leading federal agencies who will be expected to maintain close collaboration with industry and universities. Of these, however, SERI is clearly the pivot around which the whole development of photovoltaics in the United States hinges.

SERI is charged with responsibility for conducting research in photovoltaic materials (amorphous thin films, polycrystalline thin films, crystalline silicon, high-efficiency concepts and photoelectrochemical cells), while the Sandia National Laboratories deal with R&D in concentrators and power conditioning. The JPL focuses on single-crystal silicon cells and the processing of large-area amorphous silicon thin films. The work at the three centres is conducted in close collaboration with industry and university research institutes. SERI also manages subcontracted R&D, develops state-of-the-art measurement and device capabilities and arranges the transfer of technology to industry. During the 1984–5 period, SERI subcontracted major cost-shared R&D on amorphous cells to Chronar, Solarex, 3M and Spire. Xerox has been subcontracted to continue R&D on the light-induced degradation of amorphous cells, and Chevron to continue work on materials purification. In addition, the emergence of amorphous silicon as a dominant photovoltaic material has led to new forms of institutional arrangement under the Amorphous Silicon Research Programme (ASRP). The work that was previously conducted by various national research laboratories is now managed centrally by SERI. This means now that all government-supported R&D is controlled by SERI regardless of where it is actually performed. This centralization is aimed at eliminating redundancy, allowing tighter control and raising the efficiency of decision-making.

Apart from R&D, SERI also conducts the 'innovative concepts' and the 'university participation' programmes. The former is aimed at identifying new materials and device configurations. Promising innovative concepts are carried through a stage of preliminary research before they are selected for further R&D. The university participation programme is aimed at establishing and maintaining the infrastructure needed for conducting photovoltaic-related research at universities. This programme ensures that university research is conducted in an atmosphere of academic freedom. It also enables SERI to maintain contacts with universities and link them with industry. New concepts from universities can therefore be transformed rapidly into R&D projects depending on their relevance to photovoltaic goals.

In addition to its natural role SERI, in conjunction with other government agencies, has participated in aid programmes aimed at setting up photovoltaic plants in developing countries. This has been done in collaboration with the US Agency for International Development (AID) and the National Aeronautical and Space Administration (NASA). This public sector collaboration has led to the establishment of photovoltaic pilot projects in countries such as Mali, Saudi Arabia, Morocco, Niger, Nepal, Thailand, Philippines, Panama, Tanzania, Rwanda, Tunisia, Egypt, Bangladesh and Guyana. The participation of SERI in international programmes has also been extended to projects funded by the European Economic Community (EEC). For example, SERI is involved in two pilot projects set up by the EEC in Greece and French Guyana and maintains links with other projects such as the activities of NASA and the US Centres for Disease Control (CDC) on testing photovoltaic refrigeration. Some of the data from the test programmes have been used in improving subsequent components and system configurations. The refrigeration project was conducted in conjunction with the World Health Organisation's Expanded Programme on Immunization (EPI) with the aim of ensuring that areas that cannot be supplied with potent vaccines and other drugs will be able to use photovoltaics as a source of coolant energy.

7.4.2 *The European Economic Community*

While the US government has reduced its funding for photovoltaic R&D, European countries, under the auspices of the EEC, launched a major programme in the late 1970s involving state agencies, universities, industry and public utilities. Photovoltaics R&D accounted for US$15.5 million over the 1975–9 period but was increased by some 190 per cent to reach US$59 million over the 1979–83 period. The programme has focused on the construction of fifteen pilot plants with capacities ranging from 30 kWh to 100 kWh. The construction of pilot plants was aimed at gaining operating experience. Like the US, the EEC programme undertook R&D specifically to reduce cell costs by improving processing and the use of alternative materials. The work was subcontracted to universities, research institutes and industry in the various EEC countries. For example, Leuven University (Belgium) has a subcontract to look into alternative techniques of cell fabrication while work on silicon thin films is underway at Democritus University of Thrace (Greece). Other work on cell processing has been subcontracted to Photowatt International (France). Much of the research on amorphous materials is also being carried out in universities. Research on amorphous silicon is conducted at the Max-Planck Institut (West Germany), University of Dundee (Scotland), University of Sheffield (England), University of Rome and the Centre d'Etudes Nucléaires (France). Following the completion of the first set of pilot projects, the EEC has decided to establish more photovoltaic plants but with smaller capacity and on a more decentralized basis. This will provide more operating experience and promote public awareness of the technology. Amorphous R&D has become the focus of EEC work, especially after Japan and the United States have provided the lead in this field.

European countries have not reached US levels of photovoltaic research effort but the considerable support being offered by their governments through the EEC will undoubtedly strengthen their position in both R&D and commercialization. For example, the programme is supported by a project on radiation data collection for solar energy application. Already, this project has released a number of volumes of the *European Solar Radiation Atlas* on both horizontal and inclined surfaces, and the work is being extended to the use of satellite data for predicting surface solar radiation. Such information is not only useful in the design of photovoltaic modules but is also valuable in their application. The various EEC countries also support photovoltaic R&D individually. France has set aside US$154 million for photovoltaic development over the 1982–6 period, of which the government's contribution amounts to US$52 million. And West Germany spent over US$40 million on photovoltaics during the 1980–4 period. These countries are likely to increase their R&D spending as competition against the United States and Japan intensifies, but to do so effectively new institutional links will have to be established to promote the transfer of technology from universities and research institutes to industry.

7.4.3 *Japan*

Photovoltaic R&D in Japan is conducted under the 'Sunshine Project' launched in 1974, and in recent years funding for photovoltaics has been increasing rapidly. For example, the budget was raised over 140 per cent during the 1980–2 period alone, bringing the total allocation to US$30 million. By 1984 Japan was spending some US$60 million on photovoltaic R&D, an amount shared equally by industry and government. However, as we have mentioned, while the United States concentrated its early photovoltaic R&D on crystalline material, Japan turned instead to amorphous materials which were selected because they lend themselves more easily to mass production. Under the project, the government funds a dozen large companies and ten research institutes, but unlike the US, which has dedicated photovoltaics firms, many of which are subsidiaries of oil majors, the work in Japan is done by large electrical, electronics and materials companies. These include Toshiba, Hitachi, Mitsubishi, Sanyo, Fuji Electric, Sharp, Matsushita Electric, Osaka Titanium and others. Japan also devotes more of its resources to bringing viable technologies to the market as soon as possible. Many of the marketing links are established in collaboration with the Ministry of International Trade and Industry (MITI).

MITI's involvement in photovoltaics was strengthened in 1983 with the formation of the New Energy Development Organization (NEDO). Among other tasks, NEDO aims at driving down the peak watt costs of electricity from amorphous cells to below US$2.24 and at applying the technology in heavy electrical uses. The three-year project has a budget of US$13.45 million. The funds are being spent on high-performance systems, large-area devices and high manufacturing efficiency. The project aims also at reducing the performance degradation of modules to less than 15 per cent in a ten-year period. The work has been distributed to three major Japanese firms. Sanyo is working on the development of high-speed manufacturing processes while Fuji is working on large-area cells measuring at least 120,000 sq. mm. Mitsubishi is developing a way to fabricate high-performance, tandem cells (exhibiting at least 12 per cent efficiency) from amorphous material measuring 100 sq. mm. This shift to industrial application is another innovative approach by the Japanese since photovoltaic systems have hitherto been largely installed for non-industrial uses.

NEDO is also involved in setting up long-term links with foreign countries. Market surveys have been conducted in the ASEAN countries and demonstration projects, especially solar villages, are part of NEDO's activities. Already, NEDO is building a solar park at Malaysia's Kebangsaan University at the cost of US$2.1 million. The park will use solar battery equipment, photovoltaic arrays and solar drying systems. This project was set up in conjunction with the Japanese New Energy Fund (NEF), a body of private concerns, and is being implemented over the 1986–7 period. This arrangement represents an example of the institutional links betwen the Japanese government, private industry and research institutes to establish overseas markets for photovoltaic products.

7.4.4 *Other Institutional Developments*

The participation of government agencies has not been limited to financial and institutional support alone. State intervention has also been directed at the structure of the photovoltaic industry itself, mainly to consolidate existing financial and market resources so as to strengthen national competitiveness. In France, for example, the state was instrumental in the creation of Photowatt, which is a consolidation of financial and photovoltaic-related capabilities previously held by Elf Aquitaine, Compagnie Générale d'Electricité (CGE) and Radiotechnique Compelec. This merger was masterminded by the state solar energy agency, Commissariat de l'Energie Solaire (COMES) and was in response to the competitive threat posed by the United States, Japan and other EEC countries.[9] Such mergers, however, tend only to promote the efficient use of available resources. The real challenge is to support this development with major R&D programmes.

Also, it is important to recognize the role of international agencies in the promotion of photovoltaic technology. The United Nations Development Programme (UNDP), for example, has funded a World Bank-executed project on photovoltaics which has been mainly a testing project to establish the economic viability of photovoltaic systems. The findings of these tests have been used to influence the direction of R&D in photovoltaics, especially through requesting manufacturers to design components that meet particular performance criteria. Again, the impact of the World Bank has been influenced largely by the need to ensure that photovoltaic systems compete fairly with conventional systems, especially in water pumping. The industrialized countries have also used multilateral arrangements such as the Lomé Convention to promote the export of photovoltaic modules.

Under the auspices of the EEC, Belgium has installed 750 photovoltaic systems in Zaïrean schools and hospitals for lighting, radio links and vaccine refrigeration. A teachers' college which uses photovoltaics has also been set up in Zaïre. Similar projects have been set up in numerous developing countries under multilateral or bilateral agreements. In addition, the United Nations has promoted photovoltaic applications through various training and education programmes and through the provision of infrastructure for photovoltaics-related research. Although some of these activities do not have immediate effects on the market, they create awareness which may have long-term commercial effects.

Another public sector application that has not received much attention in the literature is the military application of photovoltaics. Although this end-use is still low (estimated at 0.1 MW of world module output in 1984), it is likely to expand. Armies usually rely on batteries for the supply of electricity for communication and other equipment. Photovoltaics are well suited to small-scale mobile applications and the ultra-modern rechargeable batteries will be used increasingly in conjunction with photovoltaics by the military. There are tactical reasons for using photovoltaics as well since the recharging of batteries can be done quietly. Moreover, photovoltaics can also be used to recharge vehicular batteries during periods of tactical silence or 'moth balling'.[10] The United States already sells a large share of its photovoltaic modules to the military under a government procurement programme. This is also an area which is insulated from market requirements and which can therefore be used to underwrite the initial high costs of system development.

7.5 Summary

From the foregoing analysis it appears that institutions are major facilitators of technical evolution. Not only do they provide financial support for the generation of technical variations, but they also shape the selection mechanism. Moreover, institutions help to change market environments to favour the creation of particular techno-economic niches. It appears also from this case study that institutional linkages change in conjunction with the technological dynamics at hand. These changes are also associated with dominant political and economic configurations. This is why SERI, MITI and the EEC have developed differently.

Other interesting features can be identified from the roles played by these three institutions. The role played by MITI is indicative of strategies designed to follow an already established techno-economic tradition. For example, the choice of amorphous materials was based largely on their amenability to mass production. Thus the initial choice of material was made in the context of already established engineering practices. The United States, on the other hand, has spent considerable amounts of money on establishing a technological lead. It is therefore not surprising that the United States has maintained a lead in R&D while the Japanese have been increasing their world share of photovoltaic sales. This, however, is likely to change as SERI and some private corporations begin to apply the Japanese tradition as reflected in the current linkages between SERI, research institutions, industry and universities. It is significant that the number of private firms, research laboratories and universities working on SERI subcontracts is comparable. There were some twenty-two private firms, eighteen universities, and eighteen laboratories and institutes of technology working with subcontracts from SERI in 1984.

Institutional arrangements cannot, however, be arbitrarily transferred from one country to another if only because any proposed organization will have to be consistent with the broader institutional environment. It is, for example, inconceivable that the EEC would operate a MITI-type of institutional arrangement, since it does not possess the means of ensuring tight integration between finance, industry and the state. SERI, on the other hand, has adopted some of the Japanese-type integration. This is consistent with the overall US approach to the development of advanced technologies, especially for the military sector. But even more important is the fact that photovoltaics has been the favoured energy source among the frontier technologies and has therefore received considerable government support, especially among technocrats. The reduced funding of the Reagan years has been based more on broader ideological grounds than on technological expectations.

It is likely that the institutional arrangements that SERI has set up, together with its technological lead in amorphous R & D, will restore the dominant position of the United States in photovoltaic shipments. However, much depends on how effectively the United States will undertake process innovations to match the advances being made in product innovation. As indicated, the Japanese are undertaking more photovoltaic R&D in new applications thereby opening up local market niches. The move towards industrial applications is comparable to the centralized photovoltaic farms being established in the United States. The difference, however, is that Japan has undertaken new initiatives in product innovation along lines that are not being pursued at an equal pace elsewhere.

Notes and References

1. See M. Wolf (1976), 'Historical Development of Solar Cells' in C. Backus (ed.), *Solar Cells* (New York: Institute of Electrical and Electronics Engineers).
2. F. Shirland (1976), 'The History, Design, Fabrication and Performance of CdS Thin Film Solar Cells', in Backus, op. cit., pp. 43, 44.
3. H. Kelly (1978), 'Photovoltaic Power Systems: A Tour Through the Alternatives', *Science*, **199** (10 February): 634.
4. This maximum theoretical efficiency is an intrinsic limit which also, of course, influences the limits of system efficiency.

5. J. Smith (1981), 'Photovoltaics', *Science*, **212** (June 26): 1477.
6. Photovoltaic effect in CdS was reported by Bulgarian researchers in 1954 but the photocurrents were extremely low. The main reason why the Bulgarian researchers did not report higher photocurrents was because they used gold and aluminium instead of copper as electrodes. The use of copper would have led to the Cu_2S barrier layer that was responsible for the high photocurrents reported by Reynold in the United States in the same year. See Shirland, op. cit., p. 44.
7. The view that the market environment is the dominant force that induces technical innovation is articulated by Schmookler. This view is akin to the Larmackian suggestion that the existence of a particular functional need leads to the emergence of organs that fulfil that function. The view here is that the market environment is mainly a selector of conjectural variations. But unlike in the natural environment, technical evolution is purposive and responds to environmental parameters. We therefore have an interactive view which also includes conjectural variations for which market demand does not yet exist.
8. J. Jorne (1983), 'Flow Batteries', *American Scientist*, **17**: 507–12.
9. K. Hoffman (1985), 'The Commercialization of Photovoltaics in the Third World: Unfulfilled Expectations and Limited Markets', *Development and Change*, **16** (1): 5–37.
10. P. Warwick (1985), 'Photovoltaics in the Military Environment' in R. Hill *et al.* (eds), *Application of Photovoltaics*, proceedings of the Conference held at Newcastle-upon-Tyne, September 12–13 (London: UK Section of the International Solar Energy Society).

Chapter 8

Postscript

It is useful at this stage to summarize what these case studies tell us in relation to our qualitative evolutionary model outlined in Chapter 5.

(1) *Complexity*. In both cases the evolution of technology is a highly complex process involving the interaction of a great many technical systems and subsystems, which themselves stem from a wide variety of functional units. Each such unit is constantly a focus of change which would lead to a dynamic series of system configurations, many of which in turn would need to receive a degree of economic appraisal.

(2) *Dynamic instability*. Technological complexity brings with it dynamic instability in the sense that technical change in any one functional unit induces necessary changes in other parts of the system or subsystem. This means that R&D and design activities are carried out under constant threat of necessary adaptation. It also means that efficient information flows amongst the various activities associated with functional units play an important role in reducing such instabilities.

(3) *Hierarchy*. The evolution of technologies clearly follows a hierarchical pattern through time along the lines outlined in Chapters 2 and 5, with initial competition amongst systems and subsystems gradually leading to a coalescence in favour of a smaller number of likely candidates. This process also involves progressive market articulation as various market niches are experimented with. Indeed, there is continuous feedback at all stages of development as the technology gradually evolves towards the market.

(4) *Form and structure*. The shape of the technology itself (i.e. as a configuration of units, systems and subsystems) changes through time, thus giving force to the view that a 'technology' should be seen in terms of a living, organic system rather than in terms of static factor input ratios.

(5) *Uncertainty*. Technological development is carried on under conditions of great uncertainty. Indeed, conditions of ignorance would be a better way of describing the process, and we have seen that at any point in time future states of nature are at least partly incapable of being identified. Moreover, time itself is historic or irreversible. It does not make much sense to try to model the

evolution of such technologies as if you could proceed backwards in a deterministic way.

(6) *The role of science*. In both cases, though there are some differences, the role of differentiated scientific knowledge is central to technological evolution. Science provides a theoretical framework which permits R&D to be oriented in ways that allow economic agents possibilities for envisaging future events, and it does so both at the level of what we have called functional units, as well as at progressively more systemic levels as the technology moves up the production hierarchy. Moreover, there is no clear demarcation between basic and applied research. At various stages in technological evolution recourse is necessary to the former, but there is also a continuous need to test out units and systems in a production context.

(7) *Institutions*. The role of appropriate institutions is clearly central to effective technological development. We suggest that organizations like the SERI act as necessary centres of 'information exchange' for any given technology. Their function is to gather together relevant scientific expertise, establish effective information channels, set targets, manage R&D and maintain external links with other bodies concerned with government, finance, production and R&D. Moreover, there is a case for arguing that new technology may require new institutional forms to mobilize it. Older institutions may have built up organizational structures and information channels which may have been suitable for older technologies but which need not necessarily be effective with respect to new ones. It is in this sense that technological innovation probably requires institutional innovation as well.

Part IV

Conclusions

Chapter 9

In the Long Run: Institutions and Systems

In the previous chapters on fuel ethanol and photovoltaics technology, we have tried to show how technologies articulate themselves within the economic system. The overall process is characterized as one of complex evolutionary interrelationships, taking place over long time periods, strongly influenced by events within the science/technology system and involving complicated informational networks which operate in an interactive fashion to a considerable degree independent of economic markets. It is our view that such a complex social process cannot be realistically modelled by the tools of conventional economic theory that essentially apply only to specific aspects of short-run events. Indeed, the growing complexity of socioeconomics systems is such that they cannot usefully be modelled by any *one* social science discipline such as economics, but should instead be seen in an interdisciplinary light. We see our argument in this book as a contribution to this.

It remains for us in this final chapter to do two things. In the first section we show how our approach is consistent with some of the existing modern empirical literature on innovation. The analysis will be based on microevolutionary processes and will illustrate the emergence of complexity and hierarchy in the process of technological change. It will be shown that the design of a technological system is purposive and guided by a wide range of technical, economic, social and political interrelationships, which in turn influence its morphology. The emergence of technological systems is thus closely associated with the non-linear reorganization of the economic environment. The resulting changes are both unpredictable and irreversible.

The second section then concentrates upon the implications of our approach for policy-making and institutional development. In a static neoclassical world not only are 'institutions' frowned upon (they prevent the unhampered working of 'market forces'), policy-making itself is seen in terms of bringing the whole system back to a prespecified equilibrium — in terms of 'adjustment' rather than 'adaptation'. Conversely, in a complex world where the environment is constantly changing (the *real* world, we should argue) it is clear that policy itself must take on an evolutionary character, to be seen as the purposive generation, selection, retention and evaluation of evolutionary options under conditions of uncertainty.

It is also important to recognize that technological innovation is a *social* process so that micro-evolutionary changes must be linked to macroevolutionary dynamics. In other words, our macroevolutionary analysis of social change must be done in such a way as to reflect microevolutionary reality. Any departure from this view would lead us back to the conventional situation where equilibrium analysis is superimposed on microevolutionary dynamics, a process which has resulted in the limited recognition of the role of technological and institutional change in economic evolution and hence weak long-run policy. In contrast, an evolutionary approach that emphasizes purposive action and stochastic reorganization gives a clearer perspective on technology policy issues.

9.1 Microevolution and Technological Complexity

9.1.1 *Units and Networks of Analysis*

One of the conventions adopted in conventional economics is to reduce complex systems to homogenous units and then to treat them as the central actors in the economic process. The 'firm', for example, is often treated as the fundamental productive unit, an irreducible 'whole', and what takes place within it as irrelevant. Likewise, the household is regarded as the fundamental unit of consumption so that the notion of a household acting as a productive unit, mobilizing and allocating its own resources so as to satisfy more fundamental consumption objectives, cannot be encompassed easily within conventional theory. We have shown also that 'technology' is conventionally defined in very simple terms, sometimes as a concept designed to summarize a given industry category (information technology or microprocessor technology, for example) and sometimes as the prevailing state of the art exhibited in production, for example in terms of capital–labour ratios. And even here there is often confusion brought about by lack of clear definition and agreed usage.

Abstractions of these kinds are justified, of course, in analytical terms — by the need to simplify a complex universe so as to aid logical thought. Indeed, it would be difficult to examine economic events at all were every actor considered to be a unique entity or event. However, any given abstraction is simply a tool for analysis which is designed to approximate to an ultimate reality. At some stage models built upon such abstractions need to be subjected to empirical test and progressively altered and refined so as to converge to what actually is. If they do not do this, or if they are not used in this way, then their use becomes one of ritual rather than one of scientific practice.

It is our view that this is precisely what has occurred in much of conventional economic theory — stylized models have not been given a chance to 'evolve' towards a correspondence with reality. Indeed, by assuming equilibrium it becomes very hard for such models to 'learn' to change in relation to real events. And when, inevitably, a lack of correspondence appears between 'theory' and 'evidence', there is a strong temptation to avoid the issue. Rosenberg's 'Schumpeterian paradox' is one example of this.[1] Another is the practice of ascribing 'irrationality' to economic behaviour; for example, this was the view held by many neoclassical thinkers regarding the adaptive and risk-averting behaviour of peasant communities, especially in relation to new technologies.

Returning, then, to units of analysis, we argue that these are not isolated entities but rather nodes in a complex network of activity in a socioeconomic system. Much of what goes on within the firm, both in structure and function, is integral to the process of economic change. What is significant, therefore, is the ensemble of institutional networks involving firms as well as households. In this respect, technology takes on a new character; it becomes part of the process of social learning and cannot simply be viewed in terms of factor input ratios.

Although conventional economics treats the firm as the fundamental unit of production, the textbooks define the firm in financial and legal terms. It is likely, however, that the firm is not the most appropriate unit of analysis for the study of technological change, since the very act of production itself is unstable. Only in a world where technological change is exogenous to economic change, a neoclassical and static world, is the firm a homogenous entity from a production standpoint. In all other circumstances the productive unit is a system with shifting boundaries — a world linked together by knowledge and learning networks.

This view is consistent with modern research findings. For example, Imai and his colleagues use five case studies to model productive development as a qualitative process involving the 'dynamic and continuous process of adaptation to changes in the environment'.[2] Central to such a process is the creation of an 'inter-organizational network' consisting itself of three separate subsystems (or nets); affiliate companies, suppliers and R&D institutions (public and private). Each of these may be seen as a semi-autonomous productive subsystem.

For example, a supplier network might take the form outlined in Figure 9.1, with each of the secondary subcontractors acting as a repository of specific skills or competences with regard to a set of components or sub-assemblies which are then supplied to the primary subcontractor. The production system therefore forms a nested hierarchy with horizontal and vertical linkages which are defined by the flow of information, knowledge, skills and resources. The main company may be seen as a crucial node in a network which it co-ordinates to ensure the successful development of the product in question. At the same time, networks reorganize, dividing the labour

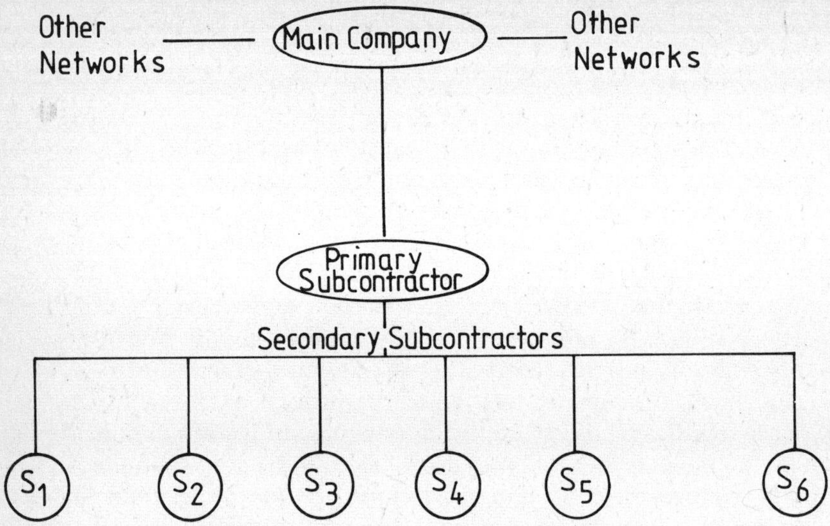

Figure 9.1 Productive units as interactive network

process, exchanging information and developing tacit codes of conduct with regard to their respective roles in the subsystem or system.

Similarly, Altshuler and his colleagues, in their study of the future of the automobile, paint a similar picture of modern Japanese methods of production organization which they contrast with traditional Western methods. Operating through industrial groups (or *keiretsu*), an assembly company will orchestrate a production system of financial houses, subcontractors and distributors which may be seen in terms of a loose (temporary) confederation of independent or semi-independent companies maintaining co-ordinated flows of information, technology and resources aimed at producing a particular design of automobile.

This ensures that many of the advantages of large organizations are utilized without the corresponding disadvantages: 'These new approaches, in combination, suggest a new definition of integration in the industry. Greater significance is attached to mutual cooperation, information flow, and *productive cross-flow among the members of a system* than to the level of finance and legal integration.'[3] Traditional methods of production, in contrast, emphasize large bufferstocks to prevent assembly-line breakdowns, vertical integration within one firm and multiple sourcing of components — leading to dedicated production equipment, lack of flexibility and lack of co-ordination between the different sections of a cumbersome operation.

And the differences in overall economic performance are considerable:

it is clear that on average the Japanese auto industry requires fewer hours of labour by factory workers, designers, technicians, and managers at all levels of the production chain to make a vehicle of any description than any other nation's auto industry. In addition [Japanese firms enjoy] . . . a very high level . . . of manufacturing accuracy, a wage level nearly the lowest (among countries investigated), a lower level of in process inventories, and greater versatility in shifting model mix and in developing new products. This contributes to lower production costs, higher product quality, and flexibility in meeting changing market conditions.[4]

The picture provided in this case is clearly a systems view in which the sum of the separate parts of systms is not equivalent to the working of the system as a whole.

A final example of the systems view is presented by the Italian garment company Benetton Brothers, which started as a small retailing business in 1968 and has since grown to become a very large multinational concern. Belussi describes this growth of what is essentially an integrated production system with a number of key characteristics.[5] The firm operates a flexible network of all production stages: designing, cutting, knitting, assembling, finishing, dyeing, labelling, warehousing and retailing, a process which involves extensive franchising and subcontracting to independent economic actors.

Centralized strategic control of the system is maintained by the Benetton family through financial, planning, marketing and production management. Peripheral operations include small firms and shops and the network is kept together by effective information flow whose efficiency is enhanced by the use of information technology. The operations also benefit from the availability of textile-related skills and the necessary labour market conditions in northern Italy.

The essential point to grasp here is that the very rapid rates of productivity change experienced by the Benetton system after 1978 depended upon a *prior* phase of organizational establishment during which production was rationalized into a coherent set of sequential operations involving semi-independent firms (from a financial and a legal viewpoint). Once the system had been put in place, however, innovations in warehousing, ordering, design, production, dyeing and marketing could then be introduced to improve dramatically total system performance. But, as Belussi notes, simply looking at Benetton R&D data on their own would provide a very poor understanding of what has really been taking place. As in the Japanese case, the most significant factor is the *organization* of a system in which the firm is not an irreducible unit of economic activity but a flexible node in a complex network of purposive economic action.

But why should firms take this rather non-specific character instead of being irreducible entities that can be subjected to the selectionism of market forces? The answer lies in the fact that firms operate in a complex environment which is constantly changing. Their ability to continue operating lies in their capacity to adapt to changing internal and external conditions through learning. The organization of the network ought therefore to reflect the need to maximize flexibility. A similar message is provided by Toffler, who argues that apart from complexity, the economic environment is dominated by non-linear processes.[6] This means that managers cannot continue using the same routines all the time. In such uncertain situations, linear and static concepts of the firm do not reflect non-linear reality: 'Under such conditions, all organizations become extremely vulnerable to outside forces or pressures. All managers must learn to cope with non-linear forces — i.e. situations in which small inputs can trigger vast results and *vice versa*.'[7] Coping with non-linear situations requires effective information flow and systemic organization in which networking plays a significant role.

Since the introduction of a new technological system in the economy represents a non-linear process, we argue that the most suitable way of analysing the evolution of complex systems is to focus on *interrelationships* and not on assumed irreducible entities. By emphasizing interrelationships, we may start to comprehend why economic actors tend to appear in hierarchical structures as the system moves through time. Moreover, this view provides a more realistic picture of the role and behaviour of institutions at the various stages of technological change.

9.1.2 *Technological Systems and Nested Hierarchies*

A second point to stress is that the evolution of technology is itself characterized by hierarchical organization. For example, the case of photovoltaic materials portrays initial competition amongst functional units, subsystems and systems which gradually leads to coalescence in favour of a small number of likely candidates. The process also involves progressive market articulation as various market niches are experimented with. Indeed, there is continuous feedback at all stages of development as the technology gradually creates a niche in the market. In addition, however, our example also shows that while the selection of suitable photovoltaic material narrows down the range of options available, the systems themselves become increasingly more complex. Hence both selection and hierarchical development are occurring at the same time. While selection is aimed at obtaining the most efficient functional units, hierarchical development aims at achieving the most desirable systems performance.

There are a number of examples in the recent innovation literature which illustrate the case of technological hierarchy. One of the most interesting is Clark's proposed model of 'design hierarchy' which is evolutionary in character and emphasizes the interactions between customers and designers in industrial morphogenesis.[8] Clark begins with the Abernathy–Utterback model in which product development is portrayed as moving gradually from a fluid phase into a more rigid standardized phase.[9] The former is characterized by uncertainty, product innovation and general-purpose machinery and skills, the latter by process innovation, standardization, rationalization and dedicated assets.

However, according to Clark, the model tends to oversimplify what is essentially a complex set of events, by portraying development in too linear a fashion. He proposes, instead, a model which emphasizes design logic and interactive feedback. Every design problem is an effort to achieve a fit between 'form' and 'context' but since both are constantly changing they require a guiding influence (or a set of influences). This is provided by Rosenberg's natural trajectories which are driven by technological imbalances (or compulsive sequences), engineering vision (Nelson and Winter), competition and consumer feedback.

Thus technological trajectories, or paradigms, should really be seen as design trajectories which develop in a hierarchical sequence very similar to Waddington's 'chreodes' along an epigenetic landscape.[10] For example, in the early stages of the automobile industry the embryonic 'form' of the automobile could be defined in terms of its functional parameters: motive power, steering, stopping, speed regulation, load capacity and so forth: 'Each parameter pertains to a functional domain, but within any particular domain, there exists a set of alternative concepts among which the designer may choose.'[11] For example, early alternatives in car engine designs included electric, gasoline and steam, while in semiconductor technology there were several rival methods in the 1950s for 'doping' base materials to create a transistor. Today there are rival organisms (viruses, fungi and bacteria) for hosting manipulated DNA. Each functional domain acts as a core which sets the agenda for subsidiary choices in an expanding hierarchy like that illustrated in Figure 9.2, for designing duct and value arrangements in a nuclear reactor.

Not only are design trajectories hierarchical but they are also reticular in the Koestler sense outlined in Chapter 2. They interact across functional domains in ways that allow for the emergence of a nested hierarchy thereby creating technological systems of great complexity. For example, Clark mentions the development of new products in automobiles in the 1930s at a time when the assembly line had become well established, particularly products associated with components made from new materials and the techniques to produce them. Another example from Chapter 6 is the improvement of feedstock preparation technology consequent on the development of continuous production of ethanol.

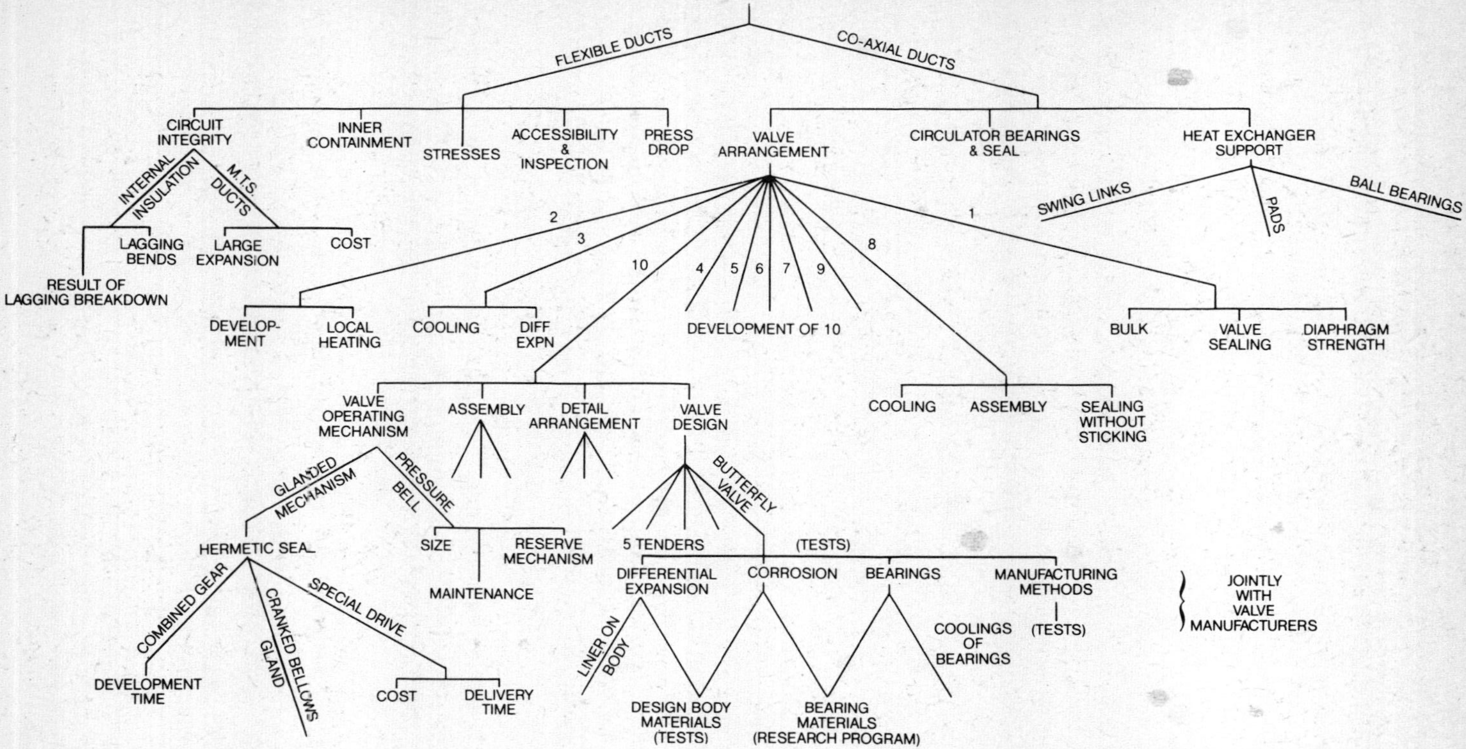

Figure 9.2 Marple's ducts and values problem. Sloping lines are alternatives; vertical lines are subproblems. *Source:* D.L. Marple, 'The Decisions of Engineering Design' IEEE Transactions on Engineering Management (June 1961), p. 60, copyright © 1961 IEEE.

Finally, the evolution of designs does not stop with the producer but goes into the domain of household consumption since consumers are faced with precisely analogous problems. Using a similar approach, Clark shows that we may view a new product as a form of consumption technology for the satisfaction of more basic needs. However, the consumer has to learn to do this, first by classifyng the product in terms of already known products (concepts), and what they can do; second, by combining the new product with other resources to satisfy needs; and third, by feeding information back to producers regarding how product design might be improved. The importance of this piece of the design chain is illustrated by the work of Gershuny and his colleagues where 'time budget' analysis has been used to show households as dynamic productive agencies, combining purchased inputs (consumer durables) with other resources (especially household labour time) to improve overall consumption efficiency particularly with respect to 'services' which were previously purchased from the market (e.g. banking, laundry and entertainment).[12]

A second example of hierarchical technological development may be seen in Aitken's detailed account of early radio communications.[13] In the pre-1912 period, radio had been conceptualized in terms of 'spark discharges' of electric energy, but there were emerging serious problems involved in energy loss and incoherence of signals at the receiving end of communications, problems of the 'presumptive anomaly' type outlined in Chapter 5. The alternative technological vector, *continuous wave communications*, took the form of three separate technologies — high frequency alternators (Fessenden, Alexanderson), electric arc generators (Elwell, Fuller) and the vacuum tube (de Forest) — each of which came from a different set of backgrounds. These technologies were subject to an uncertainty factor so that it was not clear at the beginning which option would win in the end. Indeed, the alternator and the arc each reached the stage of production and were sold in significant quantities to institutions concerned with long-range telecommunications. Moreover, according to Aitken, they made important contributions to the technical development of the radio:

The alternator and the arc were no minor contributions to the technical development of radio. The arcs proved that a commercial radiotelegraph service could survive in competition with the wired telegraph and telephone systems over land, and in competition with the submarine cables across many miles of ocean. As important, they provided the US Navy with a radio network connecting all its major bases and assuring reliable communications with units of the fleet years before any other naval power had that capability. The alternator provided indispensable communications facilities between the United States and Europe during World War I and, after the war, gave RCA the equipment it needed to equip its long distance stations in the United States and establish new stations in foreign countries. Between them, the alternator and the arc proved that highpowered continuous wave radio communication not only was possible but was, in competition with the older technology of spark, the more efficient mode. In the shift from spark to continuous wave, it was the alternator and the arc, not the vacuum tube, that broke away from the old conventions and showed what the new technology could do.[14]

However, what really led to the success of the thermionic valve as a producer and receiver of radio waves was its suitability for public broadcasting. In a sense, vacuum tube technology opened up an entirely new market, requiring a revolutionary institutional structure to operate it as a utility (under the auspices of RCA) and creating a technological trajectory which continued until the invention of the transistor in 1946. Aitken shows how all three variations constituted individual technological systems with complex roots in science and in engineering, though in each case the genealogy was different; it represented a 'different configuration of information'.[15]

From a diachronic standpoint the hierarchies were slightly different since, unlike valve technology, the alternator and the arc, once invented, tended to move along expected trajectories notwithstanding the challenging design problems involved:

the hopes and expectations of those who initiated the process of invention were closely matched by the characteristics of the devices that resulted. The big 200 kilowatt alternators with which RCA equipped its stations would have impressed and pleased Fessenden but they would not have surprised him. The 1,000 kilowatt arc Fuller designed for the Lafayette station must have struck Elwell as a fine achievement; but, if he looked at it, he would have seen a larger and more sophisticated version — which is to say, a version with greater information content — of the tiny 100 watt arc he had brought from Denmark.[16]

The vacuum tube was different:

De Forest fumbled his way to creativity, and in that respect he may more accurately typify the process of invention than does Elwell's work with the arc or Alexanderson's with the alternator. There is significantly, no single moment in the long process leading up to the triode vacuum tube that one can reasonably point to as *the* moment of invention. The one episode that looked like a classic 'eureka moment' — the gas flame experiments in de Forest's Chicago apartment — turned out to be misleading. Even the crucial step that differentiated de Forest's device from Fleming's — the insertion of the control grid — seems to have been taken without, at the time, any consciousness of radical change. It was just one more variation to try.[17]

Thus, while in each case the technology 'unfolded' through a temporal hierarchy, the vacuum tube was much more 'immanent' than the other two. Nevertheless, the difference is surely one of degree since in all cases technological emergence followed an evolutionary logic based upon a sequence of complex information exchanges. The origins of these lay in a variety of institutions and people variously associated both with markets and with the science-technology system. What was necessary for the technologies to succeed was a peculiar quality of technological entrepreneurship (or gatekeeping) required to combine vision with the capacity to put together a range of vital competences.

A final example of technological hierarchy is Sahal's portrayal of evolution through *scaling*, the analogue of morphology in biological evolution.[18] For Sahal, all coherent technological systems may be defined in terms of ratios of physical dimensions among component parts — and the development of any given system occurs through a process of physical scaling (increasing in the case of aircraft technology, for example; decreasing in the case of modern computers.) Systemic change occurs either where scale shifts run into bottlenecks, or where new technological possibilities radically alter system configurations (for instance, due to the advent of new materials), or (the 'revolutionary case') where two or more systems converge (as with the jet engine from propulsion technology and turbine technology). Such changes then create new 'dominant designs' which provide the trajectory for further technological advance. The act of technological entrepreneurship is hence that of identifying where the important bottlenecks and potential breakthrough possibilities are — a difficult task — and thence mobilizing the necessary resources, including R&D, to ensure commercial success.

Sahal likens the process to that of an 'antigravity' ball rolling along a low basin in an unknown topographical landscape, somewhat akin to Waddington's embryonic phenotypes traversing their 'chreodes'. Technological success is to be seen in terms of the ball reaching the top of the highest hill in the locality, but of course, while the ball is in the valley it does not know which pathways to choose out of those that it encounters at various points of intersection. Rather like a traveller without a map in an unknown country, the lower the valley, the greater the difficulty in choosing the right track, but in this case the topography itself is slowly changing as a result of socioeconomic and political factors (analogous, say, with a series of very gentle earthquakes). Choice of pathway is never completely uncertain, however, since the traveller has knowledge of landmarks ('technological guideposts') which give clues provided they are correctly interpreted. If they are, the traveller is successful and, indeed, becomes more certain the nearer he gets to his goal. If they are not, he may have to retrace his steps and try another track.

Sahal provides a number of cases of technological development interpreted in this way, backing up his argument by statistical analysis of relevant systems. In that of computer technology, for example, he starts with Babbage's mechanical system showing how electrical technology based upon the electronic valve allowed for much faster signalling. But as machines got bigger, they began to run into problems of overheating, frequent breakdown and fault-finding difficulties. The invention of the transistor in the form of discrete semiconductors helped to solve the problem and created possibilities for miniaturization at the same time, although to begin with there were problems related to crystal growing and switching capabilities. Eventually, progressive miniaturization led to systems failure because of the growing number of interconnections between discrete components, thus giving rise to the integrated circuit. This in turn faced early problems associated with wafer manufacture. More recently, the invention of the microprocessor (the entire processing unit of a computer on a single silicon chip) has enabled greater economies to be made in power use and mass market applications, while at present progressive miniaturization is grappling with problems associated with electromagnetic interference and heat where digital signals are moved over very short atomic distances.

9.1.3 *Purpose, System and Morphogenesis*

We have seen that a technological system is a combination of several functional technical units which evolve at different rates but which are brought together to perform a certain overall task. This makes technological evolution a purposive and not a random process since the importance of the evolution of individual units is explained by the structure and function of the whole system. Put differently, a technological system may be viewed as a convergence of co-existing functional units such that the patterns of change among the units, both functional and allometric, are governed by the purposive imperative of the whole system. The range of such technological systems is narrowed down through a selection process that attempts to match the adaptive parameters of the systems to the key features of the external techno-economic environment. The increased matching of these parametric sets may be viewed as an increase in techno-economic performance.

However, there is no technological system that is perfectly adapted to the environment or has the ultimate techno-economic performance. This is partly because of limitations in the internal structure of the systems themselves and partly because of the constant changes that occur in the external environment. What technological innovation does is to constantly improve the adaptive parameters of the system either by matching previously unmatched environmental features, or by adapting to new changes.[19] This is the logic of increased techno-economic performance, which does not necessarily mean a perfect adaptive fit. The process of raising the techno-economic performance takes on a new phase if the environmental changes are radical and disruptive enough so as to threaten the survival of hitherto existing systems, changes which may require radically new technological systems with new adaptive features.

Alternatively, the discovery of either a technical unit or a system that has a higher techno-economic performance may threaten the existing system. The displacement of technological systems is often accompanied by periods of co-evolution in which the existing system may be modified so as to enhance its adaptive parameters. Such modifications are likely to be made in those parameters where the competing technological systems have a 'competitive advantage'. For example, the introduction of continuous-flow ethanol plants forced the manufacturers and users of batch systems to introduce innovations which saved on energy, reduced inputs and improved the overall performance of the plants.

If the design of a technological system is taken as the unit of selection, then conjectural technological variants are not generated through blind or random variation. Moreover, the variants still have to be further tested in the operating environment through the process of niche realization, which suggests that the process of error-elimination continues from the point of the conception of a particular technological possibility to the stage of niche realization and beyond. Finally, shifts in the environment may require changes which can be achieved through incremental improvement and not necessarily by the scrapping of the technological system. Exogenous pressures as well as internal technical imperatives induce incremental innovations.

Hence the initial entry of a technological system into the market is not by any means the end of the story. The system will constantly be subjected to both internal and external pressures requiring constant innovation, meaning that it will remain in a state of partial success until competing systems dislodge it. The rate at which systems are dislodged is complicated and depends on factors such as the size and characteristics of the market, the economics of scrapping, costs of research and market entry, perceived profits and production scale. What is most important, however, is the process of the generation of conjectural technological variants, which is usually through research, development and demonstration.

Changes in the environment also commonly lead to the movement of technological systems from one niche to another without any form of distinctive divergence. This may happen at times of major environmental shifts, which open up new opportunities for systems which could not otherwise have survived. The fuel ethanol example is an illustration of this. The technological system evolved in the beverage environment, and although its energy potential was known, the dominance of petroleum made it uncompetitive in the energy environment. It was not until the oil shock that the potential for realizing the ethanol niche was enhanced. Another example is the Caterpillar farm tractor developed at Stockton, California, in 1904, which was later turned into the military tank and used in the First World War.[20] The two technological systems occupied different niches and continued to change in functional units. What is relevant, therefore, is not a taxonomy of technological systems and the associated dendrograms, but the process of technological variation, their selection and retention.

9.1.4 *Non-linear and Irreversible Transformations*

A final point to make about technological change as an evolutionary process is its irreversible character through time. As Prigogine and others have noted (see Chapter 4), any complex natural system undergoing irreversible change will be continuously testing the limits of its own stability as it absorbs exogenous energy. And where resultant internal fluctuations become large enough, the system will bifurcate in unpredictable ways. Allen has described the phenomenon in terms of Figure 9.3, where the value of any observed parameter of a system in far-from-equilibrium conditions can take on a number of discrete values through time depending upon its own self-organizing behaviour and its relationship to its environment.[21] However, at any given point in time it is impossible to tell precisely what these values will be. Allen goes on to argue that observations of past *average* values tend to get conflated with how the system has really behaved, with the result that a false picture of quasi-equilibrium behaviour is presented.

A good example of this in the innovation literature is shown by studies in incremental technical change at plant level. Here technical change is viewed as following a particular path associated with the accumulation of 'indigenous technology capacity' (ITC), and the fact

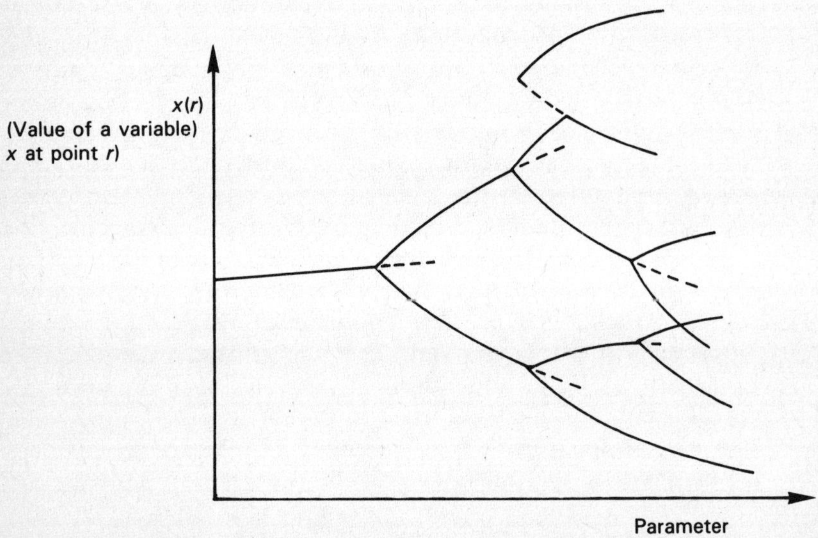

Figure 9.3 Bifurcation tree (*Source:* P.M. Allen 1985, p. 7)

that such ITC is cumulative tends to give an inaccurate picture of linearity.[22] This is partly because such studies are retroactive and hence do not capture the non-linear stochastic processes that underlie incremental innovation, but the misconception is compounded by the fact that methods employed to quantify the impact of ITC are based on aggregations and therefore reduce the complex learning process to a few average numerical values of variables such as output, down time, productivity change and input reduction. A similar tendency may be seen in the 'learning-by-doing' literature, where technical change is often simply modelled as a linear function of output growth.

In contrast, our own position is similar to that of Prigogine and Allen with the slight difference that we emphasize *informational* rather than *energetic* factors in systemic communication (though the discussion in Chapter 4 shows that both are of the same generic type).[23] Thus for complexity and hierarchy to emerge, any technological system has to undergo non-linear changes associated with the introduction of new technical information the generation of which is a constant process — say in the form of problem-solving at plant level or new patented inventions. Such continuous technical drift is both a result of varying degrees of uncertainty and a source of unexpected changes in the technological terrain, and its effects are difficult to predict. What is certain, however, is that new information, especially when embodied in technologies, reorganizes the system in non-linear ways. The reorganization may occur at plant level with minimal systemic effects, but the convergence of large quantities of technical information may also lead to major economic transformations. This is the case with technological systems associated with microelectronics as may be seen in the 'long-wave' literature.[24] Equally significant is the fact that such changes entail a qualitative shift in the knowledge and competence base.

In addition, the market environment in which the innovations compete, changes unevenly, and therefore the prospects of entry are unevenly distributed over time and economic space. Moreover, changing market environments require products to adapt to new conditions. The market therefore becomes a configuration of niches, and products have to be designed to embody those characteristics that will enable them to adapt to their respective market niche. This is the message provided by Abernathy and his colleagues in their model of technological de-maturity.

In this model, a product is viewed as a configuration of design concepts which are adapted to particular market conditions. But the introduction of an innovation may disrupt the market niche, making the existing capital equipment, labour skills, materials, components, management culture and organizational capabilities obsolete:

The stabilisation of design concepts, in which industry maturity consists, makes productive units increasingly vulnerable to changes in technology, market preference, and relative prices. As does a biological species that has become perfectly adapted to a particular environmental niche, mature industries carry with them the implicit threat of extinction or, at least, catastrophe if environmental conditions should suddenly or radically shift.[25]

If the disruptions are relatively minor, then the firm can adapt by making incremental changes. But if they are substantial, then the firm is thrown back on to a new learning process which is a source of major discontinuity in the technological terrain and which may lead to new product and process lines as new niches are created.[26] It is because of the non-linear processes associated with technical drift and niche creation that new technologies emerge. A phyletic reconstruction, however, reveals a complex flow of technical, social, political and ecological information which impinges on the emergence of new technological lines or bifurcations. Such a flow cannot occur under equilibrium conditions; the very nature of technological innovation suggests that the economic environment is in a constant state of disequilibrium.[27]

9.2 Macroevolution and Technology Policy

9.2.1. *Institutions, Information and Innovation*

We have portrayed technological evolution in the context of complex information interrelationships mediated through the socio-economic environment. The information is generated through the interaction between the science-technology system and the socio-economic environment itself, and since the environment is constantly shifting, the problem of technological entrepreneurship becomes one of great complexity and uncertainty. This is handled by tacit social 'paradigms' — agreed ways of viewing the basic nature of techno-economic relations, which in turn guide R&D. Notice that 'science' plays a very important role in this social arrangement in two senses. First, it establishes and explains the nature of physical relationships. Second, in cases where consumers themselves experience 'bounded rationality' — that is, where there is great uncertainty about the capacity of the productive system to satisfy wants — scientific authority legitimizes particular forms of economic transformation, as in the case of medical care, for example.

However, the essence of the whole process is informational. As Aitken points out:

invention is best regarded as a process by which information comes to be organised in new configurations or gestalts [and] we suggest that a useful strategy for studying such processes [is] to analyse the way in which flows of information previously separate are from time to time brought together intentionally or by chance. The points of intersection, or conference, of these information flows [are] the social locations where new combinations emerge. And . . . the areas of overlap, where different social subsystems meet and intermingle, are locations where distinct communications networks interconnect and therefore where the possibility for confluence is high.[28]

Thus 'technology' is both the means of economic transformation on the one hand and 'contextualized information' on the other. And it is the interface between these features that gives technology its complexity and instability. Contexts and information flows are constantly changing, if only because the very act of economic exchange is itself an act of learning, an act which inheres in itself the possibility for searching for alternative ways of doing things. These changes, of course, result in economic reorganizations, which lead to the generation of new forms of knowledge. This is precisely why economic change is a process of social learning.

As seen in the cases of photovoltaics and fuel ethanol, institutional organization ensures that knowledge is generated in a much less random way. In both cases it is clear that institutional support was required at various stages to provide the necessary context for further advance. Institutions such as SERI were needed to give the social context within which all the various elements of information necessary for the economic realization of a new technology, could be brought together in a coherent way. Indeed, in the absence of such institutional support it is doubtful whether modern science-based technological developments could proceed at all, and it is our argument that this makes the institution an important co-ordinating variable in our overall conceptual structure, in contrast with the neoclassical schema where institutions are seen as obstacles to the free play of market forces.

Moreover, in general, new technologies require new institutional arrangements since they involve new information configurations. For communication to take place, the information needs to be encoded, transmitted along appropriate channels and finally decoded before being received. Old institutions are usually the repositories of old codes and channels. Not only will their capacities to handle the information requirement for new technologies be limited, they may also inhibit the development of new technologies because of inappropriate channels, practices and vested interests. It follows, therefore, that in order for a society to keep abreast with rapid technological change in this modern age, it must also be prepared to permit rapid *organizational* change — an argument that has obvious implications for public policy since, in so far as its government departments and other relevant institutions (universities, for example) exhibit structural rigidity, it is difficult to see how a society can hope to develop technologically and hence maintain long-run economic growth. Instead, it is more likely to decline or remain sluggish, blaming its lack of progress on well-known shibboleths.

This argument has several policy implications. In the first place, investment in scientific research is only one aspect of the process of technological development. Although such investment may lead to the generation of large stocks of scientific information, the process by which the information is contextualized into technology-related knowledge is an institutional one. Indeed, the very process of generating technical information itself is institutional, and can be guided depending on the long-run economic policies of the various countries. For example, as the case of Japan has repeatedly illustrated, it is not R&D leadership that counts in international competitiveness but rather the ability to utilize available technical information in the process of economic evolution. This ability depends largely on the capacity of countries to establish institutions which can facilitate the process of technological development. The most important criteria for the efficacy of such institutions include the ability to smooth the flow of information and resources pertaining to planned tasks. This not only entails flexibility, it also requires extensive diversity, experimentation and relative independence in doing things.

This view already runs counter to conventional approaches, which emphasize rigid hierarchies with limited networking. Economic systems that are organized on the basis of diversity, experimentation and relative independence can only be held together through extensive information exchange, but of course the structure of most government institutions inherently restricts the flow of information, especially to non-governmental institutions. The problem may be worsened in cases where R&D activities themselves are controlled by government. This view also suggests that there are no uniform approaches which can be adopted in the development of various technological systems, if only because every candidate technological system has its own information and resource requirements which cannot be ascertained in advance. The necessary institutional arrangements will therefore be specific to a country, technology and historical period. The evolution of the institutional configuration will depend also on factors such as the available information, technical requirements, financial needs and private interests.

A good example of a field which has tended to avoid such institutional issues is that of the transfer of technology to the developing countries and the capacity of these countries to adapt the imported technologies. Most of the relevant studies have tended to emphasize firm- and plant-level innovations and to ignore broader issues of institutional organization which played a significant role in the performance of the various imported technologies. There are several reasons why institutional issues are not stressed. First, most of the studies use neoclassical tools for their analysis and use conventional indicators to judge performance. Second, their neoclassical leanings have made it difficult to recognize the role of institutional organization. Third, it is difficult to assess the impact of institutional organization on any given technological development without undertaking comparative work on a similar technology.[29]

It should be noted finally that institutional divergence is as manifest within countries as it is between countries, where it is not uncommon to find the co-existence of 'failed' and 'successful' technology acquisition projects. This is exemplified by the case of Kenya, where a fuel ethanol programme was bedevilled by numerous implementation problems leading to the loss of over US$125 million in investment in the late 1970s and early 1980s, while at the same time the country was successfully implementing a geothermal energy programme even though the technical requirements of the latter project were more complex than that of fuel ethanol.[30] This suggests that most of the knowledge that is acquired at project level does not always contribute to overall policy learning.

9.2.2 *Politics, Technology and Economic Change*

A study of institutions would be inadequate unless it is given a political context, for it is in the political arena that broad evolutionary paths are defined. Party politics or variations in political ideals are largely a reflection of differences in the way groups of people perceive the future course of their social evolution. It is at the political level that major efforts are made to change the future, and this gives politics its evolutionary character. Moreover, long-run technological development is an *in situ* process; it relates to the endogenous development of localized capability to undertake specific economic activities. This does not mean, of course, that localized learning does not have system-wide effects. Indeed, the non-linear nature of new information introduced into the economic environment is such that there are often wide variations in the ability of countries or larger economic units to learn from localized knowledge accumulation. The capacity to do so depends largely on how well existing institutions can retain and reproduce the acquired experiences. This is what constitutes 'policy learning'.

However, in most countries policy learning tends to be hampered by limited flows of newly generated information, as shown by the limited learning that has occurred as a result of the failure of many industrial projects initiated in the 1960s and 1970s in the developing countries. Conversely, policy learning tends to be more effective in areas where the political agenda is directly influenced by long-run economic imperatives or where long-term economic policies are not directly affected by changes in the political arena — in other words, where there is *continuity in policy learning*. In Japan, for example, long-term economic policies are not affected by party politics in any major way, whereas in countries where short-term party politics has a major influence on prevailing economic policies, the accumulation of particular stocks of policy knowledge may be stultified. Thus the political agenda is defined largely in terms of short-run, monetary and fiscal policy instruments, while technological change, which is the main source of economic change, tends to be ignored. And this is true even of countries that are major technological powers.[31] Moreover, often short-term political goals are used to justify projects which are likely to have long-run consequences. And since short-term objectives do not often incorporate learning requirements, projects designed under such conditions are likely to fail or can only be sustained over the long run through increased government support. For example, a recent study of five failed government projects which cost the Canadian taxpayers many billions of dollars has concluded:

> Most of the projects were begun because they had political support; their timing and location were often intended to win the support of the voters . . . the investment analyses underlying the original decisions were often superficial and biased. Government support was usually given by means of loans, loan guarantees, or letters of comfort. A variety of monitoring systems were established: government representatives on the board of directors, direct reporting to government departments, or monitoring by government lending programmes.[32]

In fact, as Collingridge and others have pointed out, there are now serious questions about the capacity of most governments to handle big projects, and arguably this is due in considerable degree to institutional structures which are inimical to learning and adaptive behaviour. Under conventional practice, the regular activities required to fulfil the requirements of the bureaucratic machinery are distributed in a fixed manner as official duties or functions. Those tasks which fall outside the jurisdictional domain are often ignored, explained away or passed on to other officials. But since, as we have seen, evolving situations tend to increase in complexity, what happens is that any new requirements for technological development cannot be met without destabilizing the bureaucratic system. The bureaucratic machinery, on the other hand, is meant to remain in a stable state, and government officials are empowered to maintain it thus.[33]

Furthermore, the bureaucratic rationality that is accorded government departments is based on the view that all knowledge required to implement investment projects is available and all necessary resources can be mobilized be government fiat. But the problems that the projects encounter are largely related to the fact that every step in the implementation process is non-linear and requires new pieces of knowledge, which is precisely where bureaucracies tend to fall down, since the manner in which government officials tend to handle information limits the capacity to learn from emerging situations and contribute to adaptive change. Thus the management of a government office is conventionally based on documents or files which are preserved in draft or original form, but the information is seldom synthesized or analysed to extract useful lessons. Furthermore, such files are often kept secret so that information cannot be subject to recombination or selection for purposes of institutional or technological innovation.

Hence in these and other ways there is a hiatus between the organizational skills required in project implementation and the bureaucratic capabilities of most civil servants. Government officials are trained to handle linear situations. There is a chain of command or bureaucratic hierarchy that has to be followed. Project implementation, however, has non-linear imperatives, and managements must be prepared to deal with a network of interrelationships which do not respect rigid hierarchical structures. As the Kenyan and Canadian cases show, since there was no provision for adaptive learning, all the financial and administrative resources mobilized by government failed to save the projects.[34]

It is for reasons such as these that we believe adequate policies for long-run economic change will only be effective where the institutional and political contexts are able to permit adaptive change.[35] In a world of increasing complexity and greater integration, our political institutions, and indeed their trained staff, must take on a corresponding character. Countries that do not will be overtaken rapidly by those who do.

9.2.3 *Ecology, Resources and Innovation*

In our ethanol case study we noted that an important reason underlying recent innovative efforts has been the need to reduce the release of stillage, or fermentation residue, into the external environment (e.g. the Biostil process produced by Alfa-Laval). This is just one illustration of our increasing but still very limited social awareness of the irreversible damage that modern economic production is inflicting on terrestrial ecology. Conventional economic thinking does not recognize this as a problem.[36] The focus on equilibrium leads naturally to the view that negative environmental effects, such as those resulting from pollutants, will gradually dissipate and the ecology will return to its previous 'balance', while the practice of 'externalizing' phenomena which cannot readily be included within conventional models all too easily allows such phenomena to be excluded from the purview of public policy.

This has not always proved to be the case. The height of the post-war industrial boom was also a period with obvious ecological problems and one which witnessed the beginnings of the modern ecological movement culminating in the holding of the 1972 United Nations Conference on the Human Environment in Stockholm. A year after the Stockholm Conference, the world experienced the worst oil crisis ever. Interestingly enough, the oil crisis occurred soon after the publication of *The Limits to Growth* by the Club of Rome in 1972, and Georgescu-Roegen's *The Entropy Law and the Economic Process* in 1971. Both studies raised major questions concerning conventional views on natural resource availability and linked the prevailing rates of industrial growth to ecological degradation.

More recently developments have shown complex interactions between environmental factors and technological change. Thus the growing diversity of industrial activities has generated options which can help abate the excessive pressure placed on particular resources. The energy crises, for example, have led to an increased search for alternative energy technologies, although the application of these technologies has been uneven and has depended on specific economic conditions. While some of the African countries have devoted much attention to biomass-based technologies, other countries have focused on high-technology innovations such as photovoltaics. In addition, however, shifts towards resource-saving technologies have introduced new systemic dimensions into the global economic environment. For example, the recent decline in world raw materials consumption has created serious financial problems for the developing countries which export them.

Problems of this type, and many others which we could mention (such as irreversible desertification of agricultural lands or the potential destruction of world fish stocks), show conclusively that the relationships between ecology and innovation are systemic and non-linear. They show also that the ecological problem is not by any means confined to the industrialized countries but affects all parts of the world economic system. But most important of all, they show that measures to deal with them require a long-run, holistic perspective whereby a short-run economic rationality is not allowed to provide the sole basis for public policy making.

9.3 Some Suggestions for Future Research

It remains for us finally to suggest some avenues for possible future research. In this volume we have tried to provide a critique of conventional thought regarding how economic systems move through time. Central to our argument is the proposition that it is the mechanistic underpinnings of neoclassical economic theory which prevent it from capturing the richness of socioeconomic transformation, where growth and structural change are inextricably linked. Conversely, an evolutionary and systemic approach provides not only greater conceptual realism but suggests also new insights for policy-making — particularly with respect to how information and learning may be handled, since it is through the introduction of new information that the system evolves.

We have argued also that economic evolution occurs under conditions of constant disequilibrium, with fluctuations brought about by the import of new information into economic systems and leading to their irreversible transformation through time. Other important features are the rise of complexity, hierarchy and diversity. These lines of enquiry should lead us to explore the findings of disciplines such as organizational theory, administrative science and, of course, systems thinking and cybernetics. Indeed, the fact that economic systems are in a constant state of disequilibrium is a significant point simply because 'learning' cannot occur in an equilibrium situation. We have, instead, conceived the process of economic change as a broad category of social learning. This line of research should lead us to a 'learning' literature which currently falls in the domain of psychology, education or biology. A further point is that since a long-run view of economic change deals mainly with the flow of events through time, we require a careful understanding of the historical circumstances associated with the units or networks of analysis. In other words, it is only by placing technological developments in their *historical* context that we can adequately understand the long-run dynamics of economic change.

Two final suggestions are first that an analysis of *microevolutionary* processes should be able to account for *macroevolutionary* dynamics. It is therefore important to understand the ways in which bifurcations emerge from non-linear processes and niches are created, maintained or replaced. Secondly, while we have argued that technological development is closely associated with institutional reorganization, our understanding of the internal dynamics of various institutions is still inadequate. There is therefore a need to analyse further the role played by institutions in the generation, selection and retention of information as well as how they relate to the larger political process.

In short, we suggest a research agenda which is both interdisciplinary and interactive. We see no future in seeking to impose homogeneous economic theories on a natural world which is increasingly characterized by complexity and diversity. To do so is ultimately a negative act not only because of the environmental consequences which we have drawn attention to, but in the deeper sense that it denies the potential for human evolution. And surely that is what the long run is all about.

Notes and References

1. See Chapter 1.
2. K. Imai *et al.* (1985), 'Managing the New Product Development Process: How Japanese Companies Learn and Unlearn' in K. Clark *et al.*, (eds), *The Uneasy Alliance: Managing the Productivity-Technology Dilemma* (Boston: Harvard Business School), p. 340.
3. A. Altshuler *et al.* (eds) (1984), *The Future of the Automobile* (Cambridge, Mass.: MIT Press), p. 138 (emphasis added).
4. Ibid., p. 146.
5. F. Belussi (1987), 'Benetton: Information Technology in Production and Distribution. A Case Study of the Innovative Potential of Traditional Sectors', SPRU Occasional Paper Series No. 25, SPRU, University of Sussex.
6. A. Toffler (1985), *The Adaptive Corporation* (New York: Bantam Books).
7. Ibid. p. ix.
8. K. Clark (1985), 'The Interaction of Design Hierarchies and Market Concepts in Technological Evolution', *Research Policy*, **14** (2): 235–51.
9. W. Abernathy and J. Utterback (1978), 'Patterns of Industrial Innovation', *Technology Review*, **80** (June–July): 40–7.
10. C. Waddington (1957), *The Strategy of the Genes* (London: Allen & Unwin), see Ch. 2.
11. Ibid., p. 237.
12. J. Gershuny (1978), *After Industrial Society* (London: Macmillan).
13. H.G.F. Aitken (1984),*The Continuous Wave* (Princeton: Princeton University Press).
14. Ibid., p. 552.
15. Ibid., p. 549. The alternator, for example, emerged from electric power engineering and wireless communication. The triode valve is closely connected with basic science in so far as de Forest's early training in mathematics and electrical theory was crucial to his later inventions (the triode audion detector, the diode amplifier and oscillator), although the eventual appearance of the 'hard vacuum tube' was also very much a triumph of precision engineering.
16. Ibid., p. 549.
17. Ibid., p. 550.
18. D. Sahal (1985), 'Technical Guideposts and Innovation Avenues', *Research Policy*, **14** (2): 61–82.
19. In other cases, firms may pre-empt the imperative to innovate by altering the external environment to suit their techno-economic performance and reduce competitive pressures. This can be done through a large number of protectionist measures. This suggests that the environment is also subject to pressures from the firm, a view akin to that of the Gaia hypothesis.
20. R. Wik (1980), 'The American Farm Tractor as Father of the Military Tank', *Agricultural History*, **54** (1): p. 126. Technological speciation is characterized by purposive divergence and is different from product differentiation. For a detailed exposition of the taxonomy, evolution and classification of organizational systems, see B. MacKelvey (1982), *Organizational Systematics: Taxonomy, Evolution, Classification* (Berkeley: University of California Press).
21. P.M. Allen (1985), 'Towards a New Science of Complex Systems' in United Nations University, *The Science and Praxis of Complexity* (Tokyo), p. 272. See also P.M. Allen (1985) 'Ecology, Thermodynamics and Self-Organization: Towards a New Understanding of Complexity' in R.

Ulanowicz and T. Platt (eds), Ecosystems Theory for Biological Oceanography', Special Issue of *Canadian Bulletin of Fisheries and Aquatic Sciences*, **213**: 9.

22. See, for example, L. Kim (1980), 'Stages of Development of Industrial Technology in a Developing Country: A Model', *Research Policy*, **9**: 254–77.
23. An interesting attempt to capture the 'entropic' implications of organizational change using conventional economic input/output data is contained in J.L.R. Proops (1983), 'Organisation and Dissipation in Economic Systems', *Journal of Social and Biological Structures*, **6**: 353–66.
24. See, for example, C. Freeman *et al.* (1982), *Unemployment and Technical Change* (London: Frances Pinter); and C. Perez (1985), 'Microelectronics, Long Waves and World Structural Change', *World Development*, **13** (3): 441–63.
25. J. Abernathy *et al.* (1983), *Industrial Renaissance: Producing a Competitive Future for America* (New York: Basic Books), pp. 28, 29. Elsewhere Abernathy and Clark state: 'As the product and process technologies evolve and develop they become more robust in the way they accommodate the full range of variety in the existing environment. Like the trees that develop an extensive root system to weather the dry season it must occasionally face, management refines and perfects a product over time to better accommodate the range of variation in the market. Yet a product and process technology that becomes more highly organised and efficient . . . also becomes more vulnerable to sudden and unanticipated variations in the environment. The highly productive, efficient and developed product unit is also more vulnerable to economic death'. See J. Abernathy and K. Clark (1985), 'Innovation: Mapping the Winds of Creative Destruction', *Research Policy*, **14** (1): 18.
26. See M. Tushman and P. Anderson (1986), 'Technological Discontinuities and Organizational Environments', *Administrative Science Quarterly*, **31**: 439–65, for an analysis of the role of technological discontinuities in competence destruction.
27. It should be noted here that the emergence of new technological lines will not always displace existing ones even if they have superior functional characteristics. Once technologies are settled into the market environment, they become so intricately linked into the social system as to resist displacement. David has shown this for example in the case of the current typewriter keyboard where the arrangement on the keyboard was made specifically to reduce the speed of typing due to technical difficulties associated with high typing speeds in the early stages of the development of the machine. However, despite the existence of numerous superior alternatives, the QWERTY arrangement has persisted. For example, the Dvorak Simplified Keyboard (DSK) would increase the speed of typing by up to 40 per cent and David goes on to claim that 'US Navy experiments have shown that the increased efficiency obtained with the DSK would amortize the cost of retraining a group of typists within the first ten days of their subsequent full-time employment'. See P. David (1985), 'Clio and the Economics of QWERTY', *American Economic Review, Pap. and Proc.*, **75** (2):
28. See H. Aitken (1984), *The Continuous Wave* (Princeton, NJ: Princeton University Press), p. 522.
29. See C. Juma (1986), 'Evolutionary Technological Change: The Case of Fuel Ethanol in Developing Countries', unpublished PhD thesis, SPRU, University of Sussex, Brighton, for a comparative study of fuel alcohol technology in Kenya and Zimbabwe in which institutional factors are shown to have

played a significant role in the divergent performance of two projects.
30. Ibid., pp. 159–97.
31. This statement would not hold in the case of military technology.
32. S. Borins and L. Brown (1986), *Investment in Failure* (Agincourt, Ontario: Methuen), p. 147. These findings are consistent with the reasons for the failure of a fuel ethanol plant in Kenya (see Juma, op. cit.).
33. This mechanistic view of institutional organization was perfected by Max Weber in his description of the ideal bureaucracy; an analogue of an efficient machine which fulfils social objectives in a rational, 'scientific' and efficient way.
34. Evidence from recent efforts to open up niches for appropriate or intermediate technologies shows clearly that technological development requires flexible, adaptive and semi-autonomous institutions which assume uncertainty and therefore emphasize learning and the flow of information (through dynamic networks). It is therefore not a surprise that non-governmental or volunteer organizations have been in some cases more effective than state institutes in facilitating the introduction of new technologies, especially for energy production and utilization. See C. Juma (1986), *Evolution of Improved Cookstoves in Kenya*, RETAIN Workshop, Manila, No. 10–14, for an evolutionary interpretation of the development of cookstoves in Kenya with emphasis on the role of non-governmental organizations' networks. See also N. Clark and E. Clay (1987), 'The Dryland Research Project at Indore: An Institutional Innovation in Rural Technology Transfer', *Journal of Rural Studies*, **3** (2), pp. 159–73.
35. An attempt to show how political factors influence the design of technological systems is given by J. Law (1986), 'The Anatomy of Socio-Technical Struggle' (paper prepared for the Conference on Technology and Social Change, Centre for Canadian Studies, University of Edinburgh, 12 & 13 June) in the case of the TSR.2, the British version of the American F1-11 plane. Law's study also emphasizes the interrelationships between the system-builders and other actors in the sociotechnical arena. The availability of particular technological options may also influence political activities; the process is not deterministic but interactive, depending on specific conditions and individuals involved.
36. There are, of course, exceptions. Those sections of the early economic literature that were concerned with resource exhaustibility dealt mainly with mines. See N. Robinson (1980), 'Classical Foundations of the Contemporary Economic Theory of Non-renewable Resources', *Research Policy*, **6** (4): 279–89.

Bibliography

Abernathy, J. *et al.* (1983), *Industrial Renaissance: Producing a Competitive Future for America*, New York, Basic Books.

——— and Clark, K. (1985), 'Innovation: Mapping the Winds of Creative Destruction', *Research Policy*, **14** (1): 3–22.

——— and Utterback, J. (1978), 'Patterns of Industrial Innovation', *Technology Review*, **80**: 40–7.

Abramovitz, M. (1962), 'Economic Growth in the United States', *American Economic Review*, **52**: 762–82.

Aitken, H.G.F. (1984), *The Continuous Wave*, Princeton, Princeton University Press.

Alchian, A. (1950), 'Uncertainty, Evolution and Economic Theory', *Journal of Political Economy*, **58**: 211–21.

Allen, G.C. (1981), 'Industrial Policy and Innovation in Japan', in C. Carter (ed.), *Industrial Policy and Innovation*, London, Heinemann, pp. 68–87.

Allen, P.M. (1985), 'Towards a New Science of Complex Systems' in United Nations University, *The Science and Praxis of Complexity*, Tokyo, pp. 268–97.

——— (1985), 'Ecology, Thermodynamics and Self-Organization: Towards a New Understanding of Complexity', in R. Ulanowicz and T. Platt (eds) 'Ecosystems Theory for Biological Oceanography', Special Issue of *Canadian Bulletin of Fisheries and Aquatic Sciences*, **213**: 3–26.

——— (1986), 'Evolution, Innovation and Economics', paper presented at the IFIA Workshop on Technical Change and Economic Theory (Lewes, Sussex, 18–20 October), mimeo, SPRU.

Altshuler, A. (1984), *The Future of the Automobile*, Cambridge, Mass., MIT Press.

Ashworth-Gordon, F. (1980), 'Agricultural Commodity Control under Vargas in Brazil, 1930–1945', *Journal of Latin American Studies*, **12**: 87–105.

Atkinson, A. and Stiglitz, J. (1969), 'A New View of Technological Change', *Economic Journal*, **79**: 573–78.

Ayres, C. (1944), *The Theory of Economic Progress: A Study of the Fundamentals of Economic Development and Cultural Change*, Chapel Hill, North Carolina University Press.

Backus, C. (ed.) (1976), *Solar Cells*, New York, Institute of Electrical and Electronics Engineers.

Barnes, B. (1977), *Interests and the Growth of Knowledge*, London, Routledge & Kegan Paul.

——— (1982), *T.S. Kuhn and Social Science*, London, Routledge & Kegan Paul.

——— (1983), 'On the Conventional Character of Knowledge and Cognition', in K.D. Knorr-Cetina and M. Mulkay (eds), *Science Observed*, London, Sage, pp. 19–51.

Beloff, J. (1972), 'The Place of Theory in Parapsychology', in R. van Over (ed.), *Psychology and Extrasensory Perception*, New York, Mentor.

Belussi, F. (1987), 'Benetton: Information Technology in Production and Distribution. A Case Study of the Innovative Potential of Traditional Sectors', SPRU Occasional Paper Series No. 25, SPRU, University of Sussex, Brighton.

Blaug, M. (1968), *Economic Theory in Retrospect*, London, Heinemann.

Bloor, D.C. (1976), *Knowledge and Social Imagery*, London, Routledge & Kegan Paul.

Bohm, D. (1980), *Wholeness and the Implicate Order*, London, Routledge.

Borins, S. and Brown, L. (1986), *Investments in Failure: Five Government Corporations that Cost the Canadian Taxpayer Billions*, Agincourt, Ontario, Methuen.

Borkin, J. (1978), *The Crime and Punishment of I.G. Farben*, New York, The Free Press.

Boulding, K. (1957), 'A New Look at Institutionalism', *American Economic Review*, **47** (May): 1–7.

—— (1962), *A Reconstruction of Economics*, New York, Science Editions.

Braun, E., Collingridge, D. and Hinton, K. (1979), *Assessment of Technical Decisions*, London, Butterworth.

de Bresson, C. (1985), 'Technological Development Poles: An Operational Concept for Policy Analysis', SPRU, University of Sussex, Brighton, mimeo.

Brooks, D. and Wiley, E. (1984), 'Evolution as an Entropic Phenomenon', in J. Pollard (ed.), *Evolutionary Theory*, Chichester, Wiley, pp. 141–69.

Brooks, H. (1985), 'The Typology of Surprises in Technology, Institutions and Development', Harvard University, Cambridge, Mass., mimeo.

Carter, C. (ed.), *Industrial Policy and Innovation*, London, Heinemann.

CEC (1985), *Solar Energy R&D Programme: Results and Conclusions*, Commission of the European Communities, Brussels.

Chamberlin, E. (1957), 'The Product as an Economic Variable', in E. Chamberlin, *Towards a More General Theory of Value*, Oxford, Oxford University Press.

—— (1962), *The Theory of Monopolistic Competition*, Cambridge, Mass., Harvard University Press.

Chemical Foundation (1935), *Proceedings of the Dearborn Conference of Agriculture, Industry and Science*, Dearborn, Michigan, 7 and 8 May 1935, New York, Chemical Foundation.

Clark, K. (1985), 'The Interaction of Design Hierarchies and Market Concepts in Technological Evolution', *Research Policy*, **14**: 235–51.

—— *et al.* (1986), *The Uneasy Alliance: Managing the Productivity-Technology Dilemma*, Boston, Harvard Business School.

Clark, N. (1985), *The Political Economy of Science and Technology*, Oxford, Basil Blackwell.

—— and Clay, E. (1987), 'The Dryland Research Project at Indore 1974–80: an Institutional Innovation in Rural Technology Transfer', *Journal of Rural Studies*, **3** (3): forthcoming.

Clow, A. *et al.* (1952), *The Chemical Revolution: A Contribution to Social Technology*, London, Batchworth Press.

Cochran, T. (1948), *The Fabst Brewing Company: The History of an American Business*, New York, New York University Press.

Coleman, D. *et al.* (eds), *Enterprise and History: Essays in Honour of Charles Wilson*, Cambridge, Cambridge University Press.

Coleman, E. (1971), 'Short Communication on the Unpublished Writings of Karl Marx Dealing with Mathematics, the Natural Sciences and Technology and the History of these Subjects', in N. Bukharin (ed.), *Science at the Crossroads*, London, Frank Cass, pp. 234–5.

Collingridge, D. (1980), *The Social Control of Technology*, Oxford, Oxford University Press.

Colp, R. (1982), 'The Myth of the Marx-Darwin Letter', *History of Political Economy*, **14** (4): 416–82.

Constant, E.W. (1980), *The Origins of the Turbojet Revolution*, Baltimore, Johns Hopkins University Press.

Cooney, C. (1979), 'Computer Application in Fermentation Technology: A

Perspective', *Biotechnology and Bioengineering Symposium No. 9,* pp. 1–11.

Cutting, G. (1984), 'Paradigms, Revolutions and Technology', in R. Laudan (ed.), *The Nature of Technical Knowledge: Are Models of Scientific Change Relevant?* (Dordrecht: D. Reidel).

Da Silva, J. *et al.* (1978), 'Energy Balance for Ethyl Alcohol Production from Crops', *Science*, **201**: 903–6.

David, P. (1975), *Technical Choice, Innovation and Economic Growth*, London, Cambridge University Press.

——— (1985), 'Clio and the Economics of QWERTY', *American Economic Review, Papers and Proceedings*, **75** (2): 332–7.

Day, R. *et al.* (eds), *Adaptive Economic Models*, New York, Academic Press.

Denison, E. (1962), *The Sources of Economic Growth in the US and the Alternatives Before Us*, Supp. Paper 13, New York, Committee for Economic Development.

Dosi, G. (1982), 'Technological Paradigms and Technological Trajectories: A Suggested Interpretation of Determinants and Directions of Technical Change', *Research Policy*, **11** (3); 147–62.

——— (1984), *Technological Change and Industrial Transformation*, London, Macmillan.

Douglas, L. *et al.* (1983), *Evaluation of Nondistillation Ethanol Separation Processes*, Boulder, Colo., Solar Energy Research Institute.

Elster, J. (1983), *Explaining Technical Change*, Cambridge, Cambridge University Press.

Essien, D. *et al.* (1983), 'Energy Conservation in Ethanol Production by Fermentation', *Process Biochemistry*, **18** (4): 31–7.

Faber, M. and Proops, J.L.R. (1986), 'Time Irreversibilities in Economics: Some Lessons from the Natural Sciences', in M. Faber (ed.), *Studies in Austrian Capital Theory, Investment and Time*, Heidelberg, Springer.

Fabricant, S. (1959), 'Basic Facts on Productivity Change', Occasional Paper 63, NBER, New York.

Fischetti, M. (1984), 'Photovoltaic-cell Technologies Joust for Position', *IEEE Spectrum*, March: 40–7.

Fransman, M. (ed.) (1986), *Machinery in Economic Development*, London, Macmillan.

Freeman, C. (1974), *The Economics of Industrial Innovation*, Harmondsworth, Penguin.

——— (1986), 'Induced Innovation, Diffusion of Innovations and Business Cycles', Paper presented at Centre of Canadian Studies Conference on 'Technology and Social Change', Edinburgh University, 12–13 June.

——— *et al.* (1982), *Unemployment and Technical Change*, London, Frances Pinter.

Gardiner, P. and Rothwell, R. (1985), 'Tough Customers: Good Designs', *Design Studies*, **6** (1): 7–17.

Garlick, L. (1983), 'Fermentation of Molasses Cane Juice Using Continuous Fermentation', *The Sugar Journal*, **46** (4): 13–16.

Garstang, W. (1922), 'The Theory of Recapitulation: A Critical Restatement of the Biogenetic Law', *Journal of the Linnean Society, London, Zoology*, **36**

Georgescu-Roegen, N. (1971), *The Entropy Law and the Economic Process*, Cambridge, Mass., Harvard University Press.

Gershuny, J. (1978), *After Industrial Society*, London, Macmillan.

Glamann, K. (1984), 'The Scientific Brewer: Founders and Successors During the Rise of the Modern Brewing Industry', in D. Coleman *et al.* (eds), *Enterprise and History: Essays in Honour of Charles Wilson*, Cambridge, Cambridge University Press, pp. 186–98.

W. Gordon, (1980), *Institutional Economics*, Texas, Texas University Press.

Gwai, K. (1984), 'Schumpeterian Dynamics', *Journal of Economic Behaviour and Organisation*, **5** (2): 159–90.

Hansen, A. (1921), 'The Technological Interpretation of History', *Quarterly Journal of Economics*, **36**: 72–83.

Harrod, R. (1939), 'An Essay in Dynamic Theory', *Economic Journal*, **49**: 14–33.

Heilbroner, R. (1967), 'Do Machines Make History', *Technology and Culture*, **8** (3): 335–45.

Hesse, M. (1974), *The Structure of Scientific Inference*, London, Macmillan.

Hicks, J.R. (1973), *Capital and Time*, Oxford, Clarendon Press.

Hill, P. *et al.* (eds) (1985), *Application of Photovoltaics*, proceedings of the Conference held at Newcastle-upon-Tyne, 12–13 September.

Hirshleifer, J. (1977), 'Economics from a Biological Viewpoint', *Journal of Law and Economics*, **20** (1): 1–52.

——— (1982), 'Evolutionary Models in Economics and Law', *Research in Law and Economics*, **4**: 1–60.

Hoffman, K. (1985), 'The Commercialization of Photovoltaics in the Third World: Unfulfilled Expectations and Limited Markets', *Development and Change*, **16** (1): 5–37.

Houthakker, H. (1956), 'Economics and Biology: Specialization and Speciation', *Kyklos*, **9**: 180–9.

Huxley, J. (1964), *Man in the Modern World*, New York

Illich, I. (1975), *Tools for Conviviality*, London, Fontana.

Imai, K. *et al.* (1985), 'Managing the New Product Development Process: How Japanese Companies Learn and Unlearn', in K. Clark *et al.* (eds) *The Uneasy Alliance*, Boston, Mass., Harvard Business School.

Inglis, B. (1982), *The Diseases of Civilization*, London, Hodder & Stoughton.

Isaacs, S. (1984), *Ethanol Production by Enzymatic Hydrolysis: Parametric Analysis of a Base-Case Process*, Golden, Colo., Solar Energy Research Institute.

Jantsch, E. (1980), *The Self-Organizing Universe*, Oxford, Pergamon.

Jones, D.T. (1985), *A Revolution in Automobile Manufacturing? Technological Change in a Mature Industry*, Papers in Science, Technology and Public Policy, SPRU, University of Sussex (No. 9).

Jorgenson, D. and Griliches, Z. (1967), 'The Explanation of Productivity Change', *Review of Economic Studies*, **34**: 249–83.

Jorne, J. (1983), 'Flow Batteries', *American Scientist*, **17**: 507–12.

Juma, C. (1983), 'Photovoltaics in Developing Countries: Techno-Economic Expectations and Strategic Responses', unpublished MSc dissertation, SPRU, University of Sussex, Brighton.

——— (1986), 'Evolutionary Technological Change: The Case of Fuel Ethanol in Developing Countries', unpublished DPhil thesis, SPRU, University of Sussex, Brighton.

——— (1986), *The Evolution of Improved Cookstoves in Kenya: A Study in Technological Articulation*, Rural Energy Technology and Innovation Network Workshop, 10–14 November, Manila.

Kamien, M. and Schwarz, N. (1982), *Market Structure and Innovation*, Cambridge, Cambridge University Press.

Kay, N. (1982), *The Evolving Firm*, London, Macmillan.

——— (1986), *The Emergent Firm*, London, Macmillan.

Kelly, H. (1978), 'Photovoltaic Power Systems: A Tour Through the Alternatives', *Science*, **199**: 634–43.

Kim, L. (1980), 'Stages of Development of Industrial Technology in a

Developing Country: A Model', *Research Policy*, **9**: 254–77.
Klein, B.H. (1977), *Dynamic Economics*, Cambridge, Mass., Harvard University Press.
Koestler, A. (1970), *The Ghost in the Machine*, London, Pan Books.
——— (1982), *Bricks to Babel*, London, Picador.
Kraft, M. and Axelrod, R. (1984), 'Political Constraints on Development of Alternative Energy Sources: Lessons from the Reagan Administration', *Policy Studies Journal*, **13**: 319–30.
Kuhn, T.S. (1970), *The Structure of Scientific Revolutions*, Chicago, Chicago University Press.
Lakatos, I. (1972), 'Falsification and the Methodology of Scientific Research Programme', in I. Lakatos and A. Musgrave (eds), *Criticism and the Growth of Knowledge*, Cambridge, Cambridge University Press.
Law, J. (1986), 'The Anatomy of Sociotechnical Struggle', paper presented for the Conference on Technology and Social Change, Centre for Canadian Studies, University of Edinburgh, 12–13 June.
——— and Lodge, P. (1984), *Science for Social Scientists*, London, Macmillan.
Lloyd, C. *et al.* (1975), 'The Market Adaptation of the Firm', in R. Day *et al.* (eds) (1975), *Adaptive Economic Models*, New York, Academic Press.
Lloyd-Jones, R. *et al.* (1982), 'Marshall and the Birth and Death of Firms: The Growth and Size Distribution in the Early Nineteenth Century Cotton Industry', *Business History*, **24** (2): 141–55.
Lundvall, B. (1985), *Product Innovation and User-Producer Interaction*, Aalborg, Aalborg University Press.
McCloskey, D. (1983), 'The Rhetoric of Economics', *Journal of Economic Literature*, **21**: 481–517.
Machlup, F. (1962), *The Production and Distribution of Knowledge in the United States*, Princeton, Princeton University Press.
McKelvey, B. (1982), *Organizational Systematics: Taxonomy, Evolution, Classification*, Berkeley, University of California Press.
MacKenzie, D. (1984), 'Marx and the Machine', *Technology and Culture*, **25** (3): 473–502.
Maclaurin, W.R. (1949), *Invention and Innovation in the Radio Industry*, London, Macmillan.
MacLeod, R. (1986), *Technology and the Human Prospect*, London, Frances Pinter.
Macomber, H. (1983) 'Status of Large US PV Systems Applications', in W. Palz (ed.) (1983), *Photovoltaic Power Generation*, Proceedings of the EC Contractors' Meeting, Hamburg/Pelluorm, 12–13 July, Dordrecht, Holland, D. Reidel Publishing Co.
McNulty, P. (1968), 'Economic Theory and the Meaning of Competition', *Quarterly Journal of Economics*, **82**, 639–56.
Marshall, A. (1925), 'Mechanical and Biological Analogies in Economics', in A.C. Pigou (ed.), *Memorials of Alfred Marshal*, London, Macmillan.
——— (1959), *Principles of Economics*, London, Macmillan.
Marthaler, D. (1976), 'Geheimmsvoller Nervenfilz', *Neue Zurcher Zeituing*, **2**.
Marx, K. (1975), *The Poverty of Philosophy*, Moscow, Progress Publishers.
——— (1976), *Capital*, Harmondsworth, Penguin.
Massell, B. (1961), 'A Disaggregated View of Technical Change', *Journal of Political Economy*, **69**: 547–57.
Mathias, P. (1959), *The Brewing Industry 1700–1830*, Cambridge, Cambridge University Press.
Maycock, P. (1985), 'The Current PV Scene Worldwide', in W. Palz *et al.*, *Sixth*

EC Photovoltaic Solar Energy Conference, Dordrecht, Holland, D. Reidel Publishing Co.

Meek, D. (ed.) (1953), *Marx and Engels on Malthus*, London, Lawrence & Wishart.

Mensch, G. (1974), *Stalemate in Technology*, New York, Ballinger.

Morris, C. (1983), 'Huge Plant for Ethanol and HFCS', *Food Engineering*, June.

Nelson, R. and Winter, S. (1977), 'In Search of a Useful Theory of Innovation', *Research Policy*, **6** (1): 36–77.

——— and ——— (1982), *An Evolutionary Theory of Economic Change*, Cambridge, Mass., Harvard University Press.

Nunberg, B. (1978), State Intervention in the Sugar Sector in Brazil: A Study of the Institute of Sugar and Alcohol, unpublished PhD, Stanford University, Palo Alto.

Pavitt, K. (1983), *Patterns of Technical Change: Evidence, Theory and Policy Implications*, Papers in Science, Technology and Public Policy, SPRU, University of Sussex (No. 3).

——— and Worboys, M. (1977), *Science, Technology and the Modern Industrial State*, London, Butterworth, SISCON.

Penrose, E. (1952), 'Biological Analogies in the Theory of the Firm', *American Economic Review*, **42** (5): 804–19.

Perez, C. (1985), 'Microelectronics, Long Waves and World Structural Change: New Perspectives for Developing Countries', *World Development*, **13** (3): 441–63.

Plotkin, H. (ed.) (1982), *Learning, Development and Culture*, Chichester, Wiley.

Proops, J.L.R. (1983), 'Organization and Dissipation in Economic Systems', *Journal Social and Biological Structure*, **6** 353–66.

Pursell, C. (1969), 'The Farm Chemurgic Council and United States Department of Agriculture, 1935–39', *Isis*, **60** (203): 306–17.

Ramos, A. (1981), *The New Science of Organizations*, Toronto, Toronto University Press.

Rapport, D. *et al.* (1977), 'Economic Models in Ecology', *Science*, **195** (4276): 367–73.

Reese, E. (1976), 'History of Cellulose Program at the US Army Natick Development Center', *Biotechnology and Bioengineering Symposium No. 6*: 9–20.

Robinson, J. (1933), *The Economics of Imperfect Competition*, London, Macmillan.

Robinson, N. (1980), 'Classical Foundations of the Contemporary Economic Theory of Non-renewable Resources', *Research Policy*, **6** (4): 279–89.

Rosenberg, N. (1976), *Perspectives on Technology*, Cambridge, Cambridge University Press.

——— (1982), *Inside the Black Box*, Cambridge, Cambridge University Press.

——— (1986), 'Schumpeter and Marx: How Common a Vision?', in R. MacLeod (ed.), *Technology and the Human Prospect*, pp. 197–213.

Sahal, D. (1979), *Recent Advances in a Theory of Technological Change*, Berlin, International Institute of Management.

——— (1985) 'Technological Guideposts and Innovation Avenues', *Research Policy*, **14** (2): 61–82.

Salter, W. (1960), *Productivity and Technical Change*, Cambridge, Cambridge University Press.

Schumpeter, J. (1934), *The Theory of Economic Development*, Cambridge, Mass., Harvard University Press.

——— (1939), *Business Cycles*, New York, McGraw-Hill.

——— (1943), *Capitalism, Socialism and Democracy*, London, Allen & Unwin.

Sen, A.K. (ed.) (1970), *Growth Economics*, Harmondsworth, Penguin.
Sercovich, F. (1983), *The Political Economy of Biomass in Brazil: The Case of Ethanol,* mimeo, Inter-American Development Bank, Washington, DC.
SERI (1984), *SERI Photovoltaic Advanced Research & Development: An Overview*, Golden, Colo., Solar Energy Institute.
Shaw, W. (1979), 'The Handmill Gives You the Feudal Lord: Marx's Technological Determinism', *History and Theory*, **18**: 155–76.
Shirland, F. (1976), 'The History, Design, Fabrication and Performance of CdS Thin Film Solar Cells', in C. Backus, *Solar Cells*, New York, Institute of Electrical and Electronics Engineers, pp. 43–4.
Sigsworth, E. (1965), 'Science and the Brewing Industry 1850–1900', *Economic History Review*, **17**: 536–50.
Simon, H. (1969), *The Sciences of the Artificial*, Cambridge, Mass., MIT Press.
Singh, J. (1966), *Information Theory, Language and Cybernetics*, London, Constable.
Smith, A. (1961), *The Wealth of Nations*, London, Methuen (Cannon edn).
Smith, J. (1981), 'Photovoltaics', *Science*, **212**: June 1472–8.
de Solla Price, D. (1965), 'Is Technology Historically Independent of Science?', *Technology and Culture*, **VI** (4): 553–68.
Solow, R. (1957), 'Technical Change and the Aggregate Production Function', *Review of Economics and Statistics*: 312–20.
Spengler, J. (1974), 'Institutions, Institutionalism: 1776–1974', *Journal of Economic Issues*, **8** (4): 877–96.
Teich, M. (1983), 'Fermentation Theory and Practice: The Beginning of Pure Yeast Cultivation and English Brewing, 1883–1913', *History of Technology*, Eighth Annual Review, pp. 117–33.
Thom, R. (1975), *Structural Stability and Morphogenesis*, Reading, Benjamin.
Thompson, E.P. (1973), *The Making of the English Working Class*, Harmondsworth, Penguin.
Toffler, A. (1985), *The Adaptive Corporation*, New York, Bantam Books.
Toulmin, S. (1961), *Foresight and Understanding*, London, Hutchinson.
Tunzelmann, N. von (1986), 'Malthus' "Total Population System": A Dynamic Re-interpretation', in D. Coleman *et al.*, *The State of Population Theory*, Oxford, Blackwell, pp. 65–95.
Tushman, M. and Anderson, P. (1986), 'Technological Discontinuities and Organisational Environments', *Administrative Science Quarterly*, **31**: 439–65.
Ulanowicz, R. and Platt, T. (eds), 'Ecosystems Theory for Biological Oceanography', Special Issue of *Canadian Bulletin of Fisheries and Aquatic Sciences*, **213**: 3–26.
UNCTAD (1984), *Studies in the Processing, Marketing and Distribution of Commodities. The Processing and Marketing of Sugar: Areas of International Co-operation*, United Nations Conference on Trade and Development, New York, United Nations.
UNCTAD (1986), *Impact of New and Emerging Technologies on Trade and Development: A Review of the UNCTAD Secretariat's Research Findings.'*
United Nations University (1985), *The Science and Praxis of Complexity* (Tokyo), pp. 268–97.
US ERDA (1977), *Program Plans*, Washington, DC, US Energy Research and Development Administration.
Veblen, T. (1898), 'Why Is Economics not an Evolutionary Science?', *Quarterly Journal of Economics*, **12**: 374–97.
Vuilleumier, S. (1983), 'World Outlook for High-Fructose Syrups', *Sugar y Azucar*, **78**: 27–47.

Waddington, C. (1957), *The Strategy of the Genes*, London, Allen & Unwin.
Walras, L. (1954), *Elements of Pure Economics*, London, Allen & Unwin.
Warwick, P. (1985), 'Photovoltaics in the Military Environment', in R. Hill (eds), *Application of Photovoltaics*, Proceedings of the Conference held at Newcastle-upon-Tyne, 12–13 September.
Whitehead, A.N. (1985), *Science and the Modern World*, London, Free Association Books.
Wik, R. (1980), 'The American Farm Tractor as Father of the Military Tank', *Agricultural History*, **54** (1): 126–33.
Wilber, C.K. and Harrison, R.S. (1978), 'The Methodological Basis of Institutional Economics', *Journal of Economic Issues*, **XII** (1): 61–89.
Williamson, O. (1985), *The Economic Institutions of Capitalism*, London, The Free Press.
Wolf, M. (1976), 'Historical Development of Solar Cells', in C. Backus (ed.), *Solar Cells*, New York, Institute of Electrical and Electronics Engineers.
World Bank (1981), *Brazil: Alcohol and Biomass Energy Development Project*, Washington, DC, World Bank.
World Solar Markets (1983), 'Worldwide Installed PV Capacity: Plotting an Accurate Picture', December.

Index